# FRACTURED LIVES

# FRACTURED LIVES

**TONI STRASBURG**

Publication © Modjaji Books 2013
Copyright Toni Strasburg © 2013

P O Box 385, Athlone, 7760, South Africa
modjaji.books@gmail.com
http://modjaji.book.co.za
www.modjajibooks.co.za

ISBN 978-1-920590-09-3

Cover design: Life is Awesome Design Studio
Book design: Life is Awesome Design Studio
Printed and bound by Mega Digital, Cape Town
Set in Garamond 11pt

Extracts from: *Another Day of Life* by Ryszard Kapuściński, Picador, 1987.
Copyright © Ryszard Kapuściński 1987

Extract from: *Reflections on Exile* by Edward W. Said
Copright © 2000, Edward W. Said
Used by permisson of the Wylie Agency (UK) Limited

*For my mother who believed in all of her children.*

# CONTENTS

## PART ONE

### 1981 THE BEGINNING — 11

1. Refugees and Exiles — 12
2. Bearing Witness — 24

## PART TWO

### 1986 DESTRUCTIVE ENGAGEMENT — 33

1. The Hidden Enemy — 34
2. Corridors of Power — 54
3. Confusão — 66
4. Harare–Mozambique — 90

## PART THREE

### 1988 CHAIN OF TEARS — 97

1. Children of War — 98
2. Zimbabwe–Tanzania — 118
3. Angola — 125
4. The End of the Earth — 132
5. Falling Apart — 139

## PART FOUR

**1990–1992 MARKING TIME**     155

1. Namibia     156
2. Angola (Going Nowhere)     164
3. Going Home     175
4. Meeting the Enemy 1     180
5. Free to Move     193

## PART FIVE

**1992 SPOILS OF WAR**     217

1. Meeting the Enemy 2     218
2. No Dead Elephants     235

## PART SIX

**1995 CHAIN OF HOPE**     249

1. Finding Franisse     250
2. Rosita's Return     265
3. The Lost Generation     277
4. Lariam Days     282
5. Heroes of Kuito     295

Glossary of Acronyms     308
References     310

# PREFACE

I have tried to describe my experiences while making documentary films about the wars in southern Africa. Over the years I made many films in many countries, but the ones described here are about a specific time in the history of the region. They portray, in particular, the effect of war on people's lives, especially those of women and children. My recollections are placed in the context of what was happening in southern Africa during those years, for if we are to understand where we are now, then we need to know what has brought us here.

The stories are also about the people I met while making the films – people who remain mostly nameless, but whose lives were destroyed beyond any comprehension.

Memory is always imperfect, however; thoughts blur and crumble over the years.

Author and crew arriving at refugee camp, Mozambique **1986**

*Photograph by:* Ivan Strasburg

# PART ONE

## 1981 THE BEGINNING

*Seeing the entire world as a foreign land makes possible originality of vision. Most people are principally aware of one culture, one setting, one home; exiles are aware of at least two, and this plurality of vision gives rise to an awareness of simultaneous dimensions, an awareness that is contrapuntal.*

**Edward Said, *Reflections on Exile*, 1984**

# 1. REFUGEES AND EXILES

The crowd milling and pushing in the dust were barely recognisable as human beings. Dressed in colourless rags, or wraps made from bark, they stared at us with blank and desperate eyes, anxious to receive anything that would help them to survive.

A man standing on a pile of sacks was shouting out names from a page torn from an exercise book. At each name, someone would surge forward to collect the family's share of the pathetic amount of aid we had brought in by tractor from the landing strip.

A ragged scrap of photograph was lying in the dust. Before it disappeared underfoot, I caught a glimpse of a family gazing at the camera wearing their best clothes. They bore no resemblance to any of these half-naked, starving and desperate people, pushing and shoving around me.

It was March 1991 and I was in Mozambique once more, making a film for the United Nations about their aid effort. For days we had struggled to reach this place. Everything possible had gone wrong: from the serious illness of the person in charge of the United Nations Disaster Relief Organisation (UNDRO) operation in Maputo, to an engine falling off the aid plane, almost forcing us to land in the sea. The heat and humidity made every movement an effort of will. All I wanted was to get out of there, go home to London, and sleep. It was as much as I could do to remain standing and try to direct my crew. I had been doing this for too long and felt only weary; the adrenalin kick was no longer there.

Tomas, who worked in the UNDRO warehouse in Maputo, felt he had suffered from the war for years. He lived with his family in one of the teeming barrios on the outskirts of the city; their poverty was worsened by food shortages and other deprivations. But in Maputo they had never experienced the real effects of the war that was fought in the countryside. Now he was shocked and distraught.

'Please, I have to do something for these people. Tell me what I can do,' he said. I tried to see the scene through Tomas's eyes. Sometimes, seeing too much poverty and suffering ceases to shock, and one's own discomfort begins to take precedence.

My own eyes saw what was going on, but I couldn't process it all. My brain was too busy trying to deal with practical matters like how to film this scene, or whether we'd ever get a plane out of here. Sometimes days or months – or even years – passed before I understood what had been going on in front of me.

I had filmed countless similar scenes over the years while covering the wars in southern Africa, but suddenly, seeing that pathetic photograph and then Tomas's real distress, and knowing there was nothing that I, or any film crew, could really do to help these people, I could bear it no longer. In all reality, I was no more than a voyeur. I felt that I could never again film a crowd of refugees and then simply walk away, having taken their images of misery and brought them nothing. Telling the world about these things didn't bring change; in the end it made no difference. It was enough. For me at least, the war was over. But as things turned out, I was wrong. There are some things that you cannot leave behind.

I went back to Africa for the first time in 1981. I had been away nearly seventeen years, and it had felt like a long time.

Until I was no longer there, I hadn't known how much Africa defined me. Growing up, I wasn't aware that the people, the light, the sounds and smells of the continent had entered me so deeply that I would never feel complete living away from it.

My political education began at a very early age. When I was only a few months old my mother, Hilda Bernstein, who was a rousing public speaker, stood as the Communist Party candidate for the Johannesburg city council. This was during the Second World War, when communism was still more or less acceptable in South Africa. She took me with her to public meetings and picked me up in mid-speech whenever I cried. This led to her being accused once of trying to get the sympathy of the voters by underhand means.

Her father – my grandfather, Simeon Schwartz – had been one of Lenin's original Bolsheviks. He had emigrated to England from Odessa in 1901, and became deeply involved in radical politics. After the Russian Revolution in 1917, he worked for the Soviets in England and was later their representative there. In 1926 he was recalled to the Soviet Union. He believed that he would be returning to his family within a year. However, the Soviets were suspicious of people who had been living in the capitalist west, and circumstances conspired against him. His family back in England were perceived as bourgeois, and although he held official positions, he was not always able to make the right contacts. In the end, despite various promises that were made to him over the years, he was unable to return to England and never saw his family again.

My grandmother, despairing of ever seeing him again, went to South Africa in the 1930s to join a sister who had gone to live there. My mother, who had grown up in London with her two sisters, went with her mother to South Africa, where she met and married my father, Rusty Bernstein, in Johannesburg. Not long after I was born, my father went to fight with the allies in Italy.

Politics was central to my parents' lives. They were well-known members of the South African Communist Party (SACP) and the African National Congress (ANC), actively involved in opposing the apartheid government. They lived a privileged, white South African existence in Johannesburg, bringing up four children, but their anti-apartheid work took place under increasingly restrictive circumstances. From the time I went to school, I was aware that my family were different from other white South Africans. We lived in white society, but our parents' beliefs and unconventional ways meant that we were also on the outside of it. My parents were unconventional in other ways too. They were atheists, though both were of Jewish origin. They were also intellectuals: my father was an architect, and my mother a talented writer and artist. Our house was full of books, pictures, music and conversations about places far away, as interesting people came and went.

I was the oldest of four children. My brother, Patrick, was born when I was five, and he was followed by my sister, Frances, and much later by our younger brother, Keith, who was born in 1956. In many ways we had a charmed childhood. Our comfortable house in a leafy suburb was a cliché of white suburbia, with its swimming pool, and large garden filled with fruit trees. We had two servants, two cars, two dogs and various other pets. After school, we were free to ride our bikes and roam the neighbourhood streets, visiting friends or swimming with a gang of children of all ages. Every Christmas we holidayed at the coast, and in the winter went camping or to the game reserve.

Growing up in the sun, Africa entered my soul and forever coloured the way I experienced the world. In the days before television and the Internet, events elsewhere barely filtered through to the tip of the continent. South Africa was out of touch with, and separated from, both the rest of Africa and the rest of the world.

But the idyll did not last. Eventually, my parents were banned, restricted and arrested by the apartheid government. Police sat outside our house all day, watching who came, and then knocked on our doors in the evenings. As children we learned not to ask too many questions, and to be careful when talking on the phone. We knew we had to keep part of our lives secret.

My parents went to mysterious meetings at night. Black friends came to our house and sat in our living room. Sometimes, especially as teenagers wanting desperately to conform, this embarrassed us and we tried to hide it from our school friends. Occasionally, our parents took us to the townships to visit black friends and we played with their children. Most of us children of politically active parents knew each other. A few of us older ones belonged to a youth group where we mixed with the children of our parents' black and Indian colleagues. We put on plays and went camping together.

We lived double lives. Our outside life was that of privileged and protected children, in the way that only middle-class, white South African children growing up in the 1950s and 1960s could be. But there was a darker side, where the clandestine activities of our parents made us aware of the injustices in our country. We grew used to the knock on the door in the early hours, of our parents being driven away while we had to go and stay with friends.

As the oldest I had to take on responsibility and step in for my parents when they went to prison. My mother told me about some of the things that were happening, which made me feel grown-up and important and helped me to understand what was going on in a way that the younger children couldn't.

I was thirteen when Keith was born, and while my mother was still in hospital, my father was arrested with 156 other South Africans and charged with treason. The trial dragged on for five years until 1961, although all the accused were acquitted in the end.

Three years later, both my parents were arrested in the State of Emergency following the shootings at Sharpeville. As usual, the police came before dawn. My mother made desperate phone calls to find someone to come and look after us. Almost everyone she called was also being arrested.

I was in my final year at school and became responsible for my three younger siblings. I wanted us to stay at home with Bessie and Claude, the servants who had been with the family for many years. But this was not something that the adults would consider. Four children were a lot for anyone to take on, so we were split up and sent to different families. Pat and Francie went to one family, while Keith – who was only three and saw me as a surrogate mother – came along with me to another. I at least understood to an extent what was going on, but for my younger siblings it was difficult, and they were all miserable.

At sixteen, I was old enough to be allowed to visit my parents in prison. I was even arrested briefly, when together with other children of detainees, we held a demonstration outside the Johannesburg city hall. I began to enjoy the 'other' status that my parents' activities conferred on me. I made the most of walking out of class, announcing loudly: 'I have to go to prison to visit my parents,' to the enormous embarrassment of the teachers.

By the time I was at college, I had joined the Congress of Democrats (COD), the organisation for whites aligned with the liberation struggle. In the COD, I made many lifelong friends and also met my husband-to-be, Ivan. Before that I'd gone out with Gerald Ludi, a member of our Congress of Democrats group, who eventually turned out to be working for the Special Branch (the security police). We travelled to Moscow and Helsinki together to attend a conference and youth festival – but that is another story entirely.

ANC membership was not open to whites; the ANC felt that the COD would be more influential if it acted as the white wing of the Congress Alliance. So, as COD members we could take part in secret anti-government activities. Many of these seem quite innocent now: painting slogans on walls at night; studying socialist writings – but at the time, any one of them could land you in prison.

This life came to an abrupt end in 1965 when my father was arrested with other leaders of the ANC and the Congress Alliance at Rivonia outside Johannesburg. The trial that followed was the one at which Nelson Mandela made his famous speech from the dock, in which he outlined the history of racial oppression in South Africa and how the ANC had tried every available method of peaceful protest before deciding to turn to the armed struggle. It was the speech that ended in unforgettable words:

> *During my lifetime I have dedicated myself to this struggle of the African people. I have fought against white domination, and I have fought against black domination. I have cherished the ideal of a democratic and free society in which all persons live together in harmony and with equal opportunities. It is an ideal which I hope to live for and to achieve. But if needs be, it is an ideal for which I am prepared to die.*

The months of the trial were an anxious time for the relatives of the accused. The legal team had warned them that the death sentence would be a likely outcome. Most days, my mother drove to Pretoria to sit in court, and sometimes I went with her.

Towards the end of the trial, I married Ivan. We were both very young, but the insecurity of my life at the time made me long for the apparent security of marriage. The wedding ceremony took place in our front garden, and all the while the security police stood outside our house, noting the number plates of the guests' cars.

All the accused were eventually found guilty and sentenced to life imprisonment. All, that is, except my father. He was acquitted on a technicality and then dramatically rearrested before he could leave the dock.

My father was given bail, but he knew that his next trial would put him in prison for many years and that it was only a matter of time before my mother would also be arrested. A few days after he came home, the police came for my mother, who escaped out of a window and through the back gardens of the neighbourhood into hiding. My parents realised that they would have to leave South Africa, and my father arranged for them to escape over the border. At a quiet spot in some public gardens in a Johannesburg suburb, my parents told Ivan and me their plans; they said we'd have to look after the younger children until they had reached a safe country. What was left unsaid was what might happen if their dangerous escape plan ended in arrest. Shortly after that my father and I took the younger children to a park to meet my mother who was in disguise, so that we could all say goodbye to her.

That night, my parents made a dramatic escape into Botswana, which was still the British Protectorate of

Bechuanaland at the time. Ivan and I were left in charge of the children, the dogs, the house and the servants. Once my parents reached safety, I was able to send my three younger siblings to join them in Zambia. A few months later, Ivan was arrested and held in police detention for ninety days. When he was released, we joined my family in exile in England. In a way, we had come full circle: back to England, the country of my mother's birth.

The similarities between my parents' lives and that of my Bolshevik grandfather fascinated me, and eventually I made a film about it. My family had dreams of a better world, for which they made choices that were not always in the best interests of their own family, yet led them to play an important role in events during the twentieth century. I was interested in the recurring pattern of exile and return, of passion and politics, of love and country, and belonging.

Exile is not unique to the South African experience; the sense of loss and dislocation it brings about is common to the condition, no matter who you are or which country you have left. It removed me from my roots, but it also brought an awareness of the outside world that broadened my life and gave me an understanding of lives and cultures other than my own. It was a very long time before I could understand both the sense of loss and the new things that exile brought me. My fractured life has helped me to understand lives that are far more broken than my own.

In my dreams at night, London and Johannesburg merged and I would awake unsure of which city I was in. If I could find the door I was always looking for, it seemed that I would be able to re-enter 'home', the magical place I was seeking. At first, I was unable to see any beauty in the English countryside. It all seemed so small, so confined. I longed for the dazzling light and the brown veld that stretched on forever. But one day, my eyes adjusted, and I began to become part of the society in which I was living.

For a while, I attempted to live an ordinary English life, although I was not English and our lives were not ordinary. It wasn't really possible to stop feeling South African or to dissociate from what was happening in my home country.

I was twenty-two when my first son, Mark, was born five months after our arrival in London. Nicholas was born two years later. We were political refugees with no money, and the early years were a continual struggle of trying to adjust to a new country that seemed grey and dark and over-full of people. We lived in a cold flat in London with the two babies; I studied part-time for a degree in sociology and psychology at London University and Ivan travelled as a film cameraman.

Later, when the boys started school, I worked as a researcher, first on a study of twins, and later on a study of children with behavioural problems. Eventually I started making documentary films for British Television.

In some ways, I think it was inevitable that I started to film wars. My early life in South Africa, growing up as the child of dissident parents, had made me addicted to adrenalin. At least, that is what the psychiatrist at the hospital in Camden Town told me when, feeling depressed, I once went to see him. Yet at the time I probably had post-natal depression, something that was not well diagnosed then. The psychiatrist said I missed the early-morning knock on the door. I missed the thrill of my parents being arrested or being on the run, visiting them in prison, having a police car outside the house. I missed our cloak-and-dagger lives. This is what he told me.

'Get a job in a shop, a supermarket,' he said, as if that would help to replace what I was missing.

I couldn't explain to him that the last thing I wanted then was constant tension. It was in fact a relief to know that the sound of a car passing slowly down the street in the early hours was not a precursor to a knock on the door.

But in one way, he may have been right. At some level it seems that I did miss some of the excitement, and needed to be involved in southern Africa.

It was years until I understood that living on the edge does turn you into an adrenalin junky, forever restless and seeking excitement in various ways. It was even longer before I realised that war contaminates everyone who comes into contact with it, and that no matter how much you might hate it, you start to need it; so you have to find a way of leaving it, before war alone seems real and you have become yet another casualty.

While filming in war zones, in a state of constant alertness, I lost the ability to switch off from it all, even when there was no danger. It was the same as when I was growing up in South Africa.

Sometimes the filming made me feel more alive than I had ever been, but there were times when it sapped my energy, leaving me utterly enervated, overcome with fatigue and unable to relax. We would come back into town after days or weeks of filming and make for our rooms at the house or hotel. I would lie on my bed, wishing never to move again. It was often only an act of extreme will that forced me to pull myself together and insist to the crew that we go out again and start filming once more.

While I was filming, I was able to distance myself from what was going on in front of me, but later the scenes would come back, and play again and again in my head. Some of them haunt me to this day.

Unlike the people we were filming, we knew that our time

in these countries would come to an end. In a matter of weeks or maybe months, we'd be flying home to a place where there were no guns, no killings.

And when I did go back home, it was impossible to explain to anyone else what it was really like, no matter how stark the images in my films. In the end, I would just say that the trip had been 'fine' or 'hard'. War has a way of staying with you long after you have left it; all these years later, it is still with me. You can only know all this when you experience it; you have to learn along the way.

When I was making the films, I believed that peace was possible and that there would be change for the better. I was not alone in thinking that despite the misery and suffering we were documenting, our films could help make the world a better place. It was still a time of hope. It was before the collapse of the Soviet Union, and the final throes of the Cold War were still being played out in Africa, Asia and Latin America. It was the time before HIV had impacted so devastatingly on Africa, before Zimbabwe had disintegrated, before we were fully aware of the impact of global warming. Before George Bush and Iraq and the world economic collapse. Long before the ANC had proved itself not much better once in power than so many other previous liberation movements.

Disillusionment is often a gradual process. It happens incrementally, little by little over time, in a series of small and larger disappointments.

But long before the disillusionment eventually set in, I still had to get on with my life in England, even though I lived with my heart turned south, waiting for news and the day we could go back.

## 2. BEARING WITNESS

Journal entry: **Chibuto, Mozambique, October 1981**

*I had a rebellion on my hands this evening when we got in from the village. Jane, my researcher, took it upon herself to give the entire bag of dried fruit we had brought from Neals Yard in London, to the hotel staff.*

*There are only two dishes available at this hotel: ravioli cooked in snot, or rotten meat, and we never know which will be the one we have to face on our return from filming. Both can be made more or less palatable with a large dose of piri piri, but the evening treat in my room, where I carefully dole out a handful of dried fruit to each of the crew, has become especially important. Now I am left with simmering bad feeling and resentment against Jane, which I know will last for the rest of the trip.*

Despite the radicalism of my parents, my generation grew up during a time when not a lot was expected from women.

I wanted to be a nurse, but that didn't work out and I trained as a teacher. It never occurred to me that I would become a filmmaker. We didn't even have television in South Africa before I left.

Like most work, making films is often mundane and boring. It's filled with longueurs of waiting, weeks of careful planning, and a lot of hard work.

But quite often it is also nerve-wracking, demanding instant decisions and changes of plan at a moment's notice. I found that my experiences growing up in South Africa had given me these skills that I'd not even known I possessed. It had also given me the ability to remain calm when things went wrong. Filmmaking provided me with a creative outlet to tell the stories that were important or interesting to me, while also giving me the kind of fear-fuelled excitement I hadn't realised I'd been missing.

Ivan's career as a cameraman meant that he was frequently away from home for weeks or even months at a time. I became used to being a single parent, managing the household and making sure that my work enabled me to be at home for the children after school or in the holidays.

By 1980, Ivan had begun to move from working on documentaries to shooting TV dramas and feature films. Mark was on the point of leaving school, and with Nick finishing his schooling at a boarding school in Devon, I was now free to begin my own career in filmmaking.

Because Ivan and I worked as freelancers in the film industry, there were long periods when either one or both of us were at home. The shooting period is a relatively short part of filmmaking, so often, while shooting in England, I was only away for a few days at a time. Even on long shoots outside the country, I was rarely away for more than six weeks. Before the shoot can begin, there are months of pre-production, fund-raising and research. Afterwards there are weeks of editing and other post-production, so I was able to juggle home, children and the other commitments that made up my own fractured life without abandoning my family. I hadn't set out to film war. I wanted to tell positive stories of what was going on in the countries bordering South Africa, despite the difficulties they were facing. My chance came in 1981 when I was commissioned to make two films about village life in two independent African countries, Mozambique and Kenya.

Mozambique had become independent in 1975, after the fall of the Salazar regime in Portugal brought an end to the liberation war there and in Angola. In 1980 Zimbabwe also became independent – and suddenly I was able to return to southern Africa.

From the moment I stepped off the plane in Maputo, and was engulfed by air that smelled of warm sea, tropical vegetation, wood smoke, old sweat and Africa, I fell in love with Mozambique and could never get enough of it. The country and the people enchanted me.

In both Angola and Mozambique, the liberation movements had taken over in a vacuum. The Portuguese had left, taking all that they could with them and destroying much of the infrastructure they left behind. They had never educated or trained the indigenous populations and these countries were left desperately short of qualified personnel.

The new government of Mozambique, Frelimo (Front for the Liberation of Mozambique), had hardly taken over from the departing Portuguese when they found themselves at war. Frelimo gave refuge to guerrillas fighting against Ian Smith's Rhodesian army and the apartheid South African government. To stop Mozambique from harbouring Zimbabwean guerrillas, Rhodesian Intelligence set up the Mozambican National Resistance (MNR), and by the end of the 1970s Mozambique was struggling with a major insurgency.

When Zimbabwe became independent in 1980, South Africa – seriously worried about yet another independent country on its borders – used its military intelligence to step in and take over the MNR. It renamed the organisation Renamo (Resistência Nacional Moçambicana), although it was mostly referred to by Mozambicans as *bandidos armadas* – armed bandits. From then on, the conflict in Mozambique began to consume the entire country.

Renamo also attracted backing from right-wing groups in West Germany and the USA, and received money from extremist religious groups in the US. The Cold War was still being played out in surrogate wars all over Africa.

Coca Missava, the village where we were filming, was in Gaza province, only half a day's drive north of the capital Maputo. On the surface it didn't look like a war zone, though proper transport was hard to come by and petrol was a major problem. We had also been warned that the *bandidos* attacked villages at night and that we would not be able to stay in the village after dark. So, each afternoon we had to drive some way over bad roads to return to the town nearby.

Food was also a problem, as the attacks by Renamo in the countryside were preventing subsistence farmers from growing crops. Forewarned of shortages, we had brought some food with us, in particular the bag of dried fruit that eventually caused so much bad feeling.

Mozambique was struggling with all the problems of underdevelopment in the wake of independence; but despite the shortages and problems, it was an exciting time to be there. Since independence, many *cooperantes*, sympathetic to the ideals of Frelimo, had arrived from Western countries as teachers, doctors, journalists, and so on. From the Eastern bloc, help came in the form of engineers and other experts. In addition, there were a number of foreign NGOs and UN agencies involved with projects there. Enthusiasm was at a high pitch, university students taught adult literacy classes in the evenings, and teams of people cleaned up their neighbourhoods at weekends. It was impossible not to be infected by the energy and optimism.

When we eventually returned to England, I was wholly in the thrall of Africa. I had met up with some ANC people in Mozambique and made many friends with Mozambican filmmakers.

After that first visit, I made many films in southern Africa, but the early hope that I had witnessed on my first visit to Mozambique was short-lived. Very soon the war grew worse, while across the continent in Angola, war had never ceased. Instead of making films about hope and change, I was engaged in trying to document South Africa's wars against these newly-formed nations.

I am not the only woman filmmaker to have lived in conflict zones, but at the time I was making these films, I was one of very few women doing this kind of work in southern Africa. Many African countries are male-dominated societies, and being a woman in charge of several men was often considered provocative. Unfailingly, those in authority would address the male members of my crew, completely ignoring me. Men in authority, policemen, and other officials found the situation particularly hard to handle and were not amenable to explanations that I was the person in charge.

Inevitably, I found myself filming people in emotional or traumatic situations. So often it was the women who, with their children, bore the largest burden of suffering as they struggled to keep families intact. Everything that women have to contend with in ordinary life is far more acute in times of war and upheaval, and more particularly so in countries where women were still largely disempowered.

In rural Africa, women work incredibly hard, bearing and caring for children, and labouring to grow subsistence crops without any form of mechanical help. Women frequently walk miles each day to fetch water and firewood. War makes difficult lives even more precarious as fighting means that crops are destroyed or cannot even be planted, and foraging for food is a constant and dangerous activity; far too many children die from lack of food and medical care.

I witnessed the effects of war beyond the physical injuries that are its inevitable outcome: families torn apart; children lost and orphaned; communities broken, the inhabitants sent scattering into the bush or to the cities. I wanted to give ordinary people the chance to speak in their own words and languages about their experiences, and it was the lives of the women and children that began to interest me the most.

When people cannot grow crops and transport links have broken down, then there is famine as well as war. It creates homelessness and waves of refugees, who wander around the affected countries, spilling over into the neighbouring ones. It leaves behind a legacy of anger, hatred and sadness that takes decades to heal.

By its nature, all filmmaking is intrusive. Documentary filmmaking also raises ethical questions common to all journalism – not only regarding the collection of material, but also how the material is used. In my films, I tried to give a glimpse of what lies beneath the surface, something that is often difficult for documentary to penetrate.

My films reflected my interpretation of what I experienced. The way I edited stories and juxtaposed them with other material meant that, in the end, I was presenting my version of the truth – but I always tried to do this with integrity.

I went to the places I went to and filmed the stories that I filmed because I felt passionate about what was happening there and wanted to bring it to public attention. For me it was southern Africa, but it could have been any of a number of other places where similar things were happening at the time.

The effects are the same wherever war happens.

I came to see that, as a woman, I had a different way of telling stories, relating them to my own experience and tending to be more subjective, oriented towards people's everyday lives and emotions. The male model of storytelling is frequently based on facts and experts: this is the tradition from which documentary filmmaking in England and America developed. But I wanted to tell my stories from a different perspective.

As far as possible, I tried to avoid 'experts' and politicians, the people who so often interpret events for us. In my early years of filmmaking, I struggled to find my 'voice', not really knowing how I wanted to tell stories.

I wasn't comfortable with the British television model of 'objectivity'. I don't believe that it is possible to witness war and remain detached, even though sometimes I thought I was detached. In any case, I was not working as a journalist or reporter, but as a filmmaker.

Finding my own way of expressing things wasn't easy. It caused conflict within myself and sometimes with my all-male crews, but more especially with commissioning editors at TV stations, who so often wanted the more accepted way of doing things. At times I lost confidence and felt undermined, but slowly I learned to allow my own voice to come through. It was many years later that the French idea of the filmmaker as *auteur* allowed me to escape from the constraints of 'objectivity' and to tell stories in the way that I wanted to.

Often I was very close to my subject matter, and, over the years, my long-suffering crews not only had to put up with witnessing the horrors of war and difficult living conditions, but also my tears and tantrums.

I knew that I wouldn't be able to change the world, but when I first began, I believed that I could make some difference, at least make some viewers more aware of lives other than their own. In the end, all I could do was bear witness.

Fapla soldiers at Ondjive, Southern Angola **1988**
*Photograph by:* Keith Bernstein

# PART TWO

## 1986 DESTRUCTIVE ENGAGEMENT

*Confusão is a situation created by people, but in the course of creating it they lose control and direction, becoming victims of confusão themselves. There is a sort of fatalism in confusão. A person wants to do something but it all falls to pieces in his hands, he wants to create something, but he produces confusão. Confusão can overwhelm our thinking. Sometimes confusão takes the form of desultory, chaotic, but bloodless haggling.*

*Confusão is a state of absolute disorientation. People who have found themselves on the inside of confusão can't comprehend what is going on around them or in themselves. There are carriers that spread confusão, and others must beware, though this is difficult because literally any person at any moment can become a perpetrator of confusão, even against his will.*

*Confusão can reign over an enormous territory and sweep through millions of people. The best thing is to act slowly and wait. After a while confusão loses energy, weakens, vanishes. We emerge from a state of confusão exhausted, but somehow satisfied that we have managed to survive. We start gathering strength again for the next confusão.*

**Ryszard Kapuściński,** *Another Day of Life,* **1987**

# 1. THE HIDDEN ENEMY

'The armed bandits came to my house on the eleventh of July last year and the first thing they did was apologise and I thought they were my people. Then I went outside. I saw cutlasses, machetes, assegais, and one of them asked: "You are Raimundo Muchalpa, the oldest teacher here? You are the head teacher here?"'

Raimundo paused and took a deep breath before continuing. Grey-haired and dignified, there was horror and outrage in his voice as he related his story.

After he told the bandits that he was indeed the head teacher of the village his captors began to taunt him.

Bewildered, he replied, 'When asked if I was a teacher, shouldn't I have said I was a teacher?'

At this, his interrogator shouted, 'Seize him.'

They pointed their rifles at him, ordering him to stand and undress.

'You know you are going to die,' they told him, 'because you are a teacher and instruct the children. You went to Maputo. You tell the children to say "down with the bandits."'

As he told the story, Raimundo demonstrated how he had responded to their orders, his face showing the horror he felt when the bandits approached him with rifles and machetes.

'What could I do? I had to accept.'

As the man struck him with the machete and Raimundo fell, he cried out, 'Oh, my God.'

But the bandits replied, 'That is useless, we are not Christians, no use asking God.'

Removing his shirt, then, Raimundo turned his back

towards us.

'They started to cut me, first here and here and there.'

His back and shoulders were patterned with deep, partially healed scars.

'Then they left me behind. I lay here all day in the sun until our troops arrived and they took me to the hospital and that was my story.'

It was 1986, and I was in Mozambique filming *Destructive Engagement*. Before that, I had made four fairly short documentaries in southern Africa. But mostly I'd been working on films set in Europe – and now I was back doing what I really wanted to do.

Frelimo's devotion to the right to literacy and health care meant that, from the start, they set up schools and clinics. In the rural areas these were sometimes no more than a thatched hut or a blackboard under a tree. High-school graduates were trained as teachers and barefoot medics, and sent into the countryside to help. Renamo centred their attacks on this infrastructure: health workers and teachers in particular were targeted, and schools and hospitals destroyed.

Everywhere, the stories were the same. Attacks took place at night. Parents grabbed children, often running in different directions and losing each other. Girls were raped, boys were abducted, people had ears or breasts cut off. They would sleep in the bush without food and clothes for days until they could reach a government-held town or refugee centre. Wearing rags or sacks or bits of bark, they arrived in advanced states of hunger and disease. Every day we heard of new attacks on villages.

I didn't know then that war was addictive. By 1987, most of Mozambique had been affected by the war. Maputo had an air of neglect, the roads disintegrating into potholes, the paint peeling from the façades of the dilapidated buildings. Along the Marginal, the paving stones were broken and there were little groups of homeless children waiting to guard cars. The enthusiasm and optimism I had experienced five years earlier had been subsumed by the weariness of war.

Three years after Mozambique and Angola became independent, South Africa's Prime Minister, P. W. Botha, announced that the country faced a 'total onslaught' from beyond its borders and therefore needed to respond with a 'total national strategy' that came to be known as 'destabilisation'. It was to be a mix of both military and economic action, different for each country in the region.

In Mozambique, military action largely took place through the use of a surrogate army, chiefly through raids and incursions. Disaffected groups were sought out, first by the Rhodesians, and later the South Africans, and then trained to fight against their own governments – in effect fighting the war for the South Africans.

In Angola, the war took place on a more conventional and far larger scale than in other targeted countries. Angola's huge oil and diamond reserves made it strategically important to both Eastern and Western Bloc countries. Also, because South Africa had never held economic influence over Angola, its approach to the war there differed from its actions elsewhere in the region. In Zimbabwe, the war was waged largely by economic means, with the cutting of transport links and the imposition of economic sanctions. And in Lesotho, Swaziland, Botswana and Zambia, South Africa used raids as well as economic sanctions.

These wars in southern Africa were often described as 'low-intensity' conflicts, to distinguish them from more conventional warfare. But low-intensity conflict does not equal low-intensity violence. And so the wars took an enormous toll on mainly civilian victims, leaving traumatised societies that are still dealing with the repercussions today. All of these countries had also to contend with poverty, disease and a huge legacy of debt. Despite emergency aid sent to Africa, to this day most of these countries remain damaged by debt repayments.

The South African-backed wars that tore Angola and Mozambique apart in the 1980s were largely hidden from the rest of the world. Media attention at the time was focused on what was happening inside South Africa, generally ignoring Mozambique and Angola. The connection between what was happening in these countries and the policies of the apartheid regime in destabilising them was rarely made. Nevertheless, the wars had a devastating effect on human life, rivalling that of the better-known conflicts in Afghanistan and Nicaragua that were taking place at the same time. South Africa was instrumental in the failure of these African countries in the early days of independence, and the repercussions reverberate through all of southern Africa today.

By the time Adrian and I met the film crew at Maputo airport, I felt as if we had been travelling between Zimbabwe and Mozambique forever. We had been on the road for a month, setting up the film I was making about South Africa's wars of destabilisation against the Frontline States, a group of countries that included Angola, Botswana, Lesotho, Mozambique, Tanzania, Zambia and Zimbabwe.

Adrian was the researcher. Tall and good-looking, he came from an English public school background. Always polite and well-spoken, this was his first experience of Africa. His cool demeanour made me feel permanently dishevelled and perhaps not quite up to the mark. He was able to make me feel clumsy and silly without saying anything at all. The English have always had a way of making me feel too loud, too outspoken, and just too African.

In Maputo we had the loan of a house that I had stayed in so many times over the years that I began to feel as if I owned it. It came with an excellent cook, whose name was John. He also knew how to find fresh food in the local markets, and his 'loasty chicken' was a firm favourite. He liked having a house full of people to look after, but one thing about us really annoyed him.

In the evenings, he and the other domestic staff in the neighbourhood would take their chairs out to the pavement to gossip. Having *estrangeiros* – foreigners – living in his house gave John extra status on the street, but we had a habit of affronting his dignity by not behaving in what he considered was the correct way: we liked to walk home after dinner with friends.

'Why you come by walk?' he would say in an aggrieved voice. 'Why you not use the car?'

I had made contact with several old friends from South Africa now based with the ANC in Maputo, and I'd made friends with Mozambican filmmakers and journalists. The house became a meeting place for friends and colleagues to drop in at all hours for a drink or a chat.

I worked with the best and most experienced crews I could get. On this film, Ivan was the cameraman, and the sound mixer was Christian, a friend of ours. Ivan and I had worked together in the past, and this was to be one of the last documentaries he worked on before becoming director of photography on TV drama and feature films.

My brother Keith accompanied us for most of this shoot, mainly doing photo stories for publication. He is a well-known photographer, and after the film was completed, we put together a book that was published soon afterwards.

Working with Ivan made my life both easier and more difficult. I never had to tell him how to frame, set things up, or get shots, but at times there were things that I knew I would need in editing that he considered dull or unnecessary. 'I am not shooting dog's breath,' he would say, and we would collapse into bickering.

It was an odd relationship in other ways as well. At one level the group was made up of husband and wife, brother and sister, friends; yet at another level we were crew and director, a professional distance that was not always easy to maintain, especially with Ivan. At the end of the day his work was done, whereas I usually had hours of work ahead, preparing my notes for the next day, trying to take stock of what we had filmed and what we'd missed, or possibly having to go and meet with someone to discuss future filming, or just deal with the protocol of gaining permission to film, confirming arrangements and being polite to local officials.

Christian was a Canadian: large, blond, and mostly genial, but with a fearsome temper at times. Although we had been friends for years, I hadn't worked with him and soon came to realise that, although wonderful at his job, he could be a bully and had little patience for any indecision on my part.

Both Ivan and Christian had lived and worked in jungles and war zones all over the world and were resourceful, used to hard conditions and had developed a good instinct for keeping out of danger. In the evenings they had a tendency to reminisce about the wonderful places they had been to and films they had worked on. The rest of us listened to interminable stories about the people they had known and the places they had seen. Christian frequently finished one of these stories by saying: 'Now there was a *real* director. He *really* knew what he was doing.'

This would undermine my confidence and, as the shoot progressed, I began to feel that the remarks were aimed at me.

Working in a remote, war-torn place like Mozambique that we hadn't been able to visit in advance meant that I often had to make quick decisions, and I probably looked as unconfident as I felt at such times. It was hard on the crew as well, as they were expected to begin filming, often without adequate guidance from me. It was all far from ideal. I felt pushed and pulled by my own plans and the pressure from both the crew and our minders. Christian was probably trying to be helpful but I read it differently, and by the end of the day I'd often be reduced to tears – which I tried to make sure he didn't see.

Permission to travel outside of Maputo had to be obtained from the Ministry of Information, and they were usually not keen on having foreign journalists and film crews in the war zones. Arlindo Lopes, the director at the ministry, was a friend and had been a journalist himself. His help in getting us the permissions we needed to travel outside of Maputo was invaluable. Whenever we were in the provinces, the government insisted on our being accompanied by a minder. Arlindo was smart enough to make this an arrangement that would benefit Mozambican filmmakers as well as provide us with the required minder, and on this shoot the Institut de Cinema sent Ahmed Ali.

We were accompanied by Bai Bai, the young Mozambican camera assistant who had been with us at Coca Missava. It was always a pleasure to have Mozambican film people with us, they were well trained and resourceful and understood the country and language in a way we never could.

Oxfam had put a small amount of money towards the film and, for part of the shoot in Mozambique, we travelled with Bill Yates, one of their senior people. Bill was a tall, thin man, with red hair and a mild manner. He never made a display of how much he knew about situations of war and famine, and he was a useful and experienced addition, tolerant of the vagaries of film crews.

Road travel was impossible due to ambushes and landmines; scheduled flights were cancelled more often than not. We arranged flights with a Canadian missionary organisation, Air Serv, which flew single-engine Cessnas around the country to help with relief work. The Air Serv pilots were all strapping, young God-fearing Canadians, who were wonderfully skilled at bush flying.

The small planes had strict weight limits. Before leaving Maputo airport we were weighed together with our luggage. The equipment and film stock were essential, so inevitably it was the personal bags that had to be left behind if we were overweight. So we'd often end up in some provincial town in swampy summer heat, with only the clothes we stood up in.

On that first trip out of Maputo, we flew for hours over endless flat green bush, the fertile interior of the country which from the air appeared to be deserted. We flew over wide meandering rivers and later, miles of unspoiled beaches stretched out below us, the coastline broken only by rivers and lagoons. There were few signs of people or villages, and no roads. It gradually dawned on me that the emptiness was largely a result of the war, which had forced the population to abandon great tracts of country.

In Zambezia province in central Mozambique, the war was all around us. We could feel it but not see it; we only ever saw the effects. The enemy was everywhere but invisible. Attacks took place at night, in the villages, in the bush. It was a silent war, but no less deadly for that.

The province had a history of banditry and was now effectively under Renamo control. Only the main towns were still held by government troops. It wasn't really clear who controlled the countryside, as Mozambique had become a country of *deslocados* – people displaced from their homes inside the country. It was estimated that more than eight hundred thousand people within the province had been forced to leave their villages. Groups of people wandered into refugee centres after escaping abduction by Renamo, often hiding in the bush for days. Many fled to neighbouring countries. To make matters worse, there was a serious famine. Fleeing villagers were unable to grow crops, and the war made it hard to get food relief to the people who needed it.

Quelimane had once been an attractive little river port from where coconut, tea and cashew had been exported. It was also the place where David Livingstone ended his trans-Africa journey from the Atlantic, and from which slaves from the interior were shipped out. Long before Vasco da Gama reached it in 1499, it had been part of the Indian Ocean trade route where various cultures intermingled. Post-war Quelimane still has a reputation of lawlessness, as a frontier town that attracts all sorts of shady types dealing in drugs and sex slaves.

But in 1986 it felt detached from the rest of the country. Our first sight of it was dispiriting. Everything appeared to be broken. All the shops were shut, their dusty, flyblown windows empty of any goods. Outside the hotel a permanent group of silent, hungry children watched us with big eyes. The town seemed to be sinking into itself, overcome by the oppressive heat and humidity. The whole place had an air of demoralisation. Besieged and isolated, it was cut off from the capital and most of the surrounding countryside.

The owner of the Hotel Chuabo was an eccentric and ill-tempered Portuguese woman, one of the few who had not left Mozambique at independence. She was tiny, with dark hair and a habit of taking out her perpetual anger on whomever happened to cross her. Her staff tried to keep a wide berth at all times. Most days there was running water in the town for only a few hours, and some days there was none. The electricity was intermittent and the lifts didn't work. Despite these drawbacks, she had no intention of allowing standards to drop. Guests had to be properly attired at meals, even if food was scarce.

Arriving with no personal luggage, this unshakeable rule presented us with a problem. I was the only member of the crew not dressed in shorts and a T-shirt, which the owner did not consider a respectable form of clothing for a provincial hotel in the middle of a war. She informed Adrian of this in no uncertain terms.

'None of you people can go to the dining room dressed like that.'

Ahmed Ali and Adrian explained why we had left our luggage behind, but she never even bothered to look up as she shuffled receipts, all the while keeping a beady eye out for any transgressions by her staff.

'These are my rules.'

'These people are filmmakers from Britain,' Ahmed Ali said. 'What do you suggest we do? They're guests in our country.'

'*Não meu problema, este é un hotel.*' Not my problem, this is a hotel, she snapped, without raising her eyes to look at him.

We had been up since five and were by now hungry and thirsty as well as very sweaty. Not being able to follow the conversation made the crew impatient, as if it were Ahmed Ali and Adrian who were at fault. Finally a compromise was negotiated and she agreed to set up screens at the far end of the dining room to shield the other diners from the horrible sight of men in shorts. It was unlikely that the handful of other guests would even have noticed. Apart from a friendly group of Russians working on a fishing project, there were some senior army personnel, and one or two others.

The Chuabo was seven or eight stories high, a typically bland 1970s-style concrete building. Our rooms looked down onto the twin spires of the riverfront cathedral that had been built by the Portuguese in 1770. In the yard, a water pump attracted a constant flow of women with buckets. Most evenings we joined the bucket queue, carrying the water up to our rooms.

I soon perfected the technique of washing myself in half a bucket of water, using my knickers as a wash cloth, and reserving the other half to rinse out my clothes for the following day. I always saved a glass of water for brushing my teeth and moistening the edge of a towel to wipe my face in the morning.

At dawn each day, we left town to film schools and clinics that had been shelled, or refugee camps where shelters of palm and straw were hastily erected for the never-ending influx of people driven from the land.

Daylight travel was only possible in areas that were still under Frelimo control. It was an eerie countryside. We would drive for hours along roads that had no cars, no people, no bicycles, no livestock, none of the usual movement of life in Africa. We drove through miles of deserted coconut plantations, where the tall palms closed in threateningly. Most of the outposts we arrived at were ghost towns, their inhabitants, who had often hidden in the bush until they could reach safety, now swelling the number of refugees in the towns and camps. The people moved at night, seldom using the roads.

One day we followed two ramshackle lorries – one of them painted a bright pink – that ferried the sacks of food aid from the warehouse in Quelimane. We came to a place in the bush where the road ended and tracks were being cleared by a group of refugees with machetes. There was a faint breeze as we lurched along the track, but once we came to a halt the heat hit us, with only the buzzing of insects to break the quiet as we walked the last few metres. The humidity made walking those last few steps almost impossible. I dripped with sweat. It was much worse for the crew carrying the gear and filming as they walked, yet they never complained. The men laid down their machetes and rushed to meet us, overjoyed to see the lorries. They were eager to get the food into the camp but waited patiently as the crew set up to film them.

'This is the first food we have had for days,' said a man in ragged shorts and a torn blue T-shirt stained with dust and sweat.

'Here, the first thing is hunger. We have been taking mangoes at night for our children. They all have diarrhoea.' The sweat ran off them in rivulets as they struggled with the sacks.

A small area of bush had been cleared where people had started to build huts. While the sacks of food were carried from the lorries to the middle of the clearing, I chatted with the drivers.

'We are constantly alert, looking out for bandits,' the taller one told me.

Behind them, women had built cooking fires and had makeshift shelters; thin children gazed at us with big eyes.

It was only too easy to imagine an enemy watching and waiting to attack, hidden in the dense green vegetation on either side of the narrow tracks.

'It is a big problem, getting food out to the districts,' the driver told us. 'We are very exposed to danger; the bandits are always trying to get our goods. Yes, we are afraid because sometimes they kill us. We must have courage, because so many people are starving.'

Many of the children wore T-shirts that had come from aid packages, and bore the most unlikely slogans. One announced: Howard School of Mortuary and Embalming.

Some days we managed to get bread and tea from the hotel kitchen before we went out filming. We had no food for the rest of the day and there was none to buy in the countryside. I was still inexperienced at filming in war and famine areas which made life more difficult for all of us. With some crazy idea that we shouldn't eat when people around us were starving, I had foolishly not made proper arrangements to ensure that the crew had sufficient food and water. This, combined with the heat and difficult conditions, made us all tired and bad-tempered. The only time we could relax for a short time was after dinner, when we'd stroll out into the cool evening air along the port area and watch children playing football in the orange sunsets.

Hospitals provide a useful way of taking the temperature of a country, allowing one to find out what the main problems are and what resources are available. Quelimane was no exception. There were many amputees at the local hospital, and the usual assortment of malnourished children. In one room I looked away in shock when I saw a woman with her head horribly split open by a machete, the wound gaping and pink, her face blank.

In a small side room, a father sat in silent despair beside the bed of two-year-old twins the size of six-month-old babies. Their mother was dead. He seemed to have no hope at all. I felt helpless; there was nothing of comfort I could offer this man. And in a way, these were the lucky ones, the ones who had somehow reached Quelimane and the hospital. What was happening out in the bush was something we only ever got glimpses of, but mostly it was anyone's guess.

Once, on the way back to Quelimane from some outlying place, we persuaded our driver to stop at Praia de Zelala, a beach resort outside town. The shabby bungalows had been abandoned, and the Mozambicans with us were uneasy, parking the Land Cruiser at the top of the dunes while we had a quick swim. It was a lonely place, and though the long, wide beach was bordered by thick bush, I felt exposed and quickly returned to the car, too nervous to stay in the warm waves.

Years later, in 1994, I was stationed at Praia de Zelala as a UN election monitor during the first elections after the war. The bungalows were still run down, but they'd been made more or less habitable for us, while an enterprising businessman had opened a small restaurant and bar there. Before driving out to our outlying election stations, a group of us would walk down the sandy track to the beach in the pre-dawn darkness to swim in the warm sea. One morning, as we bobbed about in the waves, a Russian-accented voice next to me said with satisfaction: 'Muntay morning, evervun is at vork, and ve are schweemming.'

On our last day in Quelimane, we left before sunrise to travel upriver, deep into Renamo territory, to film at little pockets of government-held centres for *deslocados*. It was difficult and dangerous to get food and medicine to these places and impossible for the government to set up proper feeding centres.

We stood in squalls of tropical rain on the deck of an ancient boat that chugged slowly through miles of mangrove swamp up the Qua Qua river. The boat was carrying beans, maize and milk powder to the refugees. The boatmen asked us for cigarettes, which they smoked with the lit side in their mouths. It felt like something out of Conrad.

At our destination, we waded through thigh-deep river mud and walked into the camp, blackened and soaking. The women refugees waiting to greet us stared in open-mouthed horror at our filthy state.

The places we visited that day were crowded with thousands of refugees. Some were on the point of death, lying unmoving on the ground. The numbers were overwhelming and it took time for me to register what I was seeing. Starving children, many of whom had been separated from their parents in Renamo attacks, lined up for cups of thin soup while soldiers stood guard. Many of them had the swollen bellies and reddish hair of acute malnutrition. Tiny girls carried even tinier babies and held out their cups silently. It was a scene from the heart of darkness. Even today, the upper reaches of the Qua Qua are remote and untamed, a place inhabited by speculators and adventurers.

There was a Frelimo presence in all these centres but none of them were secure, and were often attacked at night, sending the people there scattering into the bush once more. There used to be a saying in the countryside: 'Frelimo by day, Renamo by night.' Ahmed Ali said it most nights as we sat around and discussed the day's work.

'There are more than two thousand people in this camp, and more arrive every day,' a mournful-looking nurse told us. We followed him into a tent that had practically no medical supplies.

'Many have malaria, TB and open wounds. All of them are hungry. What can I do?'

We had no answers for him. Most of the people in these outlying areas didn't speak Portuguese, so we could only communicate with officials like the nurse. Many people were in such a bad way that it felt intrusive to film too much.

We all have ways to protect ourselves from the horrors we witness. I don't react to the misery before me while I am filming – there is always too much else to think about. But the pain of it comes to me much later. Cameramen have a tendency to hide behind the camera, so that they are seeing things second-hand, while sound recordists distance themselves with their headphones. I have seen journalists write incessantly in their notebooks to shield themselves from seeing too much.

On the trip back down river that evening, we watched as small dug-out canoes drifted past us while pelicans fished from the banks. It was a scene of such peace and tranquillity that it was hard to know which part of the day was real.

Back at the hotel, the water was off again. I stood there in my once-pink skirt now covered in dried mud, wondering how to clean myself before dinner.

Not that I really cared; I was totally exhausted. What I wanted at that moment was oblivion. I wanted to be in a place where the images I had seen that day, and all the other days, would leave me in peace. I wanted to be somewhere where I was not responsible for others.

Just then, the sound of my film crew's English voices raised in anger reached me. It had been a bad day; in fact it had been a bad week. Without realising it then, the war had got into my head: the misery of the people we had seen, and the eyes of the sad and nameless children I had filmed.

Ivan and I ran up the stairs, joined by Keith. Ahmed Ali and Bill had entered the room ahead of us. Christian was about to punch Adrian. He was almost purple with fury, a vein pulsing ominously in his temple.

'He has been swanning about town all day and did not even fill a bloody bucket for me when the water was on,' he screamed. 'He was here when the water was on and showered. He doesn't give a shit about the crew. I refuse to be treated like this. It's his fucking duty to get us some water while it's still switched on. He thinks work is making calls on the governor and the airport, he didn't go without food in the pouring rain all day, tramping in the shit and watching people die. Even the soldiers down there get buckets of water for their officers.'

It wasn't just the water problem. Our nerves had been frayed by the vague and constant threat of danger that hung over us while we worked, and the unrelieved suffering we witnessed. The dripping heat of the February rains, combined with the filth and mud and lack of food, added to the mix. Soon, everyone was yelling.

Adrian furiously shouted that he had been out all day. 'It isn't my job to fetch water for the crew.'

This only infuriated Christian more. Bill Yates tried making Christian see reason. 'This isn't Adrian's fault. Christian, you're being unreasonable.' But Chris could barely see him in his rage.

Ahmed Ali kept saying, '*Calme, calme*,' which only served to make Christian turn on him and accuse him too of not organising water.

Keith, who hated all forms of conflict, slunk out the door, while Ivan tried reasoning with them all. 'Chris, just shut up for a minute, you're going to give yourself a stroke.'

Christian couldn't hear. He did look as if he was going to have a stroke, or punch Adrian, and I was at a loss, not knowing how to handle the situation. Eventually I shouted over everyone else, trying to bring Christian to his senses. 'For God's sake, none of us has any water, we're all dirty.'

Ahmed Ali was unable to follow the shouting in English. '*Que disse?*' he asked – what did she say?

Someone tried to tell him, but it came out as: '*Diz que não pôde se lava*' – she says she hasn't been able to wash.

Ahmed glanced at me, picked up the phone, then told me to go downstairs, where the governor's car would be waiting. Confused, I assumed that this was part of the complicated protocol that we had to deal with, and protested. 'This is really not a good time, I am too dirty and we have a problem here, I'll go in the morning.'

Ahmed was adamant, '*É importante.*'

The governor's wife was standing outside her house when I arrived. To my complete embarrassment, she took me to a bathroom where a servant brought in buckets of warm water and a clean towel. There was no way I could politely refuse this luxury, even though I was consumed with guilt about the crew left to queue at the pump for a cold half-wash.

I crept back to the hotel and sheepishly joined the others who were eating in silence behind the hotel screens.

After Zambezia, Maputo felt like entering another world. It no longer seemed war-torn, but merely shabby, as we sat under the tattered awnings at the Scala or Continental cafes, sipping coffee. We had a few days to rest while Adrian and I completed arrangements for ongoing travel and shipped the rushes to England.

In those days, we still shot documentaries on film. It was before the video revolution and all the new technologies. There were no video monitors, no way to look at the material we had shot. Rushes had to be shipped back to the laboratories in England. The best we could hope for was a phone call or telex to let us know that the rushes were fine. But in places with poor communications, not even this was possible.

Each roll of 16 mm film stock ran for only ten minutes and was expensive both to buy and develop. Unlike these days of cheap videotape, we couldn't just shoot anything that seemed interesting or looked nice, nor could we run interviews for hours in the hope that the interviewee would say something interesting. Limited in this way, and with a strict budget, we were forced to work with a certain amount of discipline. Both director and crew needed to know in advance what was important and how to achieve it.

If we had a problem with the camera or with the film stock, we wouldn't know about it for days or sometimes weeks. If the cameraman had not achieved what I wanted, I wouldn't know until I got back to England and into the cutting room. There was no way to do it all again. Both of us had to have a good understanding of what I was trying to achieve and complete trust in each other, especially on long shoots like on this film.

Ivan Strasburg preparing to film, Mozambique **1986**
Production Still

## 2. CORRIDORS OF POWER

Our chartered Cessna circled Beira airport, and the Canadian pilot pointed to a small corrugated-iron building among the hangars.

'That is the best restaurant in Beira. In fact it's the only restaurant. We call it the pilots' club.'

Beira, Mozambique's second city, is built on a mangrove swamp, and it appeared to be sinking into the marsh. Unlike Maputo, which merely seemed run-down, Beira was a city in decay. Apartment blocks and offices that had not been painted in many years crumbled in the tropical humidity. All of them were scorched on the outside, as if a huge fire had raged through the city.

People cooked on wood fires on their tiny balconies, and the fires had blackened the concrete. A stream of women and girls toiled up and down the filthy, unlit stairwells with buckets of water, which they collected from wherever they could. With intermittent electricity, no water supply, and cooking fires and chickens on the balconies, multi-storey buildings had been transformed into African villages, stacked one on top of the other.

A smartly dressed man walked down the rubbish-strewn road between two high-rise blocks. He carried a briefcase in one hand and led a goat by a rope with the other.

Despite the European Economic Community money pouring in to rehabilitate the port and the rail link to Zimbabwe, the city had a general air of hopelessness.

Beira is the nearest seaport to landlocked Zimbabwe. Once, it was considered an exotic holiday resort for Rhodesians. The rail link from Rhodesia had been built a century earlier, costing many lives, and was considered a feat of engineering. It had been in decline since the departure of the Portuguese in 1975. The Rhodesian holidaymakers were long gone, too.

South Africa's policy with Zimbabwe was largely an economic one, attacking rail links with the Mozambican ports and trying to cause maximum disruption. After Zimbabwe became independent in 1980, South Africa saw it as a threat. Roughly at the geographic centre of the region, it was not only the most developed state, but was also the hub of transport links to and from Mozambique. During the war of independence, Rhodesia had become economically dependent on South Africa and now, together with other neighbouring states, it needed to find a way of breaking free of this.

The group of countries bordering South Africa and caught up in the conflict – the Frontline States – had formed their own economic alliance, the Southern African Development Coordination Conference (SADCC). There were three railway lines through Mozambique, and these were seen by the SADCC as alternatives to Durban and other South African ports.

The other two rail links were the Nacala line from Malawi to Nacala on Mozambique's northern coast, and the Limpopo line running close to the South African border and providing a link from Zimbabwe to Maputo. This latter should have been a better option than the Beira line as it had no steep inclines, but its proximity to South Africa made it vulnerable to attacks by Renamo units moving freely across the border.

The line known as the Beira corridor consisted of a road, a railway and an oil pipeline running from Mutare in Zimbabwe through the centre of Mozambique to Beira.

Considerable money and effort were being put into trying to reopen these rail links, while the European Economic

Community was investing in rebuilding the port. The Beira corridor was being rehabilitated by Zimbabwean National Railways, and Zimbabwean troops guarded the Mozambicans and Zimbabweans working on the line.

The road had recently been cleared of mines, and although still under attack, we were to be among the first civilians to drive it. To do this, we needed someone who was prepared to risk the drive, and in Zimbabwe I employed Paul and his battered Land Rover.

Paul worked in film transport. He had been a soldier in the Rhodesian army and always dressed neatly in shorts and trainers without socks. He was brown and fit, with cropped hair. Although I suspected him of spying for Renamo and the South Africans, he was efficient and reliable. As arranged, he was waiting for us at the airstrip in Beira to drive us back to Zimbabwe along the corridor.

A little way out of the crumbling city, near the beach, was the Dom Carlos. It had been the favourite holiday venue for landlocked Rhodesians before the war, and must have appealed to some bizarre fantasy they had of medieval Portugal.

Everything about it was totally unsuited to the climate. The heavy carpets smelled of damp and mildew. Unlit corridors were decorated with suits of armour. In the rooms, four-poster beds were swathed in rotting fabric, and torn strips of curtain billowed from open windows that at least allowed a sea breeze into the musty rooms. The once-grand bathrooms were mostly without water.

Despite the absence of other guests, checking in was interminable. First, we were told there were no rooms, and when we got over that obstacle, prices had to be laboriously worked out – first in meticais and then in dollars. It cost us a total of $62 for the night.

As our pilot had warned, there was no food to be had at the Dom Carlos – or anywhere else in Beira, except for the pilots' club. Paul shook his head. 'No way am I driving out there at night. If we're going to be attacked, then that will be the moment.'

But he was hungry too and finally agreed to risk it. We made our way along the deserted road with some trepidation, and after a short, tense drive arrived at the equally deserted airport. A chink of light led us to the pilots' club. Sitting outside was a taciturn waiter who spoke little Portuguese.

'Can we eat here?' we asked.

'*Sim.*'

'What can we eat?'

'*Porco e arroz*' – pig and rice, he said, and took us to a door that opened magically into another world.

Groups of people were sitting at candle-lit tables with white tablecloths. A woman wearing a black shawl and looking like a gypsy was singing fado, and her mournful folksong was accompanied by two Mozambicans playing guitars. We feasted on mounds of fresh prawns and wine.

In the morning we set off down the corridor, sitting on top of the gear in the open back of the Land Rover, and taking turns to sit in front with Paul. By lunchtime, when we stopped to film at a cotton farm run by Lonrho, we were all dehydrated and badly burned by sun and wind.

The flamboyant Tiny Rowland headed Lonrho, a British mining company. He was known to be both extremely personable and financially astute, and after independence he'd befriended many African politicians.

Lonrho ran the oil pipeline down the Beira corridor and was involved in a number of projects in Mozambique. One of these was to help Frelimo manage its agricultural resources. None of this stopped Rowland from increasing his South African holdings while sanctions against the apartheid government were still in place.

The Lonrho cotton farm was not far from Gorongosa, deep in the Renamo heartland. It was rumoured that Lonrho had an arrangement with Renamo to protect their projects and thus enable the company to continue their operations there. It seems quite likely that the landing strip they used to bring in supplies for the farm was probably also used to bring Renamo supplies from South Africa, but we had no way of proving this.

The farm manager sported a large beer belly and was burned to a deep brown by the sun. He was dressed in the uniform of white farmers in southern Africa: short shorts, veldskoene with long socks, and a battered hat. He was friendly enough and took Ivan up in the crop sprayer to film from the air, but when I asked him how they protected themselves from Renamo attacks, he suddenly became circumspect.

'They leave us alone,' he said rather morosely. 'No, you people can't do an interview. If you want to ask questions you must speak to the office in Maputo. They told me to let you film this farm, but that's all. I'm not saying anything.'

He was, however, quite happy to explain that they believed it was a good thing to pay their labourers in soap rather than cash.

'Doesn't that seem like slavery?' I asked as we walked back to our Land Rover, but he insisted that it was what the workers preferred.

At Gondola, about halfway down the line, Joe Meyers, a Zimbabwean, was waiting for us. He was of mixed race, a stout and friendly man who had worked on the railways for more than twenty years. The crew were tired, complaining about the long hours and having to constantly film in a hurry – which I took to be a criticism of me as director. Exhausted, I couldn't hold back the hot tears that rolled down my cheeks. Our sleep that night was broken by the constant whine of mosquitoes, barking dogs, and gunshots.

In the morning we accompanied Joe on a self-propelled armoured trolley that went up and down the track every morning ahead of the train to make sure there had been no attacks on the line overnight. Several years later, Joe was killed in an attack on the Limpopo line.

Whenever we stopped, Frelimo troops appeared from the bush to investigate why we were there.

'*Bom dia, camarada*, how goes the war?' Adrian called out to three ragged-looking soldiers.

'Well, thank you,' they replied, 'but we haven't eaten for some days.'

One soldier, whose name was Almada, said: 'I have been guarding this part of the line for over three years. I haven't seen my family for two years. I don't know how they are, what's happened to them.'

By contrast, the Zimbabwean troops guarding the line were well fed and properly clothed.

Mutare, on the Zimbabwean side, was another world. The roads were in good repair, the shops had painted hoardings and the choice of food in the supermarket seemed exciting. The guesthouse in the Vumba Mountains where we stayed was cool and peaceful. That night, sitting and looking at the southern sky, the war seemed very far away.

Filming in Zimbabwe had its own frustrations, but for us it was the only country in the region where things seemed to work properly. In Harare we had work to do, phone calls to place, and we had to make the rounds of ministries, embassies and aid agencies to get permissions and visas for the next round of filming. But we stayed in pleasant hotels, went out for dinner with friends, got haircuts, and relaxed.

Matabeleland in the south was in the grip of a drought and the landscape we drove through was brown and dry. The bushes and trees alongside the dirt roads were covered in dust; the leaves were grey and desiccated. We were on our way to film at a cattle ranch that had suffered several mysterious attacks.

Jock Burns's farm was deep in the bush, several hours' drive from Bulawayo. On the way there we saw no other vehicles and, once we turned off the main road, there was not a single person to be seen. The silence and emptiness felt sinister and strange.

A high fence topped with razor wire surrounded the farmhouse. Two bored, armed militiamen sat in the yard. And as Jock moved around his farm, he made sure he had a gun across his shoulder at all times.

Something strange had been happening in Matabeleland, which I believed tied in with the story we were telling about South Africa's war against the frontline states. Farms in Matabeleland had been attacked, and farmers and their workers killed.

When I interviewed cabinet ministers in Harare at the time, I did not think to question their explanations that these attacks were by South African-trained dissidents who were trying to destabilise Zimbabwe. Many other people – people I trusted – corroborated what they said. Few in fact realised what had been going on until much later, when it was already too late, and President Mugabe had already created a one-party state. I had, quite simply, failed to understand the events that I'd witnessed. It was only years later, when the truth about what the government had perpetrated in Matabeleland leaked out, that they fully made sense. At the time, I was eager to believe that countries like Mozambique, Angola and Zimbabwe were inevitably on the right side and South Africa was in the wrong. I should have looked a little deeper. Nothing is ever that clear-cut.

The liberation war in Zimbabwe had been fought by the Zimbabwean African National Union (ZANU), who were mainly Shona people, and the Zimbabwean African People's Union (ZAPU), who were mainly Ndebele. After independence, South Africa played on old rivalries as part of their destabilisation efforts. However, this was not the main story.

During 1983 and 1984, Mugabe deployed a special brigade – the Fifth Brigade – which he had formed to 'deal with dissidents and malcontents' in Matabeleland. Thousands of civilians were murdered, many of them shot in public executions and buried in mass graves or their bodies thrown down mineshafts. Homesteads were destroyed, and the impact on communities was devastating.

The government prevented anyone from entering or leaving Matabeleland. No journalists were allowed near the region. Although stories of the atrocities filtered through from people who managed to flee, it was very hard to get news of events from the area, and hard to judge the truth of these early accounts.

The liberation war had had a purpose, but what the Fifth Brigade did in Matabeleland left an unhealed wound. When we were there in 1986, few people talked about what had really happened in the area. The events of the time became known as Gukurahundi, and they resulted in the smashing of

Nkomo's ZAPU opposition party.

The authorities were not happy for us to film at Beit Bridge, the border post with South Africa. On the research trip, Adrian and I had met with hostile officials who put a number of obstacles in our way. I couldn't understand why they were so suspicious of us when I was making a film that I felt was sympathetic to Zimbabwe. In hindsight, I see how naïve I'd been. In the light of what had gone on in Matabeleland, and the government's suspicion of 'journalists' sniffing around, the hostility seems less than surprising.

We had no sooner arrived at Beit Bridge, than a message came through from Harare. Kenneth Kaunda, the president of Zambia, was only available for an interview on Sunday morning. It was Friday, and there were no flights from Harare on the weekend, so we'd have to go by road. We drove all day through heat that radiated off the car. It felt as if we were breathing fire. The crew were subdued. We didn't talk.

We seemed to drive along forever, on the same stretch of road, past the same brown patch of bush, with the same glaring sun seeming to shrivel us. The crew had an acronym for it: MMBA – more and more of bloody Africa. It was after 10 p.m. when we eventually got to Harare, and I still had to cancel all the arrangements we had made for filming there.

Driving to Zambia the following day, Paul's radiator blew up. As I sat on the side of the road wondering if we'd ever get to Lusaka, Paul came up to me, angry and frustrated, and said out of nowhere: 'You know, whites here, we're not settlers or colonialists, we're Rhodesians.' He paused while I stared at him. 'Or Zimbabweans, or whatever you want to call us.'

I didn't bother replying.

We needed ANC help to cross the border and would never meet up with them now. Miraculously, Paul managed to borrow a truck from a local garage owner for a few days, leaving his broken Land Rover as a deposit. It was after dark when we reached the border, so we were forced to sleep there.

In the morning we raced for Lusaka, stopping at the side of the road to change our clothes before going to State House.

Under the trees in the gardens of State House, Kaunda had his ubiquitous white handkerchief in his hand and rounded off the interview by saying, 'Victory will be certain – in the end.'

I used that as the end of the film.

The Kaunda interview turned out to be the high point of our Zambian filming. After that, everything went downhill. Our press accreditation wasn't ready and so we couldn't film anywhere else in Lusaka. Our permissions to film in the refugee camps hadn't come through either. Ivan, Chris and Keith sat at the hotel pool, while Adrian and I trailed from the office of one petty bureaucrat to another.

Lusaka was where the ANC in exile had their headquarters. At least we didn't need Zambian accreditation to film them, though it was hard to find anyone senior who wasn't 'too busy' for us. In the end, we interviewed both Chris Hani and Oliver Tambo. I had known Tambo since I was a child, and it felt a bit like talking to my father. He peered over his glasses at me mildly as he said, 'No amount of aggression against neighbouring countries is going to save apartheid.'

I had met Chris once before, in 1984, at the Solomon Mahlangu Freedom College, the ANC school in Tanzania. On both occasions, he wore a Cuban-style shirt over light trousers, and was one of those genuinely charismatic people who had a way of drawing people to him, making them feel that they had his full and considered attention. He had an intense intellect and a thoughtful and quiet way of answering questions. He explained briefly that the South African government wanted to hide from its white population what was in fact a civil war. 'The army is involved in Namibia and Angola, and with Renamo in Mozambique, but now for the first time it faces a serious crisis as it is actually involved inside South Africa.'

Our time with him was very short, but we left feeling both reassured and inspired.

Eventually, I extracted a letter from the Ministry of Information that would allow us to get press accreditation, and hurried off to the police to fetch it. The crew had gone to film Mozambican refugee camps at the border, leaving me in Lusaka to deal with the accreditation. The police chief was in a government building with long corridors where Adrian and I had spent long hours sitting around during the previous days. I had expected another frustrating wait, but was shown into the police chief's office, whereupon he instantly arrested me as a South African spy. A fat man, with a leather strap straining over his big chest, he sat behind a large desk. He looked at me smugly.

'How is it possible,' he sneered, 'for one woman to be in charge of four men?'

I tried charming him, but got nowhere. He was unconvinced by my argument that his president had been happy to interview us at State House. In desperation, I phoned the ANC again and they had to send someone to vouch for me. That afternoon, the crew were arrested twice because they were suspected of being South African spies.

I had only just arrived back at the hotel in the late afternoon when Adrian phoned to say that they had run out of petrol somewhere near the border.

Mr Maine had a garage that saw to all the ANC

vehicles. He was good-humoured, and seemed used to dealing with transport crises experienced by the ANC. Years later, I learned that he'd helped hide weapons being smuggled to the ANC into South Africa in overland tour vehicles. In no time at all, he arranged a car, a driver and spare fuel for us, and we set off in the African twilight to rescue the crew. One minute, the sun was still high and hot. Then suddenly it dipped below the trees that cast long shadows on the golden grass. The sky blazed orange, faded to pink and purple, and then the African night closed in. As we drove, I became increasingly anxious until we at last found the turn-off where Adrian was waiting for us. Tiny stalls, lit by lamps and candles, were selling bread and brightly coloured drinks. It looked enchanting, like a medieval market. Some kilometres further on, we found the crew huddled in the dark car at the side of the road. They were cold, and felt terrified.

'There are wild animals here,' they said, 'and bandits could have got us.'

It was 3 a.m. before we got back to Lusaka, just hours before we had to leave for Angola.

## 3. CONFUSÃO

Our plane touched down in Luanda in the dark and, for some bizarre reason, came to a halt some distance from the terminal buildings. To disembark, we had to jump from the doorway into the long grass at the edge of the runway. If I'd had time to think about this, I'd have realised that Angola was going to be a very unusual country.

Two minders from CIAM, the Aníbal de Melo Press Centre, led us to the protocol lounge, where we sat around and waited. The lounge was crowded with tired and desperate Westerners, mostly journalists, who wanted nothing more than to get out of Angola. They gave us new arrivals pitying glances, while their minders and several Angolan soldiers sat riveted by the latest episode of a Brazilian *telenovela* blaring forth from a television. It was said around Luanda that if UNITA had really wanted to win the war, all they needed to do was attack Luanda airport when the *telenovela* was on.

Our Angolan hosts took us directly to the rooftop bar of the hotel, where we soon found ourselves paying for their expensive drinks in US dollars. They ignored us until the *telenovela* finished, at which point they left abruptly and we were able to go to bed.

The Meridien Hotel was a modern tower block on the Marginal near the entrance to the port. It was far too expensive for us, but the restaurant on the top floor had wonderful views over the Marginal, the Ilha and the port. It felt like heaven every time we entered the air-conditioned marble foyer. However, whenever there was a power cut it became a nightmare: lifts didn't work, the windows didn't open, and without air-conditioning the entire building was a sealed box of heat.

Before going to Angola, I hadn't heard of the concept of *confusão*. If, beforehand, I'd read Ryszard Kapuściński account of the Angolan civil war, *Another Day of Life*, I may have been able to make sense of much that happened on my first trip there – the endless arguments, the waiting and feelings of non-existence. *Confusão* means confusion, but in Angola it has its own connotations and implies a much larger disorder than mere confusion.

As it was, we suffered from *confusão* from the moment we arrived until the time we left; only I didn't know what it was I was feeling. I had no idea that *confusão* could become a state of mind, and that we had unwittingly become infected the moment we stepped off that plane. The more we fought it and tried to stick to our schedule, the worse it became.

Nothing had prepared us for the difficulties we were to face in Angola. We'd been on the road, and in the war zone, for many weeks, and we were already physically and mentally exhausted. The weeks in the January and February heat, with insufficient food and water, the hours on bad roads, the endless frustrations and setbacks, the trauma we had witnessed, had all taken their toll.

It was late February when we reached Luanda, and the heat and humidity made any sort of physical exertion a major effort, leaving us soaked in perspiration. It was so debilitating that whenever I entered my room I would collapse on my bed and fall asleep instantly. The combination of a devastating war and the heat in that country was lethal.

Liberation in Angola had not brought fighting to an end. On the contrary, it increased, and the war went on for the next two decades. The war in Angola was unique. Angola's wealth in oil and diamonds made it strategically important to the interests of America and Russia, the major Cold War powers, and the war was fought on a far larger and more conventional scale, and carried on for longer, than anywhere else in the region.

Moscow and Cuba provided funding, training and resources to the new MPLA (Movimento Popular de Libertação de Angola) government in Luanda, while America and its proxy allies in Zaire and South Africa armed and funded UNITA (União Nacional para a Independência Total de Angola). When that support was cut off, they were funded by rightwing organisations in the United States. In the second half of the 1980s, the CIA again openly joined with South Africa in boosting UNITA's military campaign. Pretoria supplied arms, funds and training to UNITA, often using UNITA soldiers for their own war in Namibia.

A month before independence, as celebrations were due to take place, South African troops crossed the Namibian border, moving north towards the Angolan capital of Luanda. UNITA joined the South Africans in their fight. Upon hearing that South Africa had entered Angola, Cuban forces, who had been training the MPLA for some time, sent in an expeditionary force. It was this force that stopped the South Africans reaching Luanda.

The war statistics in Angola are horrifying. The United Nations estimated that Angola lost $30 billion from 1980 to 1988, with more than half a million people dead from the direct or indirect causes of war, and four million people displaced and homeless. The extensive use of landmines helped rank Angola with Afghanistan and Cambodia in the numbers of amputees: a conservative estimate reckons some ninety thousand Angolans were killed or maimed by mines.

Even today, huge areas of the country are still littered with mines. And as recently as 2009, the United Nations Children's Fund ranked Angola as one of the worst places in the world for children to grow up.

In 1986, the Marxist-style regime didn't welcome foreign journalists, and those who did go there were strictly controlled by the Press Centre, run by the Ministry of Information, and had to be accompanied by a minder at all times. We'd had to apply for visas via the Angolan Embassy in London months before we left, and before they would grant them, I'd had to provide a list of exactly where, what and whom I wished to film – which of course was impossible for me to do in a country I'd never visited. This led to many complications later on.

The principal thing we had to learn in Angola was that everything involved a lot of waiting around. This was not only because of the tribulations of a long and ugly war; it had to do with something deep in the Angolan psyche. 'African time', mixed with the bureaucratic remains of Portuguese colonialism, African Marxism, and the propensity towards *confusão*, was a deadly combination.

War and film have certain things in common, as Susan Sontag famously pointed out in her book, *On Photography*. Apart from the shared terminology of 'loading' and 'shooting', and some of the similarities between guns and cameras, there's the interminable waiting for something to happen; the hours of discomfort and boredom made worse by rumours of what might happen; and when things do eventually happen, it is often so instantaneous that it seems incoherent, and so filming is a mess.

The highs and lows often made me feel as if I might be bipolar. One minute I would be in the slough of despondency, unable to get anything done, and then out of nowhere the car would arrive, the interview would happen, or the plane would take off, and I'd be sucked along into the excitement, only to be dropped exhausted into even deeper despair sometime later.

The first morning in Luanda, we waited downstairs at the hotel for hours for someone to come and escort us to the well-equipped Press Centre. Here, Wadigimbi, the director, treated us to a lengthy and comprehensive history of Angola, from colonialism up to and including the present war. This took an especially long time because every sentence had to be translated into English.

Simeo and Mimvu were the two Press Centre minders assigned to us. Simeo was only nineteen; he was friendly and helpful, though he had little authority and seemed unable to organise anything. Mimvu was older and more senior and, I slowly came to realise, never wanted to be outside his own comfort zone in Luanda. He had a remarkable talent for turning the simplest situation into one of deepest *confusão*. Neither Simeo nor Mimvu had the slightest understanding of what filmmaking was, and they treated us like print journalists.

Most days started with a long wait for one of them to come and fetch us, and often ended without us having turned over a foot of film. We would sit with our gear in the foyer of the Meridien, and every so often one or other of the crew would get up.

'I'm going to walk to the Press Centre and find out what's going on,' they would say and stride off.

They rarely managed to go further than a block or two before reappearing, drenched in sweat, and slumping down, muttering, 'Can't, too hot.' Another half-hour would pass in bored silence before we'd start the process again.

While in Angola, we waited so long, and in so many different places, that the crew started timing the periods to see which minder or ministry could break the waiting record. It was never properly explained to us that there was no vehicle assigned to our exclusive use, and we were only vaguely aware that vehicles were in short supply, anyway. Consequently, we never fully understood these frustrating delays.

We were totally in the hands of our minders from the Press Centre, with no freedom to roam around with film equipment. They were unused to Western film crews and the process of documentary-making, as opposed to news-gathering. It was a recipe for misunderstanding, and was demoralising and created a lot of bad feeling between minders and crew.

Our first trip was to Lubango in the south of Angola. During the war, civil flying from Luanda to the provinces was pretty much a hit-and-miss affair. The routine never varied in all the years I went there. No matter where we were flying to, we always had to get up at 4 a.m., without any hope of breakfast, and then proceed to the airport in the pitch dark. Once there, we sat in the protocol lounge for hours on end, with no diversion other than watching the fighter planes leaving and returning.

There was nothing to do there. No bars or restaurants, no shops; the toilets had no water. Once we'd unloaded the boxes of gear into the lounge, the crew would become semi-comatose. They soon learned to ignore the *confusão* that raged around us. The only way to disengage was by pretending it wasn't happening.

It was in those murky pre-dawn hours at Luanda airport that we witnessed the war waking up. I saw the war come to life many times. The MiGs were always the first to be rolled onto the runway, taking off one after the other. After them came the Russian transport Antonovs, and later other aircraft flying off for a day's fighting or to re-equip the front. On days when we were unlucky enough still to be waiting for our flight after three o'clock in the afternoon, we'd see planes returning from the front.

Sometimes a small baggage truck trundled off across the runway, sparking a frisson among us. Is this finally it? we wondered. Too often it seemed that the driver was just taking himself for a ride across the airport to allay his own boredom.

At some point in the morning, we'd be handed boarding cards and begin to believe that one of the civilian aircraft would be going to our destination. There were no announcements or departure boards, just a general feeling that this was our flight.

When somehow we had a sign that the next flight could be ours, we leapt out of our slumped state, grabbed the cases of gear, and chased across the runway towards the lined-up planes, competing with a surge of other people from the main part of the airport. A motley assortment of people raced for the plane, and none of them travelled light. Among them were women wearing capulanas – the brightly-coloured cotton wraps used for everything from carrying babies to clothing – who had hired young boys to run with the crates of beer they were transporting back to the provinces, or sacks of beans or rice.

Sometimes, after a dash with heavy film gear banging against our legs in the energy-sapping humidity, the feeling turned out to have been false, and we staggered back across the tarmac. Or else we were caught up in the crowd as it surged from one plane to another, as the destinations were changed at the last minute – and the sweat dripped down our arms, legs and faces.

Even being lined up on the steps of the aircraft was no guarantee of boarding. I discovered later that apparently valid boarding passes could be bought in the market along with everything else, and so there were always more passengers with boarding passes than seats. Sometimes fisticuffs ensued. The market women pushed to get on first so that they could sit next to the windows, where they could keep an eye on their goods being loaded. They had years of practice at this and we were no match for them. If they saw that their goods were not going to make it onto the flight, they would disembark and try and get someone else's boxes off and theirs on or, failing that, leave and try again another day. We soon learned that one of us had to push ahead fast and get a window seat to watch and make sure our gear was loaded and that it stayed on board.

Some days the flight we were waiting for never left. Sometime after midday it would become obvious that no further flights would leave that day, and so it was futile to wait any longer. We would return to the hotel, lie down, and prepare ourselves to start the whole process again the next day. Most times, we did eventually take off.

And then there was the landing. The aircraft didn't make a gentle descent on approaching a town, but stayed at maximum height until the last minute. Strips of silver foil were dropped to interfere with possible enemy rockets, and then the pilot would dive, spiralling out of the sky in a few nerve-wracking seconds.

After this, we would sit on our boxes and wait for transport.

Lubango is on the *alto plano* – the high plateau – and it is much cooler than Luanda on the coast. When we arrived, the town was war-torn and run-down, the few Portuguese villas on the dusty main street were all in need of repair and paint, but the streets were brilliant with flowering trees. Mud-and-reed huts of refugees lined the road leading to town. It was only four hundred kilometres from the border, so the airfield was full of military aircraft, helicopters, soldiers and trucks. The South Africans had passed through Lubango when they had invaded, and they still frequently bombed the area.

The Grande Hotel Huile was a large, low building, with rooms opening onto a veranda around a central courtyard. It was once a stopover for tourists visiting the game parks that had existed here before the war; the walls in the public areas had faded murals of local animals, and mounted heads of buffalo and buck. Now it was shabby and filthy. The bathrooms had no plugs and the trickle of brown water ran for only a short time each morning, always after we had gone out filming. We partially solved the problem by taking small hard apples and jamming them into the plugholes so that our baths would retain some water for when we returned in the evening.

Our minders clearly disliked being in the provinces, and were determined to do all they could to prevent us getting nearer to the front than the city limits. They hooked up with some local colleagues, and spent as much time as possible drinking and having dinner with us at our expense.

Until I was presented with a huge bill at the Press Centre, I was unaware that we had to pay in US dollars for every meal that we, and anyone with us, ate – no matter how sparse or horrible the food was. That was something else that I learned to expect from the Angolan experience: the enormous bill for 'extras' from the Press Centre, which needed arguing and bargaining over, and was always handed to me as I was leaving for the airport.

Soon after arriving at Lubango, our minders told us to get ready for a trip to Namibe on the coast. Here, they said, we would be filming war damage in the port and the surrounding area. As usual, we had to be ready to leave at 6 a.m. The crew, always professional, sat ready and waiting each day as I raced about the hotel trying to get Simeo and Mimvu out of bed. I felt cross with everyone: with the stupid minders for doing this to me, with Adrian for not helping or arranging it beforehand, and with myself for even wanting to go on with this film.

The road took us past lush green farms, winding through forests and waterfalls, before spiralling dramatically through eighty-seven hairpin bends from the escarpment to the dry plains below, which soon became a rocky desert. It would have been far more spectacular if our vehicle hadn't been so crowded. Apart from the crew of four and I, there were the driver, a soldier, a local minder, and our two minders from Luanda. Ten people and our film gear in one Land Cruiser. Excruciating.

At Namibe we were left waiting in the vehicle in the heat, while the minders disappeared into an official building without telling us where they were going or why. Eventually, we wandered from empty office to empty office trying to find them.

'I feel like I used to when I was a child. My father would tell me to wait in the car while he went into a shop or business to see someone. I would sit there forever, not knowing when he would return or where he was,' Ivan remarked.

When the minders reappeared, Mimvu announced, 'The harbour master is out of town so you can't film the ships that the South Africans have sunk.'

We were all a little confused as this wasn't something

we had planned to film. Then we drove off into the desert, stopping at a bridge over a dry river bed.

'You can film here,' I was told.

'What happened here?' I asked, wondering why anyone imagined I would want to film this perfectly intact bridge.

'This bridge was bombed by the South Africans, but we have rebuilt it,' came the reply.

Five days in Angola, and we had only taken two shots. A very sulky crew squeezed back into the vehicle for the drive back up the bends.

At the bottom of the winding pass we were stopped at a checkpoint. Two soldiers in uniforms I didn't recognise peered into our vehicle. Our FAPLA (Forças Armadas Populares de Libertação de Angola) soldier was less than pleased to see them.

'Who were they?' I asked as we drove off.

'SWAPO guerrillas,' came the reply, referring to the South West Africa People's Organisation, the liberation movement of what is now Namibia.

I would have liked to have spoken to the guerrillas, but it was too late. I hadn't yet learned to be forceful enough with the Angolans.

With hindsight, and trying to see it from the perspective of the Angolans, none of it seems as idiotic as it did at the time. They were totally unused to Western documentary film crews and were genuinely showing us the effects of war in their country. But the fact remains that it simply wasn't interesting film material. Yet they did go to some risk and effort getting us to the front – something that I didn't really appreciate at the time.

Everyone was in a foul mood after the trip to Lubango. Christian demanded, 'Speak to these people about how they are treating us. This is outrageous,' and muttered on about amateurs and bad arrangements. Ivan went off to check his gear, while Adrian became more detached, withdrawing into what felt like a peeved silence. I was made paranoid by my own insecurity, and I felt conflicted about what I wanted to do with this film and what I perceived the crew were pushing me towards. I didn't yet have the courage to do things entirely my way and I was unable to convey my needs to the Angolans. But still, I knew I had to maintain control over what we were doing.

'Tomorrow we're going to the Namibian border, the frontline,' Mimvu announced at dinner.

'In that case,' I said, 'we need more vehicles or fewer people. And if we have to be ready at 6 a.m., so do our vehicles and all of you Angolans.'

'*No problemo*, Mrs Toni,' the minders assured me.

We sloped off to our rooms to see how much water the apples in our bath-plug holes had managed to retain during the day, while Mimvu and Simao entertained local friends at our expense.

Gradually, I was coming to realise that road transport in war zones was dependent on government ministries with few or no vehicles to spare, and the ones that they had were often old and in bad repair. So it was not too big a surprise when, the next day, the extra vehicle we had been promised didn't materialise. However, we were accompanied by an *escorte* of two lorries of well-armed soldiers, one to travel in front, and the other behind us.

It was always a relief to be getting out of a town or city and into the 'real Africa', so despite the discomfort, we drove off in a mood of some excitement. We knew that frustration would soon set in, but at that moment we were happy at least to be going somewhere.

Our Luandan minders, upon whom we were totally dependent to help us forage for food and water, proved useless. Once again, we set off with only the few supplies that we had brought from Luanda and inadequate amounts of drinking water. The narrow tarmac strip of road ran through an endless monotony of low, scrubby bush. It felt as if we weren't moving, with just bush and the road shimmering in the withering heat. If we opened the windows, hot wind and dust blew in; if we kept them closed, we sweltered. Dust stuck to our sweat, turning us a strange brown colour.

I retreated from the heat and discomfort by closing my eyes and going into another space in my head. The drone of the engine faded as I dreamt up menus of what I would cook when I was back home with my children: roast chicken, the skin blackened with herbs and lemon; roast potatoes, fresh vegetables, home-made desserts and salads. In my imagination, I'd wander through our London flat, seeing each item of furniture, the books and pictures, sometimes planning improvements I would make. I relived conversations that I'd had with my children, or made a mental escape to our holiday home in Wales, where I'd walk through the garden and the surrounding green hills.

Hours later, we reached the military base at Cahama, about midway from Lubango to the border. The *Comandante* was young and handsome and we joined him and several officers for a meal of goat stew and rice. My request to film at Cahama was turned down.

'It is still a long way to the border, and we have to get there to film before dark. It is too dangerous to be at the border at night. You can film here tomorrow on our way back, Mrs Toni,' Simeo said.

Somewhere on the road outside Cahama, one of our *escorte* vehicles broke down and we left the soldiers on the side of the road, a dangerous place for them to be. But it did give us a chance to film them close guarding the bush on either side of the road.

Another two hours went by before we stopped at Xangongo. A day there would have given us some good material. The place had all sorts of military activity going on, but again I was deflected.

'No, no, not here,' said Mimvu. 'You can't, we are just getting petrol; we have to get to the border and back before dark. But don't worry, Mrs Toni, because we will be sleeping here tonight and you can film as much as you want in the morning.'

There was no way of persuading our minders to deviate from our programme.

At this stage, the war was very close, and signs of the South African invasion were everywhere. Road signs were full of bullet holes; there were bomb craters everywhere; not a bridge had been left intact, and river crossings were perilous. Blank-faced people stared at us with undisguised hostility. Peculiarly, it didn't occur to me at the time that we must have looked like the South African enemy. Just before dusk we reached Ondjiva, very near the Namibian border.

'Film,' the minders ordered us. 'Quickly, quickly. We have to leave here and get back to Xangongo before dark.'

Film what? I had been here less than a minute and had had no time walk around, talk to anyone, or think. But it was already 5.30 pm and the sun sets at six sharp in that part of Africa.

It didn't seem so at the time, but we managed to film some nice long shots of vehicles negotiating the bombed bridge into the town – the bridge we ourselves had just perilously crossed. We also got some shots of people walking around, as well as a building that the South Africans had inhabited and then shelled, leaving behind traces of their racist graffiti.

Two FAPLA commanders were standing outside a shelled building on the edge of town. I rapidly explained what we were doing, and one of them agreed to be interviewed.

'Previously the population here was about eighty thousand, and they had many things, there was even a hotel here. Now, since the South Africans attacked, there is nothing. Only the sick and elderly are left,' he said.

The town lay just below us, and we were interrupted by gunfire and the sound of shelling. The commanders looked over towards the sound but seemed unperturbed, so we carried on, despite our qualms as to whether we'd get out of there. And then the sun set, a great orange ball in the sky.

Outside one of the ruined houses we met a ragged woman refugee, one of the few who agreed to speak to us. She said, 'Everybody knows the policy of UNITA against the people. Because the people know that when UNITA comes, they kill civilians. They come to rob. They steal everything – that is what they do against the population. And the people know who is defending us.'

It was dark by then, and we still had to drive back to Xangongo. When we got there, our minders again did their disappearing act. We were desperate now for something to eat and drink and a place to sleep. I went to see what was going on and found them in earnest conversation with some soldiers.

'Please, just take us to where we are sleeping, we are all exhausted. We don't care where it is, just take us somewhere,' I pleaded.

'There has been an attack nearby,' Mimvu said. 'The enemy saw us and were shelling the bridge. Didn't you hear it? It is too dangerous to sleep here, we must return to Cahama.' I made a weak protest.

'Don't worry,' he said, 'we will sleep at Cahama and return here to film in the morning.'

Then, all I could do was rage. 'Are you crazy? What are you talking about? It took us all day to get here; it will take us half the night to get back to Cahama, and all morning to get back here again, and then the rest of the day and half the night to get back to Lubango. Do you seriously think that we are going to spend the next few days driving back and forth for nothing? How on earth do you think we can film here tomorrow if we couldn't today?'

Was there really an attack? I wondered. Or were the minders just using the excuse of gunfire to get us away from there? Whatever the truth was, we drove back to Cahama in the dark – a moving target of lights for any South African planes in an otherwise pitch-dark and featureless landscape.

It was late when we arrived back, hungry and exhausted. But there were still lights on at the *Comandante*'s house, loud music, and local women. A party, in fact. The *Comandante's* face dropped when he saw us, but he courteously called for food to be brought. We were presented with a pot containing only the intestines of rancid goat.

Outside, a furious argument was raging between Mimvu, Simeo and the *Comandante*.

'What's going on?' I demanded.

'They say we can't sleep here, we have to go back to Lubango.'

Through Simeo, I addressed the *Comandante* directly, telling him that we had been driving all day and half the night and would go no further.

'Listen,' he said, 'I have been on this godforsaken border for eleven years. Many of my men have not been home in years. Every day I lose more and more of my men. Supplies of all kinds are erratic here and never sufficient. You cannot sleep here; there is a war on. This town is bombed most nights by the South Africans, I cannot take responsibility for foreign journalists here. It is too dangerous.'

'Are you telling me that the South Africans bomb this road every night?' I asked.

'Yes.' He was exasperated.

'Well, in that case, we are not leaving. Driving up the road at night would make us a moving target for their planes. We are staying here. I am responsible for these people and we aren't moving.' I felt sorry for the plight of this handsome and intelligent young man, wasted by the war.

The crew were standing nearby. 'Lie down,' I told them. 'He says we can't sleep here, but we aren't going anywhere tonight. Just lie down right here where we are standing.' All together, we lay down in the dust and refused to move.

Simeo pleaded with me, 'Get up, Mrs Toni, get up at once, you cannot sleep here.'

'We are not going anywhere now, and there is nowhere else. Good night, I am tired.'

Simeo gave a despondent shrug, and when we were alone we moved a little way off from the *Comandante*'s house, where the party was continuing at full pitch. Some of the crew crept into the Land Cruiser; the rest of us made do with the hard, dusty earth, using bits of clothing in a vain attempt to cushion our bodies.

Suddenly a lorry loomed out of the dark and stopped right next to us. Was this a warning of an attack? The driver climbed out and disappeared into the night. In this rainless place, a few large drops of rain incongruously fell from the sky.

Christian went to investigate; maybe the lorry would make a more comfortable sleeping place. He came hurrying back. 'You are not going to believe this, but that lorry is full of mattresses.'

It was one of those inexplicable things that happened in Angola. We each took a mattress and settled down under the stars – and the South Africans didn't bomb that night.

At dawn, the lorry driver arrived, woke us, picked up the mattresses and drove away.

In the early light of day, we again drove to Xangongo. Filming was difficult and unsatisfactory. It was almost impossible to do anything with the travelling circus of minders and soldiers, and every detail was argued over. By this time I was in a state of extreme exasperation with everyone. I was especially rude and abrupt with our Angolan minders, sometimes unfairly so – though Mimvu had a way of provoking me. The crew, though, had put up with the most dreadful conditions to achieve a pathetically few shots, and they had never really complained about either the conditions or the long hours.

Apart from the goat and rice, we had eaten nothing for more than twenty-four hours. We had often been hungry during those weeks, and by now we'd become obsessed with food. Driving back to Lubango, we discussed the meal we'd cook when we got home. The menu included all our favourite dishes. The dessert would be the ice cream made with condensed milk that my mother used to make for us children.

From Lubango we hitched a ride on a military flight to Huambo, Angola's second city. Though held by the government it was in UNITA territory, and who exactly the citizens supported was unclear. By the end of the war, Huambo and other central cities such as Kuito Bie had been all but flattened by artillery shells and bombing. But in 1986 the city was still largely intact.

When we arrived in Huambo, our minders were unable to find any of the local officials who were supposed to be waiting for us. It was a familiar story. When the officials were eventually contacted, they presented us with a programme that gave us only half an hour at any one place, most of them places I didn't want to film. Adrian and I became embroiled in a long and acrimonious argument with them about this. It took twenty-four hours to sort out the fiasco and finally be allowed to do some filming.

We were crossing a railway line the next afternoon, on our way to Bomba Alta on the outskirts of Huambo, when I noticed a graveyard of dead railway engines. Alongside the railway line, broken and rusting engines and carriages lay like dead giants, some of them tipped onto their sides. The Portuguese had smashed them up before they left.

'Stop, stop,' I shouted. 'We need to film here.'

'But this isn't on your programme, Mrs Toni,' the minders told me.

'Yes, but I did request filming on the railway line.' I showed them the original request sent from London.

'You didn't specify *this* kilometre of the line,' came the reply. So off we went again, arguing fiercely all the way.

Bomba Alta was a centre for making and fitting artificial limbs, run by the International Red Cross. The new brick building was set in a clean, swept yard and was well equipped with physiotherapy rooms and machine rooms where local people were being taught to make artificial prostheses.

There were appalling numbers of amputees in Angola.

Everyone involved in the fighting made extensive use of landmines. It has been estimated that more than one landmine was planted for every Angolan man, woman and child. Landmines seldom kill but they do maim, usually blowing off feet and legs. Frequently, the victims were women and children who worked in the fields. Over the years, we saw and filmed so many amputees that I was haunted by dreams of an endless stream of limbless men, women and children.

Bomba Alta was clean and well organised, virtually the only place we filmed in Angola where people were not only pleased to see us, but genuinely co-operative in helping us to film whatever we wanted to. We filmed amputees at various stages of learning to walk again, learning to balance, playing ball games. We filmed the prostheses being made and painted. We were about to interview the director when Mimvu, who had been looking bored and impatient all afternoon, suddenly called out, 'No interviews, they're not on the programme.'

I lost my temper and shouted, 'I am not making this film because I like to film victims. We are only here to try and help Angola. If I wasn't personally committed to the liberation struggle I would return to England and show on TV what a load of obstructive incompetents you all are, and that it's not surprising that UNITA gets such good press abroad.'

'Calm down, Mrs Toni, calm down.'

But I wouldn't calm down, to the embarrassment of the crew and staff at Bomba Alta. Later it occurred to me that I must have looked a spectacle, a dishevelled white foreigner shouting rudely and apparently irrationally, in front of all those Bomba Alta people. Nevertheless, what I had said was the truth.

'We are due at the next place on today's schedule,' cried the minders. The problem, however, was that the Press Centre had been set up to handle foreign journalists. Any foreign film crews that had visited up till then had been news crews; they'd never dealt with a western documentary crew. So they went ahead and drew up a list of places for us to visit each day, places they felt best showed what the press might want to see – but without understanding that documentary filming took time and thought, and couldn't just happen the moment we walked into a strange place.

I managed to ignore Mimvu, and for a while longer we continued to try and film, surrounded by an entourage of hangers-on who got into shot, crowded us, made a noise and generally irritated the crew.

One of the Bomba Alta doctors said, 'It is very difficult to look at these children. How are they going to live? How are they going to feed themselves?'

In the early hours of the next morning, I was awoken by huge explosions. The hotel shuddered and I leapt out of bed to see what was happening. I looked out of the window just as another blast shook the glass. 'Ivan, let's get out of here.'

'Where do you think you're going to go? You can go out into the street and get bombed there, or you can get back into bed and get bombed here. I'm staying. In the meantime, get away from the windows.'

When the blasts stopped, mosquitoes attacked us, whining around our ears until dawn.

Back in the Luanda heat, everywhere we went in the city, breathing felt like sucking on wet rags, and walking was like wading through damp cotton wool. When we arrived at the hotel I found handfuls of telexes from Maggie, my London secretary, waiting for me. My partner in London was anxious; we were supposed to be filming in Germany in a few weeks' time, would I be ready? Adrian and Keith were leaving, and

Christian would leave us when we got to Harare. My crew was becoming seriously depleted.

We spent our final Sunday with Manuel de Fragata de Morais, whom Christian had met several years earlier while filming in Angola. Manuel lived on the Ilha in a ramshackle house, across the road from the beach. He was overjoyed to see Christian again and treated us like old friends.

Manuel was small and wiry, his black hair was turning grey, and behind his thick glasses his kind eyes were tired. Before joining the MPLA as a student, he had travelled and worked for a time, first in South Africa and then in Europe. Manuel had a ceaseless optimism about the outcome for Angola in particular, and Africa as a whole. He was the first person with whom we could have a frank discussion about Angola and who helped us to make sense of what we had been experiencing, putting it into some sort of sensible context for us.

His small wooden house was painted pink, and he lived there with his wife and two children, Ulienge and Nyala. The house was comfortable, filled with books and set in a small garden with pomegranate trees. The one thing it lacked was running water, which he had to ferry from town in his beaten-up VW Beetle. Angolan lunches start late and go on long into the evening. We drank until curfew, arguing politics in a variety of languages.

Leaving Angola was no easier than arriving. It was fraught with anxiety, the dreadful feeling that we would not be able to leave, that we would be stuck there: the hours waiting in the protocol lounge, the security searches before boarding. Men and women were separated into curtained cubicles to be searched, which was an excellent way for those conducting the searches to confiscate unobtainable goods – such as cassette tapes and foreign currency – on the pretext that it was 'illegal' to take these out of Angola.

The woman who searched me took a bundle of dollars out of my bag, telling me in Portuguese, 'It is illegal to take dollars out of Angola.'

Those dollars were all that remained of our production money. For a while we tussled, me pulling on one end of the bundle and she on the other. I was too hassled at the time to realise that a small bribe would have done the trick.

Luckily, I had spotted a group of young men waiting for our flight who I felt sure were South Africans – MK (Umkhonto we Sizwe) soldiers on their way back to Lusaka from training in Angola. 'ANC, ANC, come and help me!' I shouted, and in an instant two of them appeared in the cubicle and shook their heads at the woman – who immediately returned my money.

On the flight back we felt the tension leave our bodies as Angola receded, and for the rest of the trip we talked with the guerrillas about 'home'.

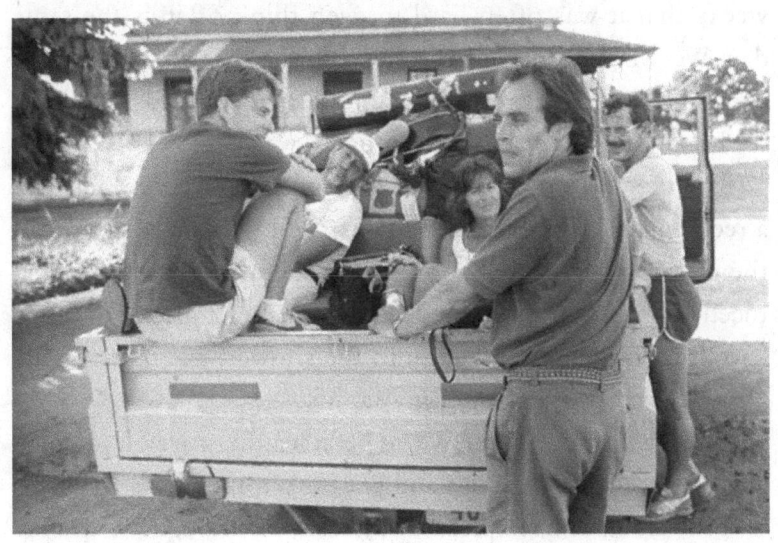

Crew leaving to go down Beira corridor **1986**
*Photograph by:* Ivan Strasburg

## 4. HARARE-MOZAMBIQUE

Every day started and ended so differently over the following weeks that it was often hard to even think of it as the same day. We would wake up in one country or city and end up somewhere else entirely. We met and made friends wherever we happened to be, and moved on.

The crew was down to Ivan and me. The Harare Sheraton, a rectangular tower with windows of gold-coloured glass, had the nickname 'Benson and Hedges', and after the places we'd recently stayed in, it seemed outrageously luxurious. I barely had time to unpack and get into the shower, when the phone rang. It was Arlindo Lopes in Maputo.

'Where are you, Toni? We've been waiting for you to come back for weeks. Get a visa and get onto tomorrow's flight.'

I should have been pleased. Instead, the thought of dealing with embassies in Harare and trying to get seats on the twice-weekly flight to Maputo, left me sitting in a heap of dirty clothes, crying with exhaustion. I was just too tired at that moment and it was no use telling myself that I wanted to do this, that I had chosen to be there.

After an air-conditioned sleep in a clean, comfortable bed, things looked slightly better. So we dashed through a torrential downpour, getting Mozambican visas and seats on that day's flight, and by that afternoon we were in Maputo. Nobody was at the airport to meet us. We hitched a ride into town and checked into the Polana Hotel.

'Things must be getting better,' I said to Ivan. 'There's soap in the bathroom.' At that moment there was a knock on the door. Ivan opened it.

'Excuse me,' said the man standing there, 'I've just moved out of this room and I seem to have left my soap behind.'

We walked to the Ministry of Information and found the waiting room full of journalists and photographers from various countries.

A large man walked over to me and asked if I was Toni Strasburg. 'Well, I'm Tim of ITN news and we are all bloody pleased to see you. The director has kept us sitting here for days, wouldn't give us permission to go out of Maputo until you arrived.'

While we had been in Angola, the footage we'd shot in Zambezia for Oxfam six weeks previously had been playing constantly on British television and had sparked off media interest in what was happening in Mozambique. I had mixed feelings about this, pleased that I'd been responsible for publicising the war, but annoyed that it had taken me four years to raise enough interest in the subject to get funding for this film.

Arlindo put his head round the door. 'Toni, come into my office.' Everyone's eyes followed us as we went through. 'I'd expected you several days ago and had someone waiting for the flights with visas,' he told us. 'I'd arranged for you to go to Ressano Garcia with the army.' Our late arrival had messed everything up. 'Never mind,' he said. 'You can go and do some filming with General Fondu near Inhambane. But this is my problem: I have a number of foreign journalists here and they all want to get to the war. We can't deal with all of them. Please can you take some of them with you? I have kept them waiting a long time.'

'Where are they from?'

'Sweden, Ireland, Denmark, England.'

'I can't take all of them with us. I can't film with all these journalists around me. We wouldn't get anything done.' I had a quick think. 'I'll take the journalist from the *Irish Times*, the photographer from the *Observer* and the ITN crew – but that's it. And I have a problem too: most of my crew have gone home, and I don't have a sound recordist.'

But Arlindo had already arranged Valentin, a sound recordist from the Instituto de Cinema, to work with us, and had set up an interview with the well-known journalist, Carlos Cardosa, that afternoon.

Ivan and Tim, who turned out to be the Harare-based stringer for ITN news, had become instant friends. Tim was tall and fat, but incredibly energetic, with a hilarious sense of humour that made even the most taciturn of officials laugh. He was a generous and fun-loving man with enormous talent, who did everything in excess. Ultimately, drink and drugs would be his downfall, but back then he was a brilliant reporter and huge fun to be around. That afternoon, he generously loaned us the ITN car and helped us make arrangements for the next day's trip.

Another 5.30 a.m. start at Maputo airport. Apart from Tim and his South African cameraman, Sam, we had with us John Reardon, the *Observer* photographer. Once again, there were weight problems loading all the gear onto the Cessna, and most of our personal luggage got dumped. I suggested we also leave behind a large carton, but Tim insisted it had to come along as it contained medical supplies.

By 8 a.m. we had reached Inhambane and were sitting despondently at the hotel as the rain poured down outside. Still, it all seemed so very easy after Angola. We had been briefed on our programme for the next few days without any *confusão* or shouting and arguing. Everything had been done in a quiet and orderly way.

When the rain finally let up, we were able to go and film at the hospital at Maxixe, across the bay from Inhambane. A large and desperate crowd had been waiting for the ferry and, as it arrived, people surged forward, pushing from behind. We almost fell down the steps and I had a moment of panic, expecting to be crushed.

That evening back in Inhambane the hotel dinner was Spartan, and more or less inedible.

Tim said to the waiter, 'What, there is no dessert?'

'No, sir.'

'No ice cream, no profiteroles?' The sad-looking waiters were all suddenly shouting with laughter.

We went upstairs and Tim broke open the box of 'medical supplies': a cornucopia of whisky, tinned tuna, caviar, cheese, crackers and nuts from the diplomatic shop in Maputo.

At dawn the next day we braved the ferry crossing again. By now, the rigours of nearly three months' travelling and filming had begun to take their toll and I had an almost constant migraine.

Tim, ever-generous, tipped some pills into my hand. 'Take one of these and two of those.'

At that stage, I didn't know Tim very well. My memory of the next two days is very hazy. We arrived at a village somewhere in the bush, and were taken to a hut to rest and have lunch. I sat outside and dozed for a while. Later on, we filmed at a re-education centre for captured 'bandits'. I remember little of the village, other than that it looked much like any other village in the area. Back at the huts, we were given buckets of water to wash ourselves and a room to sleep in. I took more of Tim's pills.

Ivan was unable to wake me the next morning, so they left me to interview some *bandidos* who had been captured in the night. Later, I found myself being half-carried onto the ferry and off again before being taken back to the hotel. Eventually, I managed to wake up and wash before having dinner with General Fondu in order to arrange the next day's shoot with the army.

Months later, I found a note in the back of my journal. It said: 'Tone – we've gone to a refugee centre – will only film if we see anything good. In the meantime enjoy your day in bed.'

When I questioned Tim two years later, he explained, 'I said two of those and one of those, not the other way round.'

After a final day filming with Frelimo troops, we waited for a break in the rains so that we could take off for Maputo. Back at the Polana, I ordered kilos of prawns and bottles of champagne, and all our Mozambican friends joined us for a farewell dinner. We opened the first bottle of champagne and, as the cork shot out with a loud bang and hit the chandelier, diners all around the room dived for cover, thinking it was a gunshot.

In the garden of the Polana, palm trees gently rattled in a breeze that wafted coolly through the open windows. On the horizon, the morning star faded as the sky lightened. We stood one more time at Maputo airport, watching the sun rise red out of the sea. The shoot was over.

Boy Mozambique **1988**
*Photograph by:* Keith Bernstein

# PART THREE

## 1988 CHAIN OF TEARS

*The world contemplates the great spectacle of combat and death, which is difficult for it to imagine in the end, because the image of war is not communicable – not by the pen, or the voice, or the camera. War is a reality only to those stuck in its bloody, dreadful, filthy insides!*
Ryszard Kapuściński, *Another Day of Life*, 1987

*What would a child of five normally draw? Playing with balls and flowers, sun, different kind of things that show how she looks at the world and how she feels. But when a child of five draws something like this: a mother crying a long, long chain of tears, this gives you the idea of how our children are really experiencing these horrors of this war.*
Graça Machel, *Chain of Tears*, 1988

# 1. CHILDREN OF WAR

Journal entry: **Maputo, 29 March 1988**

*Mozambique is an emotional see-saw. Just when it all seems hopelessly complicated, it sorts itself out, and then a few hours later you are left up in the air again.*

*What I hate about directing this sort of film is the paperwork; making lists, dealing with all sorts of logistics, bureaucracy, phone calls and discussions. How can I think creatively when dealing with these sorts of problems? I should have a PA, but of course there is not enough money.*

The element that I found most distressing and ugly about war, and that remained with me the longest, was the images of women and children. After *Destructive Engagement,* I planned to make a film concentrating on the devastating effects of war on children's lives, but wanted to do it in a way that allowed the children to speak for themselves.

After completing *Destructive Engagement*, I had taken the film to Maputo and Harare to show it locally. In Maputo, I was told that government soldiers had captured several Renamo bases in the south, freeing a number of child soldiers. There were also other children who had managed to escape from the bases, and the authorities had no clear idea of what to do with these abused and traumatised children.

At first, the children were held at military bases. Later, the Mozambican authorities, together with the international organisation Save the Children, set up a special facility in

Maputo – the Lhanguene Centre. By early 1988, there were thirty-nine former child soldiers staying at the centre.

I read up as much as I could about the effects of war on children but, other than a study from Northern Ireland, I found that little information had emerged since the Second World War. Graça Machel's study for UNICEF on the effects of violence on children had yet to take place.

Most of my previous work had been centred on children. In South Africa I had trained as a nursery school teacher, taking a course on child psychology that emphasised John Bowlby's theory of attachment, which stressed that mothers who are available and responsive to their infants' needs establish in their children a sense of security. In London I had done a degree in Social Sciences, and when my own children started school, I worked on a study of twins for the Medical Research Council in the UK. Later, at the famous Great Ormonde Street Children's Hospital, I researched children with behavioural problems. I felt convinced that this was a subject I was meant to work on, now that I was a filmmaker.

Adrian agreed to work with me again and went out ahead of us to set up the filming, while I struggled to bring in the final money needed for the project. By sheer good luck, I found myself on the same flight to Mozambique as my former boss from Great Ormonde Street Hospital's Psychiatric Department, Dr Naomi Richman. She was on her way to help advise the Mozambican authorities on how best to deal with the many orphaned, separated and traumatised children the war was producing.

The crew travelled with me. For Luke, the cameraman, this was his first big documentary. Luke looked younger than his years and, as a result, I tended to feel protective and maternal towards him. Quiet and gentle, at that stage Luke still lacked confidence. Bob, the sound recordist, was older and more experienced. He was half-Spanish and had brought a set of Portuguese language tapes with him, believing he would easily pick up the language. Almost bald, he was good-natured and amusing. We had all worked together on previous films and felt comfortable with one other. However, neither of them had worked in war zones, and although I warned them about the difficulties of travelling and working in Mozambique and Angola, and the length of the trip, I remained rather doubtful about their ability to last the course. Keith was an old hand, and came with us to do stills again.

By 1988 the war in Mozambique had intensified, with large parts of the countryside inaccessible to government forces. It was hard to know how the people survived or whom they really supported. In a country where so many children had been traumatised by war, there were only a small handful of psychiatrists. It was clearly impossible to provide these children with the sort of counselling that they needed, so the Mozambican authorities had to find another way. They did this by using traditional ceremonies in the villages, which 'cleansed' children from the acts of war and helped to reintegrate them into the community; they also placed these children with extended family or neighbours.

A UNICEF report estimated that one third of Mozambique's children died of malnutrition, starvation or preventable diseases before they reached the age of five. The situation in Angola was even worse, while in South Africa, children as young as seven and eight were being detained and tortured by the police – children who would become known as the 'lost generation'. I wanted my film to look at both the physical and psychological effects of war.

In all these countries, a large proportion of children who

did survive beyond five had witnessed killing, abuse and torture; many had been physically abused or raped themselves. In one UNICEF study, sixty-three per cent of the children surveyed had been abducted from their families.

Naomi and I discussed methods of filming the children. She was concerned about how I would do this without creating even more damage, and was especially worried about a particular group of children on whom we were focusing. She felt that they shouldn't have any further contact with the media. These were the Lhanguene boys, who had already been interviewed by army personnel, doctors and psychologists, as well as just about every journalist who passed through Maputo. The authorities were concerned that the boys were beginning to see their appalling deeds as commendable, and themselves as celebrities.

Within hours of our arrival, a stream of friends came to the house in rua Afonso Henriques to exchange news and gossip. My fiery friend, Carlos Cardosa, was first with the news of ANC houses in Botswana being bombed; Sol came to discuss his latest film idea; South African friends came by to invite me to dinner. Bai Bai was again assigned to join us as camera assistant for the Mozambique part of the shoot. It felt as if I had never left.

Filming kicked off with a football match between a group of street children and boys at the Lhanguene Centre. It was a great success. Reinaldo Mucavele was the director of the Centre. Like many Mozambicans, he looked younger than he probably was. A slightly built, gentle and self-effacing man, he had a very sympathetic manner. With his help, I was able to decide which of the children to focus on and how to film them.

The Centre was in a suburb. The building had the

neglected look that most buildings in Maputo had, and was set in a dusty field that served as a playground. We visited it most days, turning up at odd times whenever we were able to. Soon the children got used to seeing us around and became comfortable with our equipment and our presence. We gave them all a chance to look through the camera and to hear themselves on the recorder, and it wasn't too long before they ignored our presence and just got on with whatever they were doing. Whenever we got back from filming in the provinces, we visited Lhanguene.

The children went to school, played games, and were taught to dance and sing again. On the whole, there was little about the children's behaviour or appearance that seemed different to any group of children in an orphanage, but there were times when some of them displayed obviously disturbed behaviour. Many of them lacked concentration, easily became aggressive, or appeared unable to communicate; sometimes they just didn't want to participate in anything at all. One of the housemothers told me that many of them wet their beds and had terrible nightmares. But most of the time they played and learned and behaved like any other children, and it was hard to even imagine what they had experienced.

One child was so deeply traumatised that he stood out from all the others. His behaviour was painful to watch. He sidled round the building, one shoulder hugging the wall at all times. Always on the periphery, a silent shadow, he never joined in any activities with the other children. This disturbing vision was Franisse, an undersized six-year-old, with a belly enormously swollen by parasites and malnutrition. He had been mute since his arrival at Lhanguene, so it was Reinaldo who told us as much of his gruesome story as they had managed to ascertain.

Franisse had been captured by a group of Renamo soldiers who came to his village one night. They made him set fire to the hut where his parents were sleeping and as his parents ran from the smoke the soldiers killed them. Later, Franisse had been forced to eat some meat that the *bandidos* told him was the flesh of his parents. The people working at Lhanguene despaired of him and thought he might die – and we couldn't help feeling that it might be better if he did.

We filmed the children at different times of day, playing, eating and in class, careful to seem as if we were filming all of them rather than focusing on any one in particular. My crew was small and we worked with the minimum of equipment in an unobtrusive manner. Military Intelligence had assigned a man named Z to debrief the children, and he did the interviews for us. The children were comfortable with Z, who spoke to them gently in their own language, Shangaan.

One of the interviewees was Jose, an eleven-year-old whose face showed no emotion as he whispered his story to Z. But it was clear from his body language that the stories he was telling were of things that no child should know.

'Renamo captured me at night,' he said in a monotone. 'They asked me to show them where my father was and I refused, they cut my fingers and my ear and threatened to cut more if I did not show where he was.' He made a cutting action with his hand. 'Then they took me as a porter.'

His friend, Pedro, had been with him when they were found. Pedro's story was spine-chilling but he told it in an open and pleasant manner.

'They took us to a place and cut our hair like a cross,' indicating with his hand how the hair was cut, 'to show who we were, because we were the captured people. Then we started with the training while waiting for weapons.

'They captured civilians and first they cut off the fingers, then the hands, then the arms. They stabbed them in the neck and opened up their chests. They cut off heads – like this.' He indicated again, making a chopping movement with his hand. 'They put the heads on a pole in the ground, and left them there.'

Z translated the interviews for me and, later, reading through them, I found it hard to conceive how these children would eventually process what had happened to them. What sort of adults might they become?

The Mozambicans, with their few resources, had found ways to help these children, and the gentleness with which they treated them impressed us all. Many years later I learned from studies that had been made that severely traumatised children could and would recover if given the right conditions.

Other than Franisse, it was Fernando who displayed the most obviously disturbed behaviour of the children at Lhanguene. He was aggressive, forever pushing and shoving the other children, and then laughing at what he had done. He was an unattractive boy, large for his twelve years, and with a head that seemed too big for his body. His eyes weren't those of a child, and there was something extremely unsettling about him. He leaned forward with his head down, never lifting his eyes, as he whispered his story to Z.

'I was captured by the bandits at night. They tied me up and started hitting me. Then they said, "Come and show us where the soldiers are." They grabbed me and we walked until we reached their base. They gave us drugs. When I said I didn't want to take the pills, they told me, "If you ever try to escape, we will kill you." They taught me to shoot, and to prove that I had learned the lesson, they ordered me to aim at a person and kill, so I did that. They said, "Another one," and I did it again. We killed a lot of people. Big men always take pills there.

'We went out and killed some others. A bandit called Gomes fired a bazooka when we attacked a convoy, and I aimed at him and shot him dead. I shot the commander and grabbed the bag of witchcraft, so that they wouldn't guess the way I went. Then I ran away.'

Fernando said he had been a *chefe*, a chief. This seemed doubtful – in fact, no one was sure how much of this story was true. But everyone felt that Fernando thought it was real, and that they needed to find a way to help him realise that he wasn't guilty for what he may have done.

The more time we spent at Lhanguene, the more disturbed we were by the children there, and in the evenings debated endlessly their prospects for ever regaining any part of their childhood. Fernando with his evil grin, boasting about killing, and Franisse, forever hugging the wall, observing us from the sidelines, have remained images in my head that refuse to go away.

Once again we were drowsing for interminable hours in the back of a droning Cessna that was being piloted by a Canadian Air Serv pilot. Below us, the entire country was covered in a thick blanket of cloud. We were on our way to Lichinga, the capital of Niassa province in northern Mozambique.

At 4,500 feet, Lichinga felt cool and autumnal after the heat and humidity of the coast. The town was very near to Lake Malawi but it was too unsafe for us to ever go there. There was no one to meet us; maybe we were not expected that day. As we sat and waited at the only hotel in the town, I was already losing any desire to know who was supposed to make arrangements. The hotel had no electricity and the gathering thunderstorm made the dim lounge even darker.

An Angolan-style gloom descended on the crew as we sat sharing a can of tuna and some rolls Bai Bai managed to find in town. Rather unfortunately, the rolls had cockroaches baked into them.

I tried to keep everyone cheerful, but found myself succumbing to the general despondency. I'd always thought that I wouldn't really mind the privations in these places, telling myself that it was only for a few days or a week or two at a time, but still, it always got to me pretty quickly. Even under the best conditions, making documentaries entails endless waiting around for things to happen, alternating with bursts of frenetic activity. In Africa, this is infinitely multiplied. The long hours of waiting enervated and sapped any will to do anything, while the continual changes of plan, promises that didn't materialise, the swings of hope and despair, left me exhausted and angry.

In order to deal with this – especially in countries like Mozambique and Angola where the war determined where we could go, and minders and ministries controlled our filming programme – I tried to tread a fine line between practising a Zen-like patience while at the same time pinpointing the exact moment when I needed to push for what I wanted. It was impossible to get this right all the time. When things did happen, it was often in a rush. From one moment to the next, we'd be caught up in a whirl of activity and sucked into the vortex of trying to capture what was happening on film. Afterwards, we'd be washed up exhausted at the other end, and left to wait some more.

I was feeling a little worried about Luke and Bob. This was their first trip outside Maputo and already they were showing signs of strain; Luke in particular had a fragile look to him.

We had a long shoot ahead and this would be far from the worst of it.

Eventually, the rain cleared, the governor arrived to conduct the necessary protocol, and we were given permission to film virtually whatever we wanted. We spent the last part of the afternoon wandering happily around the streets of Lichinga with the camera, followed by a trail of curious children and a local news crew filming us.

The hotel was a particularly cockroach-ridden place, one of those buildings where you avoided putting your bare feet on the floor. My room was the only one with a bathroom – not that this made much difference without running water. Before dawn each day, I was woken by a soft knock at the door and a bucket of hot water was brought in. Then the decision was whether to get out of my cold bed earlier than necessary and have a warm wash, or wait a bit longer, by which time the water would be cold.

Niassa was sometimes called the 'Siberia of Mozambique', because in the early 1980s Frelimo sent various dissidents and undesirable types there. This was not a popular decision, and it created enormous resentment among the population. It was probably for this reason that Lichinga seemed to have been overcome with a degenerative form of mass ennui. People who came from Maputo, bent on making improvements and galvanising some sort of action, soon found their good intentions draining away.

The wells – the only water supply for many people – were surrounded by mud and lime that leaked into them. Nobody had bothered to build concrete lips or covers for them. To boil our drinking water each morning, we had to go to a children's project run by an English NGO.

Most hospitals outside of Maputo were poorly equipped

and run-down, but usually they were clean, despite the lack of running water. But the one in Lichinga was the filthiest I had ever seen. There were blood smears on the walls, and it stank. There was no good reason for this filth and neglect. On our second day in Lichinga, Bai Bai spent the day in bed with a sore throat. When we came back from filming, he blithely informed me he had taken himself off to the disgusting hospital for an injection of antibiotics. I froze in horror. 'Bai Bai, why didn't you tell me? I would have given you one of the syringes and needles that we have with us.'

We travelled with a pack of needles and syringes in our first aid kit for just this sort of emergency. Now I was consumed with worry that he would have contracted AIDS or hepatitis, but Bai Bai seemed to think it was fine. One early morning, we accompanied an ancient truck piled so high with aid parcels that it took ages to navigate the twenty kilometres from Lichinga to the village of Moussa, where we were going to film the aid distribution.

The countryside we drove through was green and carpeted with pink and white cosmos flowers and orange African marigolds.

Moussa was little more than a camp set up for *deslocados*. Being fairly well established and relatively near to Lichinga, it received a reasonable supply of food, so it was far from the worst place we visited. Most of the people there were gathered under a tree, waiting for the aid to be distributed. This was an efficient procedure. The camp authorities had a list of all the families there, and called them up one at a time to receive their share. Adrian and I left Luke and Bob to film the distribution, while we went off to look around the village.

It is not always the worst things you see that stay with you forever. Sometimes there are small incidents that you don't think of for years – and then there they are again, flooding you with pain and guilt because you know you should have done more at the time.

A young man, reasonably well dressed in a cotton shirt and well-worn trousers, approached us hesitantly. Two tiny children clutched his hands. 'I have just arrived here,' he told Adrian. 'I have nothing to give my little children. Renamo attacked and kidnapped my wife and I am left with my three little children. Please can you give me some food for them?'

He had not yet been registered and so was not yet entitled to any aid. I felt my heart breaking at the sight of the children, but neither Adrian nor I had anything with us other than a packet of cigarettes, which we offered to him. He thanked us with quiet resignation and walked off. His air of resignation left me feeling frustrated at not finding a better way to respond to his need. I tried to hide my tears as I rejoined the crew. Later, I burned with hurt and anger at myself for not finding a way to do more. This sad young man, holding his two ragged and silent children, walking away from me in quiet acceptance, has haunted me ever since.

Mozambique had long been a country of refugees. People lived in the bush, many of them surviving on a diet of leaves. Small groups, close to starvation, arrived in government-held towns. Many had been wandering for weeks; others escaped abduction by the *bandidos*, who used the men to fight and the women as prostitutes and servants.

By end of the 1980s, it was estimated that there were three and a half million *deslocados*, and a further million refugees in neighbouring states. Between 1980 and 1988, 978 rural health clinics, almost half the total number in the country, had been destroyed. During that period, nearly half a million

Mozambican children under the age of five had died of war-related causes. A US State Department report by Robert Gersony in 1988 held Renamo responsible for ninety-five per cent of abuses to civilians during the war. He pointed to what he called 'extremely high levels of abuse': Renamo was well organised and murderous; it put slave labour to work in the fields, raised taxes and indulged in 'systematic forced portering, lootings, burning of villages, abductions, beatings, rape and mutilations' – an orchestrated terror.

Augusto was one of these victims. He was living in Lichinga with Rica, who was caring for him. While he played with some toys we had brought with us, Rica told us his story. 'Augusto is only seven years old,' she said. 'He is not like an ordinary child; as you can see, he is very shy and scared. His parents' village was attacked and he was separated from them, but he escaped with some of the villagers, who looked after him. Sometime later they were attacked again, and Augusto now has nobody. We have adopted him and are trying to give him some sort of security. This little boy carries all his belongings with him, he even sleeps with them under his pillow, and he often talks of revenge.'

In Lichinga, an English NGO was running a play project for children. This gave us a chance to film children doing some of things that children do everywhere. In two thatched huts in a field of long grass, a group of girls skipped and chanted rhymes; some boys pushed an old cart about, while others played football. The star attraction in the field was an old propeller plane that had crashed sometime before – it was always covered with clambering children pretending to fly it. The 'pilot' gave us the thumbs up as we filmed him preparing for 'take-off'.

Good documentary filmmakers make their own luck,

sometimes by sheer doggedness, but also by developing a sixth sense – an instinct for what might work – and the courage to be flexible enough to take advantage of the serendipitous things that happen outside of one's schedule. Frequently, these seem unrelated to what one is supposed to be filming, but they are often the bits that make the difference between an ordinary good film and one that has a bit of magic. One of these times happened in Lichinga.

An older man, more heavily built than most Mozambicans, and smartly dressed in a white cotton shirt and ironed trousers, came up to me while we were filming the children playing.

'Are you English?' he asked.

I said we were and told him what we were doing.

'I am a Malawian, that is why I speak good English.' He went on, 'I am a piano teacher. You have to film Billy, he is my star pupil.'

I was not keen on this idea but he persisted, and in the end I agreed to go and look at the piano in one of the huts. Inside the hut it was almost completely dark with only a shaft of light coming through the doorway. Somewhere in the shadows stood a piano.

'I can't do this,' I told him. 'It is impossible to film in that light.'

'No problem. We will move the piano outside,' he said. I protested again, but he was determined, and in the end it seemed easier to film than resist further. Two men carried the piano into the long grass, while someone went off to find Billy.

Billy was a grave little boy of six, who walked up to the piano carrying his music under his arm. He sat down on a rickety chair without looking at us or saying a word.

'My master plan,' the teacher announced, 'is Johnson's

piano method.' He looked at me expectantly, and when I didn't react he said, 'It is English, you *must* know it.'

He opened the top of the piano and Billy began to play a Scott Joplin ragtime piece. The hammers were damp and didn't return when Billy hit a note, so the teacher had to keep up with the tune, returning the hammers by hand. It was a surreal scene and eventually became one of the most poignant moments in the film we were making.

Nearby was a group of children who had formed a band. They had no instruments, just replicas made out of cardboard and foil. The guitars were all made to look electric and had complicated wires made of coloured wool that needed to be plugged into the correct plugs, which had been drawn on make-believe amplifiers made from cardboard boxes. The saxophone was made from gold foil and had all the correct buttons. Setting up took us as long as it would have if this had been a real band. The amplifiers and microphones needed to be wired and instruments tested. It was all done with the utmost seriousness and gravity. Then they played. One boy hummed into a comb, while the others mimed to their instruments. A small girl in a tank top danced and sang into a paper microphone.

We left Lichinga in yet another downpour to do some work on Adrian's story. Bob complained he was suffering from 'sunburn, worms, mosquitoes and general bad conditions'. Luke didn't complain, but was clearly less than happy. I still found Adrian's ever-polite but cool demeanour, which appeared to emanate disapproval of my directing methods, discomfiting. I never managed to find out what he really thought.

Cuamba was a pleasant town, with avenues of mango trees.

It was on the Nacala railway line and was being rehabilitated by DSL, a British company, represented here by three former SAS soldiers. DSL was partly funded by the mining company Lonrho. They were training a battalion of Mozambicans to guard the line.

Adrian hadn't succeeded in getting permission to film the troops, and so we spent most of the few days in Cuamba sitting around, frustrated. Bob had a cold, and both Adrian and Keith came down with dysentery – which continued to plague Adrian until he got back to London.

From Cuamba we went to film some children in Quelimane. That year, it surprised us. Quelimane had improved since our 1986 visit: Frelimo had secured the town and surrounding area – and the war had moved on. There were a number of aid vehicles driving about and, although still dusty and flyblown, the shop windows were filled with cheap clothing and plastic items. One evening, walking around the town, we found a lively area populated by an Indian community. They were traders and businesspeople who had managed to leave Quelimane when it was under siege, but were now back. Most days, there was running water and electricity at the Hotel Chuabo, and the food was well prepared. However, the owner's bad temper and insane rules had not changed, and we still couldn't wear shorts in the dining room or push two small tables together to make a larger one.

Before returning to Maputo, we spent a day filming in a small town called Morrumbala, which Frelimo had recently retaken after nearly eighteen months in Renamo hands. Morrumbala looked like one of the towns that UNITA and South Africa had destroyed in southern Angola. Not a single building was intact. This was not because of bombing or shelling; Renamo had systematically forced the townspeople to strip all the houses of their corrugated iron roofs, electric cables, wooden doors and window frames. Then they had force-marched them thirty kilometres to Malawi, where the soldiers sold everything. What they didn't take, they totally vandalised. The hospital had nothing but a wrecked operating table lying in a roofless operating theatre.

Every day, *deslocados* were pouring in from the bush, in need of food. We filmed some of the seven hundred orphans who were living in the ruins of the electricity station. One little boy spoke to us in a language I hadn't heard before. His piping voice made him sound like a little bird as he told us a hair-raising story of how his family had been attacked, and of his long journey through the bush with other children. Because of the war, people were still unable to venture to the river to fish. The Italians were paying for food to be airlifted into Morrumbala, using South African pilots. What an irony that seemed.

An old cook, still wearing the remains of a torn white jacket, provided a good lunch of maize porridge and beans for us at the house of an official. 'I have cooked for the Portuguese,' he told us, 'I have cooked for the bandits. Now there is nothing to cook, no oil, no flour, no fish, no *nada*.'

Back in Maputo, on the last leg of the Mozambican part of the shoot, Bob spent a considerable amount of time 'learning Portuguese' – his code for taking a nap. I spent my free time with friends or swimming at the Polana. Everyone was eager to call home and talk to their families. For me, this proved to be a mixed blessing. My younger son had broken up with a long-term girlfriend and was depressed and upset. I felt helplessly far away and unable to give much support. Maggie, our PA in London, was unavailable due to a personal crisis of her own, leaving me with no back-up from there.

To make matters worse, I was given the devastating news from Angola that not only had our trip there been cancelled, but Simon, a filmmaker I knew from Harare, had been allowed to go there and film some of the things that I'd intended to cover. I could feel myself spiralling into depression but knew I had to find a way to salvage the rest of the shoot and complete filming in Maputo. The pain of everything I had witnessed was inside me, but I had to postpone recognising it until the filming was complete. I simply didn't have the time to deal with it then.

A Russian doctor at the Central Hospital allowed us to film him removing a bullet from the back of a ten-year-old girl, Chuma, who had been shot running away from an attack. As he removed the bullet from her spine he handed it to me. It lay in my hand, a perfect, small, bronze bullet. Somehow it seemed to me symbolic of the war we were covering. I kept it in my bag for years and years, until it was finally lost. Perhaps I needed to lose it in order to move on and away from war.

In Maputo we filmed at an art project for children run by the famous artist Malangatana. In the sand, a little girl had traced the outline of a head with eyes that wept tears made of small stones.

All the pictures at an exhibition of children's art that I visited in the city were of war: guns, shooting, helicopters, dying people. In one, a small figure lay dead, while above it, a larger face cried a long stream of tears.

I took some of these drawings to show Graça Machel when I interviewed her soon afterwards. Graça was the widow of Samora Machel, the first president of Mozambique who had died in a mysterious accident when his plane crashed in a remote area of South Africa in October 1986. At that time, she was Mozambique's Minister of Education.

Graça was still in mourning, and though always elegant, she wore black. Her face was drawn, marked by the shock of what had happened to her husband. I had met Graça previously through Mozambican friends, but I still felt slightly in awe of her. Later, we came to know each other far better.

It hadn't been easy to get an interview with her, but she greeted us warmly and showed a clear understanding of what we were trying to do. She expressed anger at the way in which, by and large, the international community ignored the war in Mozambique.

Struck by the tears in the drawings, she said, 'What would a child of five years normally draw? Playing with balls, and flowers, sun, different kinds of things that show how she looks at the world and how she feels. But when a child of five draws something like this: a mother crying a long, long chain of tears, this gives you the idea of how our children are really experiencing the horrors of this war.'

*Chain of Tears* became the title of the film we were making.

Child's drawing of a chain of tears, used for film title **1988**

## 2. ZIMBABWE–TANZANIA

The bar at the Trout Inn in Nyanga, Zimbabwe, was full of the VIPs who had been on our flight from Maputo, when we staggered in with our piles of equipment, travel-worn and weary. The Brigadier and Colonel Jones from the British army were drinking with Jim Allen, the British ambassador.

'Ready for the bang bang tomorrow?' the ambassador asked us cheerfully.

We were in the Eastern Highlands, not far from the Zimbabwean border with Mozambique, amid misty pine forests and trout lakes. The British Army had been training the first battalion of Frelimo troops here. We were there for their passing-out parade in the morning. We had stopped in Harare only long enough to say goodbye to my brother Keith who was returning to London, have lunch at the Sheraton, and pick up our filming accreditations and a rather ancient VW Kombi, before setting off to drive to Nyanga.

It was relaxing driving out of Harare, with the late-afternoon sun turning the roadside grasses pink, and Luke's moans about coming down with flu were easy to ignore. But nothing was ever predictable in Africa. Without warning, the drive to Nyanga turned into one of those depressing African journeys. Along the way, we stopped for a drink, and the van wouldn't start again. By then it was dark and very cold. Arranging two very decrepit taxis to drive us the last 113 kilometres took some time. The taxis were slow and overloaded, and the winding road to the Trout Inn proved too much for one of them, which broke down, leaving the other to ferry us the final ten kilometres in relays.

The Trout Inn was a comfortable old colonial hotel, with log fires, and, for us, the greatest luxury after a month of freezing showers or bucket washes in Mozambique: en suite bathrooms with unlimited hot baths.

Late that night I called home and was given a message that one of my sons had written down for me: 'Tell Toni that she has permission to film in Angola.'

The message threw me into a state of complete disarray and I was unable to sleep. What now? How to arrange all this from up here?

In the morning, things improved. We filmed the Mozambican troops going through their paces at the training camp. As they were loaded onto vehicles to return to their war, they sang haunting songs.

We had lunch in a marquee with all the VIPs and met up with Tim, who was covering the story for ITN. Tim generously suggested we all stay at his house while we were in Harare. I was also introduced to Jeremy Harding, a writer from England who was working on a book about the region. Jeremy was tall and lanky with amazing blue eyes and thick, curly brown hair. He had a way of turning his eyes on you and engaging in deep discussion as if you were the most interesting person he had ever met. I took to Jeremy immediately, finding him stimulating, intelligent and very well read. He was a deeply thoughtful, respectful man – one of the few men I have ever met who had a woman's capacity to discuss emotions and thoughts.

Luke called his cold 'the flu' and took to his bed, while Bob fussed around him like a mother hen. Adrian went off to play golf and I walked in the forest with Jeremy and his friend Margie. She and I enjoyed each other's company and have been close friends ever since that afternoon. Jeremy was interested in what I was doing and we discussed the film, the children we were dealing with, and the planned trip to Angola. By the end of the afternoon I had invited him to join us on the Angolan part of the trip – one of my better decisions.

Tim had not curbed his excesses since we had last met in Mozambique. He kept an open house, supplying us with an unlimited amount of food, drink and entertainment, and composing funny songs about each of us. He lived in a pleasant Harare suburb, in a house big enough to accommodate all of us, with a pool and large garden. All sorts of people drifted in and out, something that began to worry me slightly. Many of the foreign correspondents at that time passed on information to their embassies; it was known as 'brokering', and it disturbed me that Tim was able to go in and out of South Africa so freely. One day, as I was leaving to visit some ANC friends, he asked me where I was going.

'Oh, just to see some old friends.'

'Toni, does G still think I work for MI6?' he asked, indicating that he not only knew where I was going, but also knew who my friends and contacts were – suggesting also that he knew more about them than I did. Or maybe he was just pretending that he did.

On our last evening in Harare, we invited old and new friends to dinner. Simon, Margie and Jeremy were there. Margie was planning a study trip to England and the crew competed with each other with offers of places for her to stay while in England. Simon and I were both interested in filming the effects of war in the frontline region. Two years previously, we had clashed over commissions from Channel Four. Now we started discussing what we were filming, and soon became embroiled in a childish argument.

'Listen, Toni,' Simon said, 'You can have Mozambique, but Angola is mine.'

'Don't be bloody ridiculous, neither of us owns these countries, we can film wherever we like.'

Rivalries like this were fed by the competitive nature of documentary filmmaking. We were all chasing the same money from the same commissioning editors, and at times it left friendships in tatters. Fortunately, though, Simon and I were soon laughing at ourselves.

Adrian left to go to South Africa as a 'tourist', to do some clandestine filming with children who had been detained. Having left as a political refugee on an exit permit, I was banned from South Africa, and so, in case Adrian was unsuccessful, Luke, Bob and I decided to go to Dar es Salaam to film South African children at Mazimbu, the ANC school near Morogoro.

Despite numerous phone calls, telexes to Dar es Salaam, and visits to the Harare ANC office, I had had no confirmation from the ANC in Dar es Salaam before we left Harare. Consequently, there was no sign of ANC immigration at airport arrivals. The Tanzanian immigration officer took one look at me and said, 'I remember you from last time. I didn't let you in then, and I won't let you in now.'

Oh, for heaven's sake, I thought, as my heart sank.

Last time had been four years previously, when I had visited Tanzania to make a film about the ANC school there. The ANC had failed to send their immigration officer to clear me, so I'd spent my first night at the airport, which was then newly built and had beds in a special transit section, complete with showers and running water.

Now, though, the airport was dirty and run-down. The

immigration officer's white uniform was crumpled and grubby and, apart from a wooden desk, his office was bare. The unswept floor was piled high with toppling heaps of entry forms that passengers entering Tanzania had to fill in. What became of these forms, I wondered. Whatever was the point of forms if there was no process of filing them, no filing cabinet to put them in?

We were trying to argue that, as British citizens, we didn't need visas to enter Tanzania, when the ANC immigration comrade arrived, full of apologies. He took up the argument, but the immigration officer kept changing the rules. 'If they are British citizens, then why do they need ANC clearance?'

'Because they are working for the ANC.'

'OK. Well, if they are ANC, why did they just tell me they are British? Anyway, they can't be ANC – look at them, they're all white.'

Realising we'd have to spend the night at the airport, I raced to the transit section. But all the beds had already been taken. There was no longer running water in the toilets. In the past four years, the airport had succumbed to the general dereliction of Dar es Salaam. I went to find Luke and Bob in the snack bar.

'Bob, go and have a peek in the first class lounge,' I suggested. 'They have more comfortable chairs, maybe you can persuade them to let us sleep there.' He was gone for a very long time.

'The bad news,' he said when he eventually reappeared, 'is that they are locking the first class lounge for the night. The good news is that I have been chatting to Apasaria, the Air Tanzania stewardess on duty, and I have a date with her for when we come back through Dar.'

Neither Luke nor I was impressed with this – though we

should have been.

I spread my *capulana* – my sarong – on the none-too-clean marble floor, and spent the night fending off clouds of mosquitoes. A continuous tape of music played all night, featuring especially the group UB40. To this day, I can't bear to listen to their song 'Red, Red Wine'. I couldn't wait for ANC immigration to arrive with the correct papers the following morning.

Dar es Salaam was a bustling port town, and the mix of cultures on that Swahili coast gave it an exotic air. No one moved fast in the heat and humidity; men mostly wore short-sleeved cotton shirts, while the women dressed in brightly coloured *capulanas*. Many of them were Muslim, and wore matching *capulanas* draped over their heads and shoulders.

The drive to Mazimbu took us over roads so riddled with potholes that vehicles had to manoeuvre slowly around them. The roads were an indication of the general state of decay in Tanzania, a run-down, broken country that shocked the South African students at Mazimbu.

'So many years of independence,' they said, 'and this is all they have managed to achieve.'

The delay in getting to Mazimbu meant we had very little time to film, and had to do everything in a rush once again. Nevertheless, we did interesting interviews with children who – harassed, arrested and tortured in South Africa – had managed to flee across the border and join the ANC.

A day later, we were back in Dar es Salaam. Bob met up with Apasaria from Air Tanzania; she had brought her cousin as chaperone, so Luke chaperoned the cousin.

Landmine victims at Bomba Alta, Angola **1986**
*Photograph by:* Keith Bernstein

# 3. ANGOLA

This time, Angola was going to be different. I knew about *confusão*, I knew what it was like to fly to the provinces, I knew what I wanted to film and had sent them a detailed outline; but more importantly, I had requested that the Press Centre in Luanda assign Katia to me.

A stocky, middle-aged woman, Katia was a naturalised Angolan from Finland who spoke fluent Portuguese and English with a Finnish accent. She had the blonde hair, short, plump stature and slanted eyes typical of many Finns. Katia knew how to stand her ground, and she had no time for the usual shenanigans of the Press Centre minders. More than that, she could deal with Wadigimbi, the director of the Centre, and understood the needs of foreign journalists. Katia never left us sitting for hours without telling us what the delay was. Often, she was able to bypass the waiting entirely. I came to believe that she could even cut through *confusão*.

Watching Katia deal with recalcitrant officials, or any person displaying any form of stupidity, was a great pleasure. Her stubborn manner and way of questioning idiotic decisions nearly always resulted in the discomfiture of the person involved, and success in what we planned to do.

We were sitting at the Press Centre one afternoon when Pascal, a journalist from Reuters, shouted excitedly, 'I knew it! I knew there were Russians in FAPLA.'

'Where are these Russians in FAPLA?' Katia wanted to know. 'There are plenty of Russians here advising us, it is common knowledge, but they are not in our army. They do not wear our uniform.'

'There, down there,' Pascal pointed out of the window. 'Look, there are two Russians in FAPLA fatigues in that Jeep.'

Katia glanced down. 'Don't be ridiculous,' she said. 'Those aren't Russians, they're my sons waiting to take me home. They are Angolans, born here.'

But even with Katia helping us, we didn't manage to get out of the airport without a certain amount of *confusão*. One piece of luggage had not arrived – a box of film stock. Today, with easily obtainable small cassette tapes that slot into lightweight video cameras, it is hard to imagine what a disaster it was to lose a box of film stock in a place like Angola. We immediately arranged for more to be shipped from London.

At the Press Centre the next morning, Katia was in a foul mood: journalists who had arrived before us had commandeered all the vehicles, and this infuriated her. Angola was big news at this time. In the eighteen months since we had last been there, the war had moved to a different level. The battle of Cuito Cuanavale had taken place in the few months before our arrival, but it wasn't entirely over yet. The Press Centre was alive with foreign journalists. Everyone wanted to get to Cuito.

Cuito Cuanavale has been claimed as both a victory and a defeat by all the sides involved. It was the biggest conventional battle that had been fought since World War Two, and it was also part of the beginning of the end for the regime in South Africa.

It was certainly the defining battle of both the civil war in Angola and the South African border war. It set the stage for independence for Namibia and for the first short-lived peace negotiations in Angola. It took place just before the collapse of the USSR, and so was perhaps the last battle of the Cold War.

In it, UNITA was supported by the South African Defence Force (SADF), while the Cuban forces helped FAPLA turn the tide. Although it was not exactly relevant to *Chain of Tears*, I desperately wanted to go to Cuito. The end of the liberation war seemed close, and I wanted to be part of it.

It was late May, and much cooler than when we had been in Angola filming *Destructive Engagement* in February 1986. We could walk around without being overcome by heat, and for the first time I saw shops selling various household goods. There was a cholera epidemic in Angola that year and a yellow powder, some sort of disinfectant, had been sprayed against all the benches and pillars of buildings along the Marginal. Walking around Luanda reminded me of scenes from *Death in Venice*. I wore sandals because of the hot weather, and I was anxious that I'd catch cholera or worse through my toes!

The hotel bathrooms had notices saying: 'Do not drink the water.'

Despite the yellow powder, the streets seemed cleaner than before. And despite the cholera, it all felt better, partly because it was now familiar and partly because I had lower expectations.

In the late afternoon a car materialised, and Katia and I went to the dollar shop, known as the *loja franca*, to buy water for the crew. It was a crazy system: go in with trolley and get supplies, add up the total, and convert into US dollars; leave supplies and go to bank to change the exact amount; queue and hand over voucher for goods; queue again, this time with trolley load of goods; queue again for security check. Collect handbag from front of shop.

After a few days in Luanda we flew to Kuito Bie on the central plateau, about seven hundred kilometres northwest of Cuito Cuanavale and not far from Huambo. Kuito was once known as Silvo Porto and had a history of violence going back to the slave trade. More recently it had seen terrible fighting.

As always, we were told to be ready to go to the airport at 5.30 a.m.; whether or not a plane would leave for Kuito Bie that day was not clear at the time. But our flight did take off, and Katia had arranged for two vehicles to meet us there. While we sat through the formalities, she gave us a brief rundown of what was going on.

The town square in Kuito had once been imposing, with baroque pink-and-white government buildings on three sides, and a church on the fourth side. Near the town centre was a wide boulevard lined with large villas, their ice cream colours of painted stucco now fading and peeling.

The boulevard had become a street of orphanages – an indication of just how many children this war had affected. Five hundred children lived in these houses, along nearly two blocks. They were organised into age groups: the first house was for the babies, the next house for the next age group, and so on.

'Isn't there a programme to reintegrate children into villages here?' I asked Evangalista Charmarle, who worked for the local authority. 'I have seen this in Mozambique and it is much better for the children.'

'The war has been so disruptive here, that whole villages are destroyed. People disappear, no one really knows where a lot of these children are from,' she replied. 'When we put children into families we quite often find that the older children are used as servants.'

I was not convinced.

At the hospital we met a young woman with her leg encased in plaster from thigh to ankle. While heavily pregnant, she had been badly injured by a landmine, but fortunately she had safely given birth to a little girl.

As we were leaving the ward, she called out to Jeremy, 'You haven't asked my baby's name.'

The baby was called Fracturada – which means fractured.

In the same room, two terrified eyes peered from a tent made of grey army blankets. Inside was a little boy so traumatised that no one in the hospital had yet been able to coax him out. Some soldiers had found him wandering around with a gangrenous foot and brought him to the hospital. So many of these children were orphaned, abandoned, displaced, injured, traumatised, and no one knew who they were or where they were from. Again, I wondered how a country whose children had been so terribly scarred would ever become whole again.

One morning, the waiter produced only dry bread and hot water for breakfast. Katia called all the waiters over and berated them: 'Isn't there a market here?'

'*Sim.*'

'And does it have maize or flour? Bananas, tomatoes?'

'*Sim.*'

'Well, then, why don't you buy maize meal for porridge, and bananas? This is not proper food – you are not under the Portuguese any more, and there are other things to eat at breakfast besides bread and tea.'

After breakfast, Katia went to the market to investigate what was available, and came back with two little figures for me: a man and a woman. They were the saddest carvings I had ever seen, made of soft balsa wood with all the details burned into the wood. The man carried a gun and wore a military cap; the woman carried a hoe on her head. I have kept them in my office ever since to remind me of that terrible war.

In Kuito, I found that the impossible had happened: I had fallen in love with Angola. The provinces seemed like something out of a Gabriel García Márquez novel. I began to like many of the things that had driven me crazy last year. Suddenly, I was enamoured with the FAPLA camouflage, and the Angolan sense of style and elegance. Despite the soldiers' arrogance, one couldn't help admiring them.

No matter how attuned I now felt to Angola, there were still the realities of filmmaking to deal with. Waiting around one day to begin filming, I looked at the crew sitting on the boxes of gear and noticed how completely exhausted they had become. Adrian had been unwell on and off for weeks, and looked strained and even more distant; Luke had succumbed to everything going, and looked pale and listless. It was hard for me to distance myself from my own drive to tell the story of the children, so I wasn't always fully aware of how the crew were holding up. But looking at them then, I worried about how they would deal with the rest of the time in Angola.

Back in Luanda, we were told that the authorities would be taking some foreign journalists to the frontline. This was the first time in many years that they had allowed this. We had to prepare for Cuito Cuanavale, where there were still pockets of fighting in the battle that had raged since January that year.

With Katia and Mimvu as minders, a group of us were to be flown to the front. We would be travelling in a group that included Pascal from Reuters, well-known Italian journalist Augusta, a Swede, and some members of a Brazilian crew who were making a film about music in Angola I gave my crew the option not to come if they didn't want to: it was not strictly in their remit to attend a battlefield. They all agreed to come, though I sensed that both Luke and Bob would have been happy if the trip was cancelled.

I wrote a note in my journal to my family if, for any reason, I didn't come back, I wanted them to know that there were few wars I was prepared to die in, but because this one was part of our own struggle, it would be all right. And that I loved them.

## 4. THE END OF THE EARTH

We were going to the End of the Earth. It was before dawn, and once again we were at Luanda airport. Everyone was wearing a small piece of combat chic – a khaki shirt or a photographer's jacket – except for the Brazilians, who were dressed as if for a day at the beach in headbands and flip-flops.

This time was different to other mornings when we'd waited at Luanda airport. We didn't have to watch the war waking up. We ourselves were off to the front, and we boarded one of the first Antonov transport planes to leave.

We flew over the endless nothingness of Angola, and finally we were there. Or somewhere. Although this looked like the front to us, it wasn't quite the front. We weren't sure when we were going to get there; it could be soon, or tomorrow, but it wasn't right now.

At Menongue, some way from the front, we were left to wait on the airstrip, sitting on our gear in the shade of the Antonov's wing. A constant haze of aviation fuel hung over the landing strip. It was both exciting and boring as we watched Cuban troops loading planes and flying off to the battlefield; MiGs, helicopters and transporters all showered anti-missile devices as they climbed. It all looked very professional and serious.

I could feel déja vu setting in as we entered a period of *confusão*. The helicopter was supposed to be leaving in fifteen minutes. Only it wasn't ready yet. Mimvu wanted breakfast and was trying to manoeuvre us into town for a 'briefing' at the Command HQ where he believed there would be food.

We wanted to get to the front; it was after 11 a.m., and we all felt more than usually impatient with this time-wasting exercise. The day was getting old; maybe this was a tactic to keep us from the war?

Mimvu got his way and we were driven into town, where we were ushered into a room at the Portuguese villa serving as Command HQ. A table groaning with every kind of alcohol known to mankind confronted us: bottles of whisky, brandy, gin, vodka, beer, rum. This was hardly what we wanted after the usual pre-dawn start and no breakfast, although Jeremy later claimed there were two tins of nuts there as well. We looked at each other in horror – how to deal with this?

It seemed forever that we sat making small talk, trying not to drink anything. Eventually, we were taken back to the airstrip where we boarded two helicopter gunships and were introduced to Lieutenant-Colonel Ngueto, the *Comandante*. He was a tall, dark man, extremely courteous; he would be flying with us. Ngueto was accompanied by several soldiers, one of whom was a lovely girl with tightly-braided hair. All the journalists instantly fell in love with her. Aware of the attention, she tossed her braids seductively.

We rose up in a haze of heat, skimming the treetops, sometimes grazing the uppermost branches while the soldiers aimed their guns through the open door. Nearer to Cuito, I could just make out huge areas of camouflage nets that hid the many Angolan troops dug in there. They had suffered months of almost continuous heavy bombardment, a visceral sound that shakes the earth, blotting out everything. Many who experience this do not come back sane.

After about forty-five minutes, we landed in the middle of a road. A peasant woman walking by with a basket on her head ignored us, as if it were normal for helicopters to land in the road. We jumped out and the helicopters flew off, their rotors spattering us with a stinging storm of sand and stones.

From there, an open truck and armoured personnel carrier (APC) drove us through this nowhere of shell craters, bombed-out vehicles and the odd group of waving soldiers, to Cuito. Only, there was nothing remaining of Cuito: it had been bombed to rubble. There were empty mud huts, but the town itself was in ruins – there were no civilians other than two small children who stood on a street corner. So, I thought to myself: this is the front.

It was eerily quiet, and hot with the searing, white, still heat of southern Angola. Groups of soldiers stood alert with crackling radios as we walked around what was left of the main street. A bombed-out school, an empty clinic with a few skeletons of hospital beds. It was ironic that this remote outpost in the featureless wilderness of southern Angola – which the Portuguese used to call the 'End of the Earth' – was the place where the history of southern Africa, in the dying years of the twentieth century, had been shaped. I couldn't help feeling slightly disappointed that this silent ruin was the only evidence of the biggest battle.

Many FAPLA brigades were still engaged in the battle and thousands of Cuban fighters, some PLAN (People's Liberation Army of Namibia) fighters, and some MK fighters all took part as well. At least three thousand SADF soldiers were involved, as well as a number from UNITA. It was hard to think of the lives wasted in that desolate place. And in some ways it is still hard to understand what had been defended there, and why.

The journalists crowded round *Comandante* Ngueto, asking questions. We were not news reporters, so did not bother to film this. Instead, I sent Luke and Bob off to get some of the shots I had seen around town.

A little while later I found the two men inside the shell of a house, removing thorns from their socks. Luke had been increasingly hard to motivate for some time now, but today it seemed they were both determined to keep from doing anything at all. I insisted that they start filming, which they did reluctantly.

All the journalists wanted something to happen.

'If this is the front,' one asked, 'then why is it so quiet?'

'Where are the Cubans?' they chorused.

'Have the South Africans really withdrawn the seventy k, as they have agreed?'

'*Que passa?*' What's happening?

Pascal wandered over to where Jeremy and I were standing. 'The *Comandante* is keeping something from us,' he said. 'It is too quiet here. Something is happening, I can feel it.'

They were all willing something to happen.

Ngueto asked if we wanted to visit the bridge. Of course we did. It was the point where the South African forces had been stopped, and it served as the most important symbol of this battle. The Cubans had control of the bridge, but there were still South Africans south of it.

'The South Africans are still around on the other side. Their artillery, G5s, have a long range. We will only have a few minutes there before they get us in their sights. When I say "go", we go. Understood? There will be no time,' Ngueto warned us before we left.

We bumped down the steep road to the river and got out of the vehicles before they turned around, so that they faced back up the way we had come. This broken bridge was the place of defeat or victory.

'You have five minutes before the South Africans start

shelling,' the *Comandante* shouted.

Everyone wanted to talk to the Cuban soldiers they could see on the other side of the bridge, and some groups started picking their way across it. I told my crew to remain on this side: we would be near the vehicles, and our lenses were long enough to film whatever we needed from here.

After a short while, Ngueto clapped his hands. 'Time's up. Back into the vehicles. Now. Hurry, hurry.'

Katia and Augusta were already in the front seats of the truck. We started climbing in, but others were slower or determined to stay longer.

Ngueto ordered everyone into the vehicles once more, as the engines started to rev. People were still scrambling to get into the vehicles as they began to move off. As the APC roared off ahead of us, our truck stopped for a moment so that we could pull up one of the Brazilians who had been running alongside it.

Then 'Whump!', the first G5 landed. The sound reverberated through my body, blotting out the world for a moment. Sand and smoke and shrapnel were flying around me. I saw a crater open up in a great fountain of mud as we lurched forward. Luckily, the marshy ground absorbed much of the impact.

The truck screamed up the sandy slope, jouncing and bouncing. The Brazilians were shouting and camera gear was all over the place. Jeremy was still half-standing, and I almost strangled him with the Palestinian keffir he was wearing as I tried to stop him flying off the open back. With my other hand I caught small bits of camera gear that were flying about.

Then another shell landed. The South Africans were very accurate – it was sheer chance that it wasn't a direct hit. We continued up the road at high speed, stopping only when we were well out of range.

Pascal came running towards us from the APC. 'Are you all right? Is everyone OK?'

Yes, we were – but what about him? He was covered in blood.

'It's only a small shrapnel scratch,' he said. 'I'm fine, but we have some wounded with us.'

I stood up and in the other vehicle I saw a soldier being supported by his comrades. He was bleeding profusely from his side. Two others had less-serious wounds. The APC had taken a hit in the first explosion. We'd been saved by the delay caused by the Brazilian. As our truck was both overcrowded and exposed, the effects could have been much worse. Everyone was subdued.

We roared off to take the wounded to the nearby field hospital and, while they were being attended to, we jumped out into the road to try and collect ourselves. The Brazilians looked pale and shocked. Luke, Bob and Mimvu were also terribly shaken. I wandered off a little way and lit a cigarette, feeling hugely exhilarated by the rush of adrenalin. I was too excited to wonder why this had not frightened me. Jeremy was standing nearby, also lighting up. He was staring ahead, but had a smile on his face.

'What are you grinning at?' I asked.

'The same as you,' he replied.

Many people get off on war in some perverse way. There is nothing like it to make one feel truly alive. This was something I'd felt for a long time, but not acknowledged until now. It is why journalists and photographers follow wars, going from one to the other, unable to settle down when they are at home. And this is why they become crazy or unstable if they don't give it all up before they can no longer settle down into normal society.

The helicopters landed in the road and the wounded were brought back, bandaged and on drips. In silence we got into the helicopter and skimmed over the trees again, faster and faster, while the wounded lay on the floor, one with his life seeming to ebb away. We held their drips all the way back to Luanda.

To the ends of the earth, Angola, **1988**
Production Still

# 5. FALLING APART

Back in Luanda, dead beat and filthy, we tried to collect ourselves. Unable to sleep, I wrote in my diary. I used it on these trips as a way to release the anger and frustration I felt about my crew, myself, and everything else. I felt sad for all of us fighting this beastly war. I hated the South Africans for what they were doing to these countries and I was sad for the boys who were needlessly hit while accompanying us today. They had been wounded while 'showing' the war to a bunch of journalists.

Snapshots from the day raced through my head as I lay in my room at the Meridien. The unnatural stillness of Cuito, the white-hot sky, the Cubans walking across the bridge, the thud as the shells landed, and that poor boy in the *Comandante*'s arms, dripping blood.

Bob and Luke were not happy about having been taken to the front and put in danger. I didn't really blame them, even though I had given them the chance to opt out; they had not expected to come under fire from South African shells. I wondered if perhaps I hadn't made it clear enough that they really didn't have to come, or if I had made them feel obliged in some way. Still, they had made no effort to film anything at all, and that was wrong. We had a story today, a drama before our eyes, and they either couldn't or wouldn't get it.

I realise now that just because I felt personally involved in the war, this was no reason to expect them to feel the same about being in danger. Maybe I had been wrong, but I wouldn't have missed it for anything.

In retrospect, I see that the day in Cuito almost cost me the rest of the film. Everyone was already tired out by the weeks in Mozambique and the amount of time we had been on the road. The shoot had been dogged by illness and, after Cuito, we struggled to film in Luanda as we all fell apart in our own ways. We still had three weeks to go, and a lot to do.

The next day, I was struck down by a severe migraine and had to wake someone in the early hours to take me to a private clinic for treatment. Adrian was very unwell again and I worried about his health; I needed him for this last part of the shoot in Angola and was unsure whether his illness was a reaction to the long haul of this shoot and the stress of the day before at Cuito, or something more serious.

The filming was cancelled while we all recovered, and Luke and Bob walked to the beach on the Ilha to swim. Bob somehow managed to injure his ankle and was now hobbling about. But things weren't totally disastrous. Katia was a pleasure to work with, even though it seemed that she and Mimvu were rivals at the Press Centre. She had set up some good stuff for us to film in Luanda, and UNICEF had arranged a van and driver for us, so we were no longer dependent on the Press Centre for transport. Carlos, our new driver, was from Sao Tome and knew all the problems in Luanda. He was appalled to hear what it cost to eat at the Meridien and arranged for us to eat at a good local restaurant. This was a huge relief. Drivers are key in places like this.

We struggled through the next few days, all of us feeling more or less under the weather. The many minor discomforts of life in Luanda were getting to us. My lighter was broken and Jeremy had run out of matches; neither seemed to be obtainable in Luanda, so we chain-smoked through the days lighting fresh cigarettes off the ends of the previous ones.

We had been puzzled by the shots we heard fired in the

street below the hotel most evenings, so one afternoon Bob went down and chatted with a woman sitting on a bench nearby. He came back with the explanation. Workers from the port smuggled out tins of oil and other commodities as they came off shift. The market women hung around on the benches, waiting to receive these goods. The soldiers knew the game, drove through, fired a few shots to frighten the women, took their cut, and then left.

We were discussing this in the car one day when Carlos explained it further. 'You know that Angola operates on the *kandongo*, the parallel market?' he said. 'Kwanzas are worth nothing, and anyway, people don't get paid many. You need dollars or something else to trade with.

'If you go to Roque Santeiro, the big market, there is nothing that you can't get. All you need is some currency. So if you have a few dollars or a bottle of beer or vodka or some cigarettes, even fruit or cloth, you can use these to trade. They aren't hard to get.'

At the time, the official rate was thirty kwanza to the US dollar, but on the parallel market dollars were worth much more. People who had access to US dollars went to the *loja franca* and bought a few cases of beer. These they could sell at an inflated rate at the market and make many times their original outlay, or they could barter them for other goods. If you knew someone going to the provinces, a case of beer would open up all sorts of possibilities to obtain the fruit, meat and vegetables that were virtually unobtainable in Luanda.

We were due to leave for Huambo again. It would be our last trip to the provinces before going home. I had permission for only three days there and knew that this wouldn't be enough. The first and last day would be taken up with travel and protocol, and we wouldn't have enough time to shoot anything meaningful. I requested an extra day and was refused. Katia took Jeremy aside and explained that it was dangerous for journalists to spend very long in Huambo. UNITA controlled much of the countryside around the city, and no one knew who in the town was UNITA. Also, she said, 'UNITA knows that Toni's film crew is in Angola and they are likely to attack the hotel. Her last film was too influential, you see.'

When Jeremy told me this, I felt worried and depressed. I knew the crew was not up to any further serious risk, and I certainly didn't want to be responsible for an attack on Bomba Alta. But I needed my story.

Jeremy and I discussed it, but I felt that what Katia had said didn't entirely make sense. Lots of journalists went to Huambo, which UNITA attacked all the time, anyway. I was sceptical that UNITA knew that I was in Angola, and in any case, did they really care about the influence of a documentary film? Also, why should Huambo be any more dangerous than Kuito Bie, for example? We decided to speak to Carlos Enriques, a filmmaker friend, but I had trouble getting hold of him.

At 1.30 a.m. Jeremy called my room. 'Carlos is here to speak to you.'

I got dressed and we went to the bar to explain our concerns to him.

He laughed. 'Come on, Toni. I thought you were a filmmaker. What are you afraid of? It's much more likely that Katia hates climbing all the stairs at that horrible Almirante Hotel in Huambo.'

Right, I thought.

Jeremy, Adrian and I sat up far too late with Carlos, discussing what exactly it was that exhausted one so much on these sorts of films.

'Being in war zones is number one,' Jeremy reckoned. We all agreed. 'Trying to communicate and work in a language one doesn't know too well,' I said, 'and the constant need to find the energy to push and drive for what one wants. Also, being bombarded by new people and experiences every day.'

'It is my opinion that all the illnesses your crew are getting are caused by too much war and too much Africa. They are psychosomatic – they are scared,' Carlos said.

Adrian and Jeremy were sceptical, but I tended to agree. 'I just want to go home right now,' I said. 'I know how they feel.'

'Home,' said Carlos. 'Where is that? You've got a good few years before that is possible.' Meaning South Africa, of course.

Bob's leg was still bad so we decided to leave him in Luanda while we went to Huambo. Jeremy kindly agreed that he could manage the sound if Bob would give him a crash course. Jokingly, we insisted that as we were going to Bomba Alta, the centre for artificial prostheses, he must also be one-legged. We spent the evening killing ourselves laughing while Jeremy hopped up and down the corridors of the hotel on one leg, trying to work the Nagra tape recorder. It was probably unkind and definitely stupid, but it was one of the bizarre ways that we relieved the pressure of being exposed to all the sad and bad things in war. Laughing was good for us, and after that evening the crew felt like more of a unit again.

Before leaving for Huambo, I sent furious telexes to Maggie in my London office.

**HOTEL LE PRESIDENTE MERIDIEN LUANDA 30.05.88**
**ATTN MAGGIE COATES – OR ANYONE WHO CARES WHETHER WE STILL EXIST.**
**I'M HERE IN THE MIDDLE OF WAR AND CHOLERA, STRUGGLING TO MAKE A FILM, DO ANY OF YOU CARE? OR HAS ENGLAND CEASED TO EXIST? ANGOLA IS PART OF THE WORLD YOU KNOW.**
**WHY DON'T YOU TELEX ME? I'VE HAD NO RUSHES REPORT, REPLY TO LIST OF QUESTIONS SENT WITH LAST RUSHES, REPLY WHETHER STOCK WAS CANCELLED.**
**BETTER STILL TELEX ME AND PHONE TUES 6PM. PLEASE ASK IVAN TO DO SAME ANYTIME OF NIGHT, TUES.**
**HOW ARE MY CHILDREN? DOES CENTRAL TV STILL EXIST? DOES MY COMPANY HAVE ANY MONEY?**
**ARE ALL THE ACCOUNTS ETC UP TO DATE FOR MY RETURN? IS ALAN SYNCHING UP, VIEWING RUSHES? IS THERE ANYONE THERE AT ALL? WHAT THE HELL IS GOING ON? PLEASE MAKE CONTACT. TONI**

Eventually, I got a reply:

**FOR THE URGENT ATTENTION OF TONI STRASBURG.**
**MANAGED TO STOP SHIPMENT OF STOCK IN PARIS.**
**HAVE TRIED MANY TIMES TO TELEPHONE YOU, NO JOY.**
**RUSHES REPORT FROM LABS EVERYTHING IS OK.**
**NICK IS FINE – PUTTING A BRAVE FACE ON IT.**
**DON'T FEEL TOO LONELY YOU'LL BE BACK SOON. KEEP YOUR HEADS DOWN. LOTS OF LOVE.**

Katia fell ill and the Press Centre assigned Simeo to accompany us. He was still very junior and, unlike Katia, carried no weight. He consistently failed to get anything organised in advance. As expected, we spent the first day waiting; first at Luanda airport for the plane to leave, then at Huambo airport for transport, and then at some hotel where we were temporarily dumped. Simeo wandered off to try and arrange transport and protocol.

A long afternoon of nothingness ensued, which felt as if it would never end. It was 6 p.m. before we ended up at the dreaded Almirante, where we'd stayed before. The smell of sewage and goat meat had not improved since our last stay. Unsurprisingly, there was a power failure, and the policeman who guarded the hotel decided he had to show us he had a job to do – in the pitch dark.

'I need to inspect all these cases, so open them,' he ordered us.

'No,' said the soldier accompanying us. 'They are here with us, you don't have to open them.'

And so they continued to argue until we were eventually taken to our rooms. Weirdly, I found myself in the same room Ivan and I had shared in 1986.

There was an uneasy feeling in Huambo this time round, with notices on all the trees telling local brigades to be extra-vigilant. The place was an agony. Every minute that passed seemed to take an excruciating age. Nothing could push time on. All I could think about was getting through the days and going home. I hated Huambo. I hated it last time and I hated it now.

In the morning, we were ready and waiting with the gear at 8.30. Two hours went by before Simeo informed us that the car was broken, and that someone from protocol had gone to get it repaired. The morning drifted on in a haze of boredom.

We waited inside. We waited outside in the sun, smoking. Finally, someone said to Simeo, 'Let's go and talk to them at protocol.'

'You can't,' he replied. 'They are with the car and I can't get them on the phone.'

At half past twelve we gloomily went upstairs for lunch. The food was disgusting and none of us was really eating. Only the Vietnamese, who were teaching philosophy at the local college, smiled and greeted us. They seemed to think that the food was edible and were clearly not bothered by the fusty smells in this dining room. At the table, I tried to make an effort to resume control over the film.

'Simeo,' I said, 'after lunch we are walking to protocol to demand a car from somewhere. I don't care if it is not from protocol, it can be from Bomba Alta or OMA (the Women's Organisation of Angola), or anywhere. And if we don't get one, then we are going to find a flight back to Luanda in the morning. This trip is a complete waste of time and money. And remember – I'm paying for this trip and I am going to put in a complaint to the Press Centre.'

'You are quite right, Mrs Toni, I think it is better if we do that.' That was his standard reply to everything I said, and it was driving me mad. Still smiling, he went on, 'But Mrs Toni, no one is in the protocol office until 2.30 p.m.'

'Fine, we will start walking at 2.15. We all need the exercise and something to do.'

At 2.15 we were waiting outside the building. So was Lara, a Cuban journalist who had come to Huambo with us. She was as pissed off as we were, but she, at least, was able to stay at the Cuban mission.

Where was Simeo, we asked.

Lara grimaced. 'Oh, it seems he went off to make or receive

a phone call, but he said he would be back by 2.15. '

Adrian and I sat on the dusty kerb in the sun while Jeremy and Luke returned to their interminable game of chess.

'It's war weariness,' Adrian said. 'No one can be bothered even to come and tell us what is going on.' He was probably right. It seemed as if the war in Huambo was not going well and the great victory of Cuito Cuanavale had made little impact here.

Then finally, the handsome soldier from protocol arrived. 'We are unable to get another car,' he told us. 'There are no tyres in Huambo, but the van has been repaired. It will pick you up at eight o'clock tomorrow morning.'

'What about today?' I asked.

He gave a lovely smile. 'Bomba Alta closes at 3 p.m. and it is now after three, so no point.' He was handsome and charming, and indicated that he understood the problem of our not being able to do our work. Somehow, I was won over and placated.

Simeo had still not returned and I hoped that he had been arrested for incompetence, knowing not only that this was not possible but also that there were many others far less competent than he. Lara hurried back to the Cuban mission. I continued sitting outside, writing in my journal and wondering if I could bear to wash my hair in a bucket of cold water. The crew's chess game went on.

We spent the evening in the gloomy bar of the hotel, drinking a bottle of wine that Jeremy had somehow managed to find. We also amused ourselves with silly word games that Jeremy taught us – at least we were laughing once more.

The following day we managed a full day's filming, despite a certain amount of *confusão* to begin with.

While working on *Destructive Engagement*, we had filmed at the hospital in Huambo, and nothing much had changed since. The dark wards were still overcrowded, understaffed, and lacking in many of the basics. We were told that there were nine Angolan doctors working in the area and eighteen Soviets as well as sixteen Cuban doctors. Dr Vladimir was one of the Russian doctors. He had a perpetually worried look.

'It is hard here,' he told us. 'There are constant UNITA attacks and the hospital has little in the way of supplies. We are short of proper analgesics for all the wounded.'

He took us into a ward full of children: limbless, wounded by bullets, feverish, some were being attended to by family members. The wards were bare except for old iron hospital beds; the children lay on stained mattresses; most didn't have sheets – only rough blankets. Dusty light filtered through shutters closed against the sun, and the air smelled sour with sepsis.

'It is very difficult to cure this kind of thing,' Dr Vladimir said. 'There are children who have had their limbs amputated. These people who can do this to women and children are completely heartless. It is very, very sad.'

He took us to see two tiny boys. They were brothers whose mother had been killed in the attack in which they were wounded. The two-year-old was a pretty, trusting child who held Dr Vladimir's hand and looked up at him appealingly as we filmed. The baby was only six months old and had a horrible, festering bullet wound on his tiny leg. As Dr Vladimir and the nurses struggled to change the dressing, the baby screamed, and all the while a woman with withered breasts attempted to nurse him. She seemed to be an aunt of the children, or maybe their grandmother, and was apparently their only surviving relative. The doctors were not sure that this baby would recover, or, if he did, whether he would ever be able to walk. They hoped that the woman would start lactating soon.

'The bullet hit him close to the knee. It's very difficult, there are always germs and pus, and his general state of health is bad because of poor nutrition. He is only a little baby, he lost a lot of blood, and the mother was killed. He can't get the milk and food he needs. His future is uncertain. He is going to be physically handicapped.'

When, later, I put this scene into the film, the commissioning editor from Channel 4 said that it was too disturbing and that I must remove it. I refused.

'War is not just a little bit nasty,' I said. 'Children don't just get a bit wounded. It is *very* nasty and this is what war does to children. People need to know.'

I'm still not sure if I was right.

After the hospital in Huambo, the relative cleanliness and order of Bomba Alta came as a relief, despite the unending flow of amputees. Here, at least, one felt that something positive was happening, and we resumed our filming.

Josefa was a cheerful-looking little girl with a wide smile, despite her missing leg. She was too shy to talk, but was happy to show us how she was learning to skip. She skipped around the room on one leg, with her skirt flying out behind her, while Armando Jamba, the physiotherapist, told us her story.

'Josefa is twelve. Last year this little girl was walking home from school with her sister and niece. When they were about halfway home, this little one, Josefa, stepped on a landmine. It went off, wounding all of them. Josefa lost her leg; the other girls received bad facial injuries. Some men working in the fields came to their aid and took them to hospital.'

Armando sighed as he paused in the story to watch Josefa

practising her skipping.

'As for her future, once Josefa gets her artificial limb, she will go back to school. She is doing well now and will soon be able to go home. Hers is a fairly typical case.' He dealt with cases like this every day, an unceasing parade of legless people.

We then filmed a poignant scene of Josefa in the workshop, watching the technicians working on her new leg. Her little face shone with a touching expectation as she watched the prosthesis being made. It all seemed fairly optimistic, but afterwards I wondered what would happen to Josefa later in life. Would she get new prostheses as she grew taller, or would she end up on crutches? Who would marry a woman without a leg in Angola, where women are expected to do such hard work?

Jeremy and Adrian had found some more wine, and again that evening we sat around playing silly games until late. This kept our minds off the gunfire and explosions that we could hear – it was clearly not a good time for foreign film crews to be in Huambo. The fighting was very close, and though we knew something was going on, we were not told what it was all about.

'Who undresses completely at night?' Luke asked.

We confessed that we all slept half-dressed so that if we did have to run for it in the night, we'd be ready.

Back in Luanda after three days in Huambo, I heard news that UNITA had attacked a place we were supposed to have visited the previous day, but which I had cancelled in order to get to Bomba Alta. Lara told me that while we'd been in Huambo a convoy of trucks bringing food from Benguela on the coast was attacked just outside the town. The trucks were burned and many people were killed, including a Cuban doctor from the hospital. No wonder there was so little food in Huambo, and no wonder we'd felt something big was happening there.

Jeremy was about to return to Zimbabwe, and we were also due to leave in the next few days. But we had one more Sunday to spend on the Ilha with Manuel and his children. Half-asleep in the hammock at his house, I reflected on the weeks that had passed, and couldn't help feeling guilty about pushing everyone so hard.

I discussed this with Jeremy.

'I think that Cuito was the breaking point for all of them,' he slowly said. Then, looking straight at me, he went on, 'Although, I know we both feel that, even with the shelling, it was no more dangerous than many of the other places we've been to, both here and in Mozambique.'

We discussed our mutual obsession with war.

'I reckon nothing makes me feel more alive than danger, and the struggle to get something done. Maybe that psychiatrist in Camden Town was right,' I told him.

The telephone in my hotel room kept ringing, but when I answered there was no one there; sometimes there was a dial tone, sometimes I heard noises being made. This had been going on since we'd returned from Huambo, and now it was freaking me out. I lay there, waiting for UNITA to come and shoot me, yet knowing that it was more likely just some sort of mess with the hotel phone system.

On the morning we were supposed to leave, we were told there was an airline strike. Bob's leg suddenly mended when he heard the news, and he showed enormous energy going from airline office to airline office, trying to get us onto a flight. I telexed Jeremy in Zimbabwe:

LUANDA 08.06.88
IS IT NICE TO BE BACK IN HARARE? OUR FLIGHT WAS CANCELLED, SO WE ARE STUCK FOR AT LEAST ONE MORE DAY. I THOUGHT YOU WOULD LIKE THIS QUOTE FROM CHE GUEVARA:
'WE ARE ALWAYS AGAINST WAR, BUT ONCE WE HAVE FOUGHT IN A WAR, WE CAN'T LIVE WITHOUT IT. WE WANT TO GO BACK TO IT ALL THE TIME.'
DON'T GO BEYOND THE LIMIT, AND KEEP YOUR HEAD DOWN. MUCH LOVE AND THANKS FOR EVERYTHING. TONI

Almost immediately, I received the following reply:

**ATTN TONI STRASBURG ROOM 111**
YES, AND LOOK WHAT HAPPENED TO HIM.
SORRY TO HEAR ABOUT DELAY.
TREMENDOUS SHOW FROM CIAM LEAVING LUANDA.
HOUR LONG SEARCH FOR MIMVU IN MOST OBSCURE PLACES INCLUDING DECREPIT VW FACTORY PRODUCES NO RESULT.
SO MAURICIO DECIDES THE TIME IS RIGHT TO FIX PASSENGER SEAT OF PRESS CENTRE CAR.
BREAKNECK JOURNEY TO AIRPORT INTERRUPTED BY THREE CONVERSATONS WITH STREET GIRLS.
THAT'S LIFE HE SAID.
I THOUGHT LIFE WOULD CERTAINLY COME BETWEEN ME AND THE PLANE BUT BOARDED AS IT WAS CRUISING DOWN RUNWAY. SOME OF THIS IS EXAGGERATED.
LOVE TO YOU ALL, MISS YOU ALL. J

On the ninth of June we left. It was three months since we had arrived in Mozambique. I knew that I would have to find a way to go back eventually, to find out what had happened to all those children.

Bob was in an unusual state of excitement when we landed in Paris in the early morning. As we waited at Charles de Gaulle for our flight to London we discovered why. Apasaria was waiting for him in the departure lounge. They got married a few weeks later.

Soldier holding landmine, Angola **1988**

*Photograph by:* Keith Bernstein

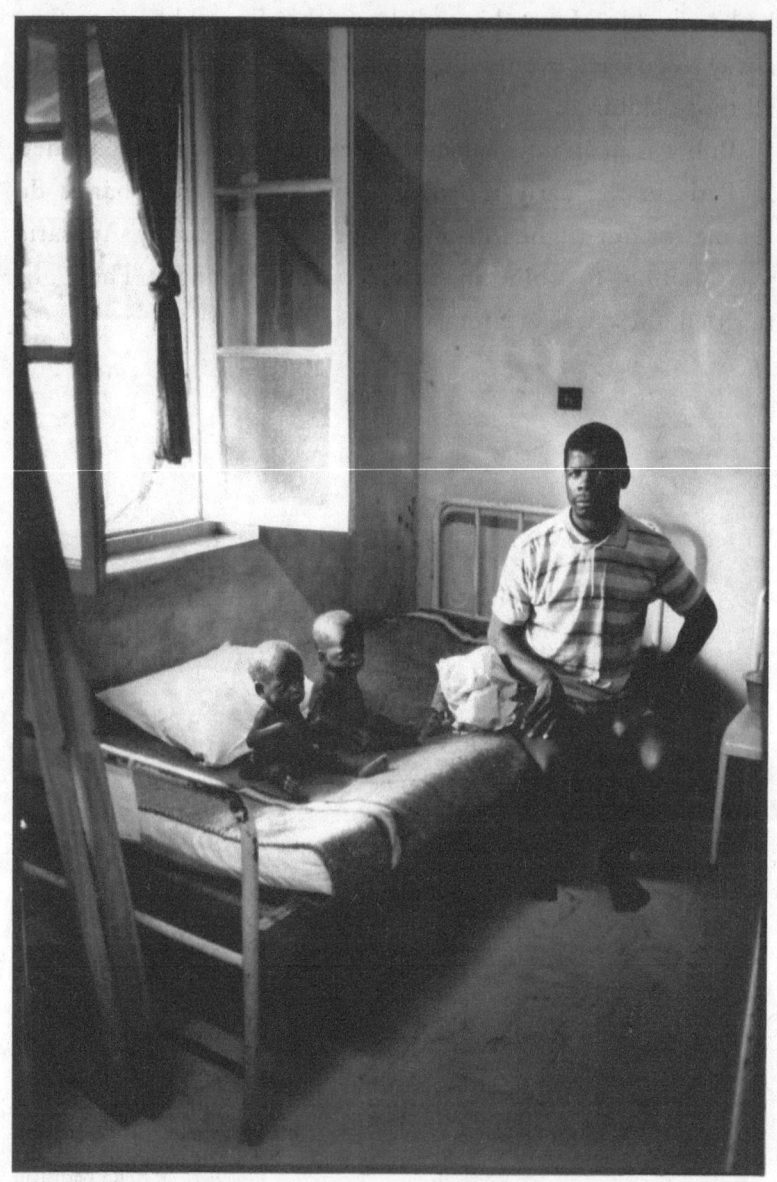

Twins, Quelimane Hospital, Mozambique **1988**
*Photograph by:* Keith Berstein

# PART FOUR

## 1990–1992 MARKING TIME

# 1. NAMIBIA

Jeremy and I were sitting at a dusty table, eating dry little oranges. We had run out of conversation, and the only sound was the angry buzzing of wasps. We were in a mobile home set in treeless gravel at the far end of a tourist campsite at Etosha Pan. This was not the part where tourists stayed.

'I feel like I'm in a scene from a Wim Wenders movie,' Jeremy said as he peeled another orange.

I nodded drowsily. Namibia was a country that lent itself to the surreal. Then I reminded him that the next day we'd be driving north to Oshakati in Ovamboland.

In the two years since we'd filmed *Chain of Tears* in 1988, southern Africa had begun to change radically. The ending of the Cold War meant that the surrogate wars being fought in southern Africa had lost their US and Soviet backers. In Mozambique, attempts were being made to broker peace talks, and the defeat of the South African forces at Cuito Cuanavale had ushered in peace negotiations with the Angolans. The central negotiation issue was UN Security Council Resolution 435, which concerned South Africa's withdrawal from Namibia and that country's independence. A settlement had been signed in New York in December 1988, and Namibia became independent in March 1990.

An event that dramatically affected the entire region was the political unbannings announced by the South African government in February of 1990. The ANC and other liberation organisations could now begin to operate freely, and Nelson Mandela was released after twenty-seven years' imprisonment.

It was still early days and I had not yet tried to get permission to go back to South Africa – but nor could I stay away from the region. In March I was offered a consultancy by TVE (Television Trust for the Environment), a UK charity supported by various UN agencies and other NGOs, which supplied documentaries in developing countries. My brief was to visit six southern African countries, informing broadcasters and local NGOs about TVE and offering films to them. It was a perfect way for me to revisit the region while not being involved in producing a film myself. The work was quickly done, leaving me plenty of time to research future films, see friends and observe the changes.

Jeremy and I had agreed to meet in Namibia and travel together from there. He'd worked with me on *Chain of Tears*, and was now working on a book about the region. After our past experiences in Angola, neither of us relished being in Angola on our own.

Namibia's population was tiny, with only a million people, most of whom lived in Ovamboland in the north. Windhoek, the capital, felt like a toy town: a small, clean city set among brown hills, it appeared to be stuck in a time warp. It was as though the dying days of colonialism had frozen it in an era from which the rest of the world had long moved on.

In those early days of independence it was easy to get an appointment with almost anyone. Jeremy and I had gone to the parliament buildings to arrange some meetings, and within minutes we'd found ourselves with the Deputy Minister for Wildlife and Conservation. We mentioned an interest in anti-poaching, and before we realised what he was doing, he picked up the phone and had a rapid conversation in Afrikaans.

'That was my anti-poaching squad in Etosha,' he said,

turning to us. 'They will take you with them. But you must leave immediately if you want to get to the gates before nightfall.'

We made a few weak noises of protest, but obediently set off on the long drive.

Etosha National Park is part of a vast depression in the north of Namibia that was once a huge lake. Although dry, and in places desert-like, it has abundant game. Nowadays it has luxurious tourist camps, but when we visited in May 1990, the facilities were old-fashioned and run-down. During the war years, SWAPO guerrillas were hunted down in the park, conservation was neglected, and poaching was rife.

We reached the gates just before they closed and were introduced to a bunch of uniformly fit, tanned young men. Dressed in khaki shorts and socks, they were hard-eyed and tough with a focused look to their eyes. I saw them glance pityingly at us – two Londoners dressed in city clothes – but they were polite and said nothing, other than to tell us to be ready at 6 a.m.

Later that evening, as we sat at the camp waterhole watching springbok and elephants come down to drink, Jeremy said, 'They're all probably ex-Koevoet. They hate us, don't they? Do you think they're going to torture us by making us walk for miles in the bush in the blazing heat?'

I did suspect as much – but we needn't have worried. Alan, the young man assigned to us, had indeed done his military service in Angola, but whatever hardened attitudes he may have left the army with, seemed to have softened. He was interesting to talk to and very considerate, taking us to his house for breakfast and explaining the changes in conservation policy since the war had ended. The emphasis now was on game preservation and the prevention of poaching, he told us. They were all pleased with the new policies that were being introduced in the national parks.

We drove with him along part of the perimeter fence, which covered an endless stretch of mopani trees and scrub. There was nothing soft in this landscape. It had a relentlessness to it that hurt the eyes, and the climate was withering. After nine hours' tough driving, we were back in camp, covered in white dust.

At the end of the First World War, South Africa had taken control of the German colony of South-West Africa and run it as a mandate. Then, after the Second World War, South Africa annexed the territory, making it a de facto province of the country. In the early 1960s Britain granted independence to several African colonies, and in countries all over Africa movements arose that fought for independence. SWAPO began its fight in 1966. Things became easier for SWAPO when Angola became independent in 1975, and its guerrilla force, PLAN, was able to operate from southern Angola.

The SADF fought against SWAPO and made direct incursions into Angola from huge bases in Namibia. One of their more notorious battalions in the region was Battalion 32 or Buffalo Battalion – which was known to operate under South African military intelligence, specialising in torture and terror tactics.

The South African Special Forces also ran a police counter-intelligence unit called Koevoet, which was known for its use of brutal and indiscriminate methods of torture. These methods included slashing off victims' ears and stringing them into necklaces, and dragging victims' bodies behind vehicles.

In 1978 the United Nations adopted Resolution 435, which

called for a ceasefire between SWAPO and the SADF. It took another ten years before 435 eventually came into effect. By then, South Africa was severely stretched, both at home and throughout the region, and the Cold War was almost over. UN-supervised elections were held in March 1990, and they resulted in the independence of Namibia under a SWAPO government.

We knew we had reached Ovamboland when the vast, fenced ranches vanished and the bush became even scrubbier than before. The area had been declared a 'homeland' by South Africa in 1968, and it had borne the brunt of the war. It felt as if we were crossing into another country. Until then, the almost-empty road to the northern border had been an excellent, tarred one, built for tactical reasons by the SADF. Now it was filled with the ceaseless traffic of donkeys, goats, cattle and children.

A motley mess of tin shacks and tracks stretched into the scrub. Only those living near the road had access to water. Nearly all of the shacks were *cuca* shops – a combination of general store and bar. Many of them had ironically amusing names like 'Peace Comes Bar', and 'Broadway'.

We drove past recently abandoned South African military camps. Their metal watchtowers stood empty, yet they remained sinister-looking as they protruded above sandbags still piled up around the perimeter fences. It wasn't difficult to see the extent of the South African occupation. The atmosphere of war hung in the air and was reflected in the blank stares of the population, who studiously failed to meet our eyes.

At Oshakati we met up with Penny Hango who had recently returned from sixteen years in exile. A mutual friend had put us in contact with her in Windhoek. She was an attractive and friendly young woman, fluent in a number of languages. Penny had many skills that she'd learned in exile, but she'd not yet found a job back in Namibia. She was happy to accompany us up north as she had relatives there, and wanted to show them her eighteen-month-old baby who had been born in Angola.

As a teenager, Penny had left Ovamboland together with a group of school friends who wanted to make contact with SWAPO. They crossed Angola, making a journey of over a thousand miles to Zambia, walking and hitching rides. SWAPO sent her to school and then to Leipzig in Germany to study agriculture. Afterwards, she had worked on SWAPO farming projects in both Zambia and Angola. Penny was fluent in English, Portuguese, German and Afrikaans, as well as her native Oshivambo, and she appeared to have taken in her stride all the changes she'd had to face.

Through Penny we were able to meet with SWAPO officials and ordinary Ovambos, avoiding some of the hostility and suspicion that was directed at whites – for until recently, whites had been the main enemy, although several of the battalions that fought in Namibia included black soldiers too. Penny's relatives welcomed us into their homes and were keen to tell us what they had suffered under the South African regime.

One afternoon we were taken to a group of cement buildings, far from anywhere, that housed a centre for disabled PLAN fighters. Jeremy wanted to interview some of the ex-combatants. Most of the people there had been injured fighting in Angola – some of them horribly: we met men and women with disfiguring burns, some of the people were blind, and many of them were amputees. They had been dumped there and virtually forgotten, with no jobs, no plans, no programmes for improvement, and little hope. It was here that I was brought face to face with the realities of the aftermath of war.

Though I had spent all those years filming refugees and victims of war and had been so concerned about orphaned and abandoned children and the break-up of families, I had never really considered what happened to all those young freedom fighters after the conflict. I hadn't properly thought about how they would be reintegrated into civilian society, or whether there would be a way to find jobs for them. This was an especially difficult problem for the disabled in countries like Namibia with so few resources.

One of the people we met that afternoon was John, a depressed young man who had lost his sight in a landmine explosion. His wife also had dreadfully disfiguring injuries from burns she'd suffered during a bomb attack on a refugee camp where she had been staying. I found it hard to look at her face. Here, there was no possibility of reconstructive surgery, and little hope of being able to find work.

I was reminded of the many amputees we had filmed or seen wandering the streets in Angola. I had spent so long trying to show the effects of war, but this visit brought home to me the need to start thinking about what happens to people once war has ended.

Ovambo civilians had also suffered under the South Africans, but they had had little acknowledgement from the returning exiles. A UN official told us that he felt many of the people who had stayed behind had suffered far more than the returning exiles. There was much fear and suspicion among both groups, especially of outsiders.

The talk was all of reconciliation, but I wondered if those who had fought for liberation could really forgive their own brothers who had fought on the other side. And how would those who had been tortured, imprisoned and humiliated by the South Africans feel towards the exiles, who in their opinion had enjoyed all sorts of privileges? I began to see that peace was merely a beginning. Dealing with the problems of ex-fighters from both sides – the wounded, the maimed, and the tortured, as well as the returning exiles – was a gargantuan task. And to me, it seemed already to be failing.

One afternoon we found ourselves at a village right on the Angolan border. Beyond the Angolan flag that drooped in the oppressive heat at the border post, I could see bombed-out buildings. Then suddenly, I knew exactly where I was. I was looking at the area just south of Ondjiva – a village we had driven to from Lubango in 1987.

Angolan soldiers stood with civilians and children at the border post. Penny said the civilians were probably farmers who had crossed into Namibia to sell cattle and were now on their way home. As she spoke, Penny pointed to the frontier and said to her baby, 'Angola.'

Jeremy wanted to stay in an 'authentic' African hotel, and chose one that was no more than a corrugated iron shack behind a garage and a *cuca* shop. It was full of cockroaches and mosquitoes; the beds were lumpy, there was no hot water, and dogs barked all night. I sulked, unable to see the point of roughing it when there was no need, but Jeremy, all English boarding school, seemed not to care. After two days with nothing said between us, he suggested that we move to the hotel in Oshakati. A lot of the time in Ovamboland I felt quite redundant. This was Jeremy's story and I was just tagging along.

## 2. ANGOLA (GOING NOWHERE)

Only one other poor soul stepped off the plane with Jeremy and me in Luanda. The Press Centre had sent Tona to meet us.

'Madame Toni,' he said, and we were through and off to the Hotel Turismo – a Russian-run hotel that had a desultory Eastern European air about it. However, it was at least in the centre of town and we could walk to most places we needed.

Tona, an especially stylish Angolan who always wore a black beret at a rakish angle, was more competent than the usual Press Centre minders. The problem for me was that he spoke virtually no English. He and Jeremy conversed in French, which left me dependent on Jeremy for communication.

He took us to see Wadigimbi, the director of the Press Centre, who looked even more weary and jaded than usual.

'What do you have in mind as a programme here?' he wanted to know from us. And in particular, 'What are you doing, Toni?'

This was a good question, and I fumbled and floundered and clearly didn't make much sense in any language. Tona shuffled anxiously and suddenly produced Simeo to translate, and I was able to make myself sound less muddled.

Wadigimbi plainly thought, and correctly so, that doing a consultancy for TVE was not 'real' journalism, so he turned his attention to Jeremy. Although Jeremy's mission sounded much more serious, he too began to sound disjointed and faintly silly.

'What happened in there?' I asked Jeremy once we were outside again.

Jeremy had obviously been thinking about it. 'It's the Wadigimbi effect,' he said. 'I think he wields quite a lot of power, you know, just through the looks he gives you. You know the way he has of holding your eyes for as long as *he* wants to?'

'I reckon he has a private system for deciding whether journalists are worth going to any trouble for, and that it has nothing to do with how they report on the MPLA, but rather something else.'

We didn't know what this 'something else' was, but whatever it was, I felt we had passed the test – me, partly because he had some admiration for my films, and Jeremy, for his broadcasts. But also because we had passed the secret 'Angola test': we'd come back, proving that we could take whatever shit Angola, the war, and the Press Centre threw at us.

As it turned out, Wadigimbi had organised a good programme for us and suggested several things that he thought 'Madame Toni' would be interested in.

That year, there was a peace of sorts in parts of Angola. Yet even though the South Africans had withdrawn, the Cubans had left, and the Soviet Union had collapsed, it still felt very precarious. People had had enough, and I really couldn't see what good would come from this prolonged war between UNITA and the MPLA.

The streets weren't piled up with rubbish as they had been previously; nevertheless, Luanda was still filthy, the roads fatally potholed, the pavements broken, and the water situation dire. Open sewage still ran in the streets and settled into stagnant pools, alive with mosquitoes. Some buildings along the Marginal had been done up, but mostly they were decaying beyond belief; lovely old buildings and houses disintegrated under the tide of teeming families who spilled onto the streets.

The Press Centre no longer seemed interested in keeping a close watch on us. In fact, beyond the programme they had arranged for us, they didn't appear to give a damn about what we did. This left us to our own devices much of the time, free to wander around and make our own contacts.

Jeremy had requested a trip to Benguela, to see the rehabilitation of the rail link to Zambia's copper belt. But in the meantime we were marking time, waiting for the trip to materialise and beginning to wonder if it would indeed take place. I had finished my consultancy work, but had no intention of leaving while there was the possibility of trips outside of Luanda. So I traipsed around with Jeremy, accompanying him on his appointments, or walking to the Ilha to swim in the sea and relax at Manuel's house.

The football World Cup was taking place in Italy, and the Marginal was full of children playing very serious soccer games. In the evenings, while Jeremy watched the matches with the crowds in the hotel bar, I retreated to my room where I could hear the shouts from Brazilian commentators yelling 'GO-O-O-O-AL.'

Osei Kofi was a dashing Ghanian working for UNICEF, who I'd met up with over the years in various parts of southern Africa. At that time, he was the UNICEF information officer in Luanda. One evening at dinner, he gave us his view of life in the city.

'No one,' he said, 'gives a shit for anything except their own survival: "Have I got enough for myself and my family to survive?"'

It explained a lot about the filth and decrepitude of the surroundings and environment, always such a stark contrast with Mozambique. Here people openly despised the MPLA and the blatant corruption; and of course, there was the *kandongo*, the black market. Everything stolen from the port found its way into the big markets.

The biggest was Roque Santeiro, named for a popular Brazilian *telenovela*. The market lay in a slum section full of refugees from the countryside, on the outskirts of the city. We had heard legendary tales of it but had not been allowed to visit it before.

If you stood on the road above the market, it stretched further than the eye could see; a city on its own. And diving into it, you entered a different Angola. In Roque Santeiro you could buy all those daily necessities hard to find elsewhere in Luanda; from small things like toothpaste and shampoo, through *capulanas*, T-shirts, travel bags, CDs from Zaire, right up to fridges, freezers, even trucks. Virtually anything could be had there.

On the morning of our visit, Osei had asked me to look out for Kodak photographic paper for him. I found a huge stack of it and went to his flat after work to tell him about it.

'The bastards! I knew it!' He had ordered the paper from the US, but when he went to the port to fetch it, it was gone. And now, here it was – being sold in the market. This was all unofficially sanctioned, he told us. The harbour master had actually said on TV that every worker should be entitled to 'take' a certain amount from the cargo they unloaded, to sell at the market. The official exchange rate was still 29.6 kwanza to the dollar, but nobody used the official rate: the practical rate was 25,000 kwanza to the dollar.

'Corruption in Angola,' said Osei, 'doesn't work like in a "normal" African country.'

Jeremy and I decided to do some further research into the

relationship between beer and money that we had first learned about during *Chain of Tears*. So one Saturday morning we went the Jumbo supermarket, formerly the dollar shop. People came out of the store with six or ten cases, and sometimes even whole pallets, of beer crates. It was the equivalent of a bank. This was where people came to get the 'currency' they needed to survive.

There were forty-six brands of beer imported into Angola, many of them packaged solely for the Angolan market. Each brand had a value, the most desired one being Heineken. And, as we learned later in Benguela, cold beer was more valuable than warm beer. With a case of cold Heineken you could buy almost anything.

When we finally got there, Benguela was a surprise. The attractive port city had a central square and even a garden with flowers and benches. The colonial-era buildings sparkled with new paint – something I'd not seen in Angola before. We strolled around the town and sat in an open-air café that sold beer and snacks. I was seeing another Angola, one where the war had ended and things generally worked.

Our hotel had also been freshly painted on the outside, and had flowers in the foyer. But sadly, this proved deceptive. The rooms were hung with frayed curtains and the carpets retained ancient odours and stains of all kinds. Despite the bucket of water provided, the problems of non-flushing toilets and no running water made for an indescribable stink that grew during the night.

As I was falling asleep, Jeremy came into my room. 'Do you have any perfume?'

I was baffled, and offered him a small bottle of essential oil.

'I need to sprinkle it in my room,' he said. 'The carpet smells as if a herd of buffalo have vomited on it.'

The next night he came back for the by now nearly empty bottle. 'I didn't sleep a wink last night. The smells in there freaked me out.'

I offered him the spare bed in my room, 'That is, if you can bear the smell of the toilet,' I said.

'Toni, compared to mine, your room smells delightful.'

We lay there and discussed the things in the hotel that bothered us. Jeremy was obsessed with the filth and the odours that collected in the soft furnishings of these hotels, especially the carpets. He was nauseated by the dining room with its fabric-covered pillars, and couldn't eat the food, which filled him with disgust. He said he was revolted by the way the food was served, 'without respect', in a famine region. In places like this hotel, the food we were given was ill-prepared and as often as not dumped in front of us in an off-hand manner. I was not without sympathy, but my problems were different. I couldn't bear being without clean clothes and water. I had had it with freezing bucket-washes in stinking bathrooms and being unable to wash my hair.

Luckily for Jeremy's health, Tona surprised us by taking us to one of the new restaurants that had recently opened in the spirit of free enterprise and glasnost sweeping Angola. We had a passable meal of steak, egg, chips and beer.

Tona was a trained journalist. He was from an MPLA family who had fled from Uige to Zaire, where he had been educated at a Catholic mission station. He'd gone to Cuba for further education, and from there to Europe. At dinner that night, he gave us an impassioned speech about Cuba's sacrifices in Angola.

Then he turned to me. 'What is wrong with the ANC?' he

asked. 'I see them singing and singing, they sing and dance, we in Angola shoot. You can't make a revolution without shooting.'

Well, yes — but I wasn't sure which was the better option just then.

Our aim had been to travel the short distance between Benguela and Lobito at the coast — the only part of the Benguela railway that had been rehabilitated. We walked to the railway station but had somehow missed the 6 a.m. train to Lobito. At seven thirty a train made up of twenty cattle trucks, all packed with people, arrived. Even before it had halted, a mob of people began jumping off: dozens of little boys carrying loads and shouting '*vai, vai, vai*', women with baskets and babies, amputees hopping on crutches — they all surged forward. There was no possibility of boarding, so we left to go back into town where we interviewed Paulo Jorge, the governor of the province, about the famine. He suggested that we visit the local TV station to view some of the news footage from villages where people were starving. He told us that getting food to these outlying areas was difficult, as UNITA attacked food convoys.

In the evening he arranged for us to be taken to a small house at a beach resort just outside Benguela. Jeremy was keen to interview some UNITA 'elements' who had been 'reconstructed'. Four blank-faced men filed into the room to tell their stories. They were very constrained, as if doing what their captors demanded of them.

It felt so uncomfortable that I tried to reassure them by saying, 'We aren't here to make judgements. We understand that there has been much suffering in Angola.'

They nodded, and one of them asked: 'Do you know if this is the only country where such things happen?'

This gave Jeremy a chance to talk about Mozambique and Eritrea, and in the end it was not so bad. All of them had been abducted after UNITA attacks on their villages and had served in UNITA for several years. Unable to put up with the conditions any longer, they had eventually handed themselves over to FAPLA.

I couldn't find a way to properly express to them how I felt about their predicament, and came away feeling sad.

On the way back to our hotel in Benguela, we spotted little fires between rows and rows of trucks that were being loaded. It was a food convoy preparing to leave for Huambo in the early hours. Few convoys got through – it was tremendously dangerous – but in the light of the fires it all looked romantic, like a caravan preparing for an arduous journey. It was enticing and I could see that Jeremy would have given anything to go along with it, although I wasn't so keen; I was afraid of a UNITA attack, and for me there'd be no purpose to the journey, since I wasn't making a film at the time.

On our last Sunday in Angola, we had lunch at Manuel's. He was still optimistic about the future. 'I am convinced there will be peace soon,' he said, 'and Angola will become one of the main countries in Africa, together with South Africa. You will see I am right.'

I was not so sure of this.

'You will go home soon to South Africa,' he told me. 'How can you want to live there in England, when you could have all this?' he gestured at the beach.

Loud music was competing with a TV on full blast while Cameroon played Colombia in the football World Cup. Children scrambled underfoot while the adults sat around drinking and debating politics. Every time Cameroon scored a goal – they eventually beat Colombia – the music was turned to a deafening level and everyone jumped up and danced.

Manuel's other guests were like characters out of a surreal film: a rather camp young man, whose father had been one of the founders of the MPLA, sat with his silent, rather wasted-looking boyfriend; several attractive women from another well-connected family were as neurotic as over-trained whippets. One of the women had a little girl who was deaf, a genetic defect in this interbred clan, Manuel later explained.

Another silent young man sat in a corner; one of the many Angolans traumatised by the war, he looked decidedly disturbed. It turned out he was the younger brother of one of the whippet women, and was partially deaf. He had recently returned from eighteen months on the southern front, where he'd suffered daily bombardment and fighting. His job was to test for mines by walking through the bush with a rod. Inevitably, he'd seen many of his friends blown up along the way. Unlike American Vietnam war vets, or Russian soldiers returning from Afghanistan, there was no help for these Angolan boys suffering post-traumatic stress.

The afternoon slowly descended into chaos. It was dark by the time one of the very drunk guests drove us back to town, and he raced at hair-raising speed, swerving around cars and people and coming to a sudden halt some blocks from our hotel. Jeremy and I shook with relief at getting back alive.

But we still had Monday to get through.

Journal entry: **Luanda, 27 June 1990**

*Today's my last day and it started badly. Hotel charged for the two nights that we were in Benguela and when I argued I was told not to leave the hotel until I paid. They had my passport. I was a hostage.*

*Jeremy chased to the Press Centre to look for Tona. Couldn't find him anywhere, but did find out that they were charging us $750 for the meal we had in Benguela which actually only cost $10 at the unofficial rate, but of course they charge the official rate. Left Jeremy hostage in my place and went to find Manuel, who called Wadigimbi and the cat was among the pigeons.*

*Now everyone with very long faces. Tona arrived in a filthy temper as he had got into trouble with the chefe, Wadigimbi. Jeremy mad at me as I had got Tona, 'a poor Angolan', into trouble. No one is talking to me, but I did get the bills sorted out.*

Soon after lunch that final Monday, we set off on a visit arranged by OMA, a women's organisation. We were due to meet with a traditional midwife in a village about fifty kilometres away, set among huge baobabs and mango trees. It was horrifyingly poor, with few facilities, despite its relative proximity to Luanda.

The midwife was an elderly woman in a filthy black dress. Thick clusters of flies clung to the parts of it that were soaked with blood. Her eyes were tired and she apologised for being late.

'I lost a mother and baby early this morning,' she said sighing. 'Here, the mortality rate is very high. We're far from the clinic, there is no doctor.' She did all the deliveries. No drugs, no anything.

I sat with her and a group of village women and we talked of the things common to all women and they told me their problems. They were fascinated to hear about my family. Only two children? Why was that? Why did I not have more? And my husband? Did he have a job? They thought *my* life was strange, while I was appalled that a village that was not in a war zone, and within easy driving distance of Luanda, could be so lacking in basic amenities. By this time, I no longer naively believed that it was a simple equation of one side good, the other bad; I had spent too long in the region and learned too much, and increasingly I saw the failures of the MPLA in looking after the people.

Much later, in the departure lounge, I felt that I had finished with Angola. However, I should have known better.

## 3. GOING HOME

It was a quiet Sunday night at Heathrow, and the immigration officer who looked at my British passport asked if I was going anywhere exciting.

'I think so,' I replied, 'I'm going to South Africa.'

'Let me see your passport again.'

I handed it to him and he flicked through, stopping at the page with the big black South African stamp.

'My goodness,' he exclaimed, 'you must have done something very bad.'

'How do you know?'

'Look here, and I'll show you,' he said, pointing at the black stamp that was the visa. 'See all these letters and numbers printed across the top and bottom of the visa? Well, this here shows that you were a banned person; and this shows that you were barred from entering. And this one indicates that you work in media. How long are you going for?'

'I hope about two weeks,' I said.

He looked doubtful. 'Well, be careful when you enter the country. It looks to me that they have only given you three days. Any longer will be at the discretion of the individual immigration officer.'

It was October 1990, and I was on my way 'home' for the first time in twenty-five years. I was feeling both apprehensive and very excited.

World events that had affected the war in Angola and the independence of Namibia had begun to bring change to South Africa. In February 1990, F. W. de Klerk had unbanned the ANC. From my home in London, I had watched with joy and amazement the television footage of Nelson Mandela walking out of Pollsmoor Prison, and following on from this, the unfolding events that would eventually lead to the elections of 1994.

The apartheid government was still in place, but once the ANC was unbanned, exiled South Africans were no longer debarred from visiting. Many of us in England had begun to make arrangements to move back to South Africa, some to find jobs and homes while waiting to take up official positions, but there were also those of us who found it difficult to uproot ourselves once more.

I had been invited to show one of my films at a small film festival at the University of Witwatersrand in Johannesburg. It seemed like a good way of going back to South Africa for the first time. To apply for the special visa I needed in London, I had had to enter South Africa House – a building that had been enemy territory for so many years.

I arrived in Johannesburg feeling sleep-deprived, dazed, and strangely empty. I don't know what I had expected, but this felt like just another anonymous airport arrival. Outside it was hot, and the thin air of the highveld gave the light a glaring intensity. I didn't remember Johannesburg being this hot and this bright.

By strange coincidence, the festival organisers had arranged for me to stay with Lawrence, a local filmmaker who lived only three blocks from my old family home. Everything was so familiar, I could find my way around as if I had never left. But it was also very different. I felt disoriented. This was not the home that I had been fantasising about all those years. Everything looked shabbier, smaller, less perfect than I remembered. The idea of home that I had held in my head was no longer connected to the reality of South Africa nearly thirty years later.

The UK immigration officer had been right: I was only given three days and would have to go to Home Affairs, in Rissik Street in the centre of town, to apply for an extension. The route was so deeply imprinted in my brain that I didn't even need to glance at the map before driving there. But the downtown area of Johannesburg had changed beyond all recognition. The streets were still the same, the buildings were there, but everything else was different. It was no longer the sanitised, whites-only city of my childhood, with smart department stores and suburban women dressed up for a day in town; instead, it was a busy and buzzing African city.

At Home Affairs, I was treated with deep suspicion. 'Mrs Strasburg, where is your husband?' the woman behind the desk asked repeatedly in an Afrikaans accent, as if I had done something wrong by going there alone.

'He is in England,' I kept answering, without any idea of what she was trying to find out.

Many of the white people who were in official positions seemed to be stiff and hostile. Not just to me, but to anything that crossed their paths. Everything appeared to be a threat to them.

On the way back to Lawrence's house, the car seemed to drive itself and I found myself parked outside the house I'd once lived in. It looked curiously small and unattractive. The garden where we had played as children was no longer beautiful: the jacarandas lining the driveway were gone; all the fruit trees had been cut down and the swimming pool filled in; the large windows that looked out onto the garden were shrouded in curtains. The long-remembered home was home no more. I sat in the car and wept. Maputo and Harare felt more like home to me than this place.

There were changes taking place everywhere, but it was too early to really be aware of them. I didn't know who I was any more. I decided to phone my mother.

'What's it like?' her voice rose in expectation.

'Mommy, it's horrible, horrible,' I cried. 'It looks all wrong. I don't understand it any more.'

I couldn't explain what was 'horrible'. I don't know what I had expected to find or feel, I simply felt disconnected. Johannesburg was both familiar and deeply foreign. The light was too bright, the people too 'other'. The city had changed. This was not the place of my dreams. What had I expected? To revert to a place that existed only in the rosy memories of childhood?

I drifted into a nightmare in which I had no control over anything. I wasn't ready to return to London, I needed time to make sense of South Africa, and so I flew to Maputo to spend a few days with my friend Pam. She was also originally from Johannesburg, but in exile had married one of the leaders of Frelimo and now lived in Maputo. There at least I felt at home. We had dinner with Graça Machel, who asked me how South Africa had been.

'I didn't like it,' I said. 'You cannot imagine how awful it felt, it didn't feel like my country at all.' I was unable to explain what was wrong, because I didn't really know.

Graça was sympathetic, but chided me gently. 'Don't keep saying it's horrible,' she said. 'You have been away a long time. Think about it and give yourself time to relearn your country.'

Her words stuck with me, I needed time to relearn where I had come from. But after a long exile there is no going back – only forward.

A year later, at the end of 1991, Ivan and I returned to South Africa and spent six weeks driving around the country, laying old ghosts to rest and meeting old friends; remembering the sounds, smells, places and people; all the reasons we loved South Africa. For many years afterwards I was torn: England remained my home, the place where I lived with my family – yet Africa was the home of my heart.

## 4. MEETING THE ENEMY 1

In January 1992, I met the enemy face to face.

One hot Saturday afternoon in Maputo, I went for a swim. The Hotel Cardoso is on top of a bluff. The pool and garden have a wonderful view onto downtown Maputo and across the harbour. I needed a break from Jon, who was travelling with me; he had not been to Mozambique before and his enthusiasm was tiring.

It was quiet at the pool that afternoon, with only one or two people sitting around. Among them was a man reading under a tree. He was an attractive man in his forties, with a good muscular body, brown hair and a full beard. I couldn't place him. He was definitely not a Mozambican, nor was he the usual expatriate or co-operant. I took my time settling down, so that I could observe him better. I knew he was watching me. What was it that made us both so instantly aware of each other, as if everyone else at the pool was out of focus?

I lay and read and watched him. He lay and read and watched me. When I went to swim, he came over to speak to me. Had I been willing him to do this?

'You must be careful lying in the sun here, it's terribly hot and you'll get burnt.'

The moment he spoke I knew who he was: a South African; an Afrikaans-speaking South African – the accent is unmistakable. What the hell was he doing here, sunbathing openly at the Cardoso pool, when South Africa was still funding the Renamo rebels, and South Africans couldn't easily travel to Mozambique?

And who did he think I was? A reasonably attractive woman

to chat up in the absence of anyone younger?

He didn't immediately pick up my South African accent, which had softened after many years in England. We chatted a bit and he asked what I was doing in Maputo. I told him the partial truth, that I'd come from London to help set up a small film festival. And what did he do? He took my answer at face value and gave me a half-truth in reply.

'Well,' he said, 'I work for Electricidade de Mozambique.'

Could this possibly be true? A South African, an Afrikaner, the enemy, working for the Mozambican electricity board, a national utility company, while the war was still on? White South Africans weren't yet roaming the streets of Maputo, and this man with his heavy accent tells me he is working for Electricidade de Mozambique. Not possible.

'Really, and what exactly is this work, then?'

Slowly, he told me a little more. 'You may have noticed,' he said, 'that there aren't power cuts any more.'

This, he explained, was because he and his team were clearing the mines from the pylons that carried electricity to Maputo from Ressano Garcia on the South African border. Once cleared of mines, an Italian company would mend the pylons. He and two colleagues had been busy for some weeks now. They were using two ex-SADF Casspirs – now painted white – and they'd been given a squad of Frelimo soldiers.

I played the innocent. 'Goodness, what a dangerous job, how interesting.'

I believe that, at that moment, he truly didn't know who I was and wanted to act the hero a bit, to impress me. He began to boast about his job. How dangerous it was, the ambushes that he had missed by luck, the things he saw out in the bush. He seemed flattered by my interest and feigned awe.

I could barely contain my excitement. This conversation

would have been unimaginable only a few months earlier. And now, without warning, I was talking to the enemy. There was a frisson that went way beyond mere physical attraction or the flattery of being chatted up.

We exchanged names. I go under my married name – but in any case, I felt sure that he would have recognised my father's name immediately. His is name was Stefan.

This is what I discovered that afternoon; some of it he told me, the rest I put together from my knowledge of the situation in that region: Stefan had been a soldier in the SADF and had fought in Rhodesia before independence and in Namibia, and therefore almost certainly in Angola, for the past fifteen years. Now the war seemed to be over and South Africa had capitulated to the ANC (and possibly also the communists); he would need another job, but his only skills were war.

He had formed a company with some other ex-SADF colleagues; it had the rather extraordinary name 'Explode Incorporated'. Their aim was to lift landmines in former war zones. Clearing Maputo's electricity pylons was their first assignment.

I exclaimed again about the dangers of his work, and eventually he said, 'If you came with me to Ressano Garcia, I could show you a thing or two.'

Ressano Garcia was on the border with South Africa. Electricity in southern Mozambique came from the South African grid. Normally it would be a three-hour drive from Maputo, but the road had become notorious for vicious attacks by Renamo. The buses and trucks that were the main users had been attacked so often that few people travelled on it voluntarily. No foreigner was allowed to risk it.

I had always wanted to see the place, and here, suddenly, was a chance for more than just a drive to the border; I'd be travelling with the enemy, in an armoured vehicle. How could I possibly resist?

'Could I really come with you? I would be so interested.'

'Yes, but it's not that simple here. You can't just go out of Maputo; you have to get permission,' he said.

'Well, if I could get permission, then would you take me?'

'*If* you got permission,' he repeated, 'but it's not that easy.'

'OK. If I get permission, could you take me on Wednesday? It's my only day off.'

'If you got permission, I would.' He had a lovely and mischievous smile. I knew he didn't believe I'd get permission, and that is where we left it.

I was determined to see this man again, and not only because of the possibility of the trip to Ressano Garcia in his Casspir. And I believed he was determined to see me again, too.

It was a strange time in southern Africa. South Africa was moving towards democratic elections, but in Mozambique the war dragged on. It had gone on for so long that it seemed to have become the normal condition of the country. Peace talks with Renamo were being brokered in Rome, but the fighting continued in the provinces, and life continued in a desultory fashion in Maputo. The early years of idealism were long gone, as was the worst of the misery, but although things were physically easier, the heart seemed to have gone out of the place.

Yet there were signs, in Maputo at least, that the war might be drawing to a close. There were fewer shortages and it was possible to buy most things in the shops or marketplace. In little ways, the city was also beginning to look less shabby. The electricity worked. Lights went on all over the city each night, and for the most part, stayed on. One could count on having working lifts in the high-rise buildings, as well as air conditioning.

During the bad years, when the pylons bringing power from South Africa were blown up for the umpteenth time, people would shrug and say: '*Não temos energia*' – we have no energy. Often it meant more than simply that the electricity was down; it also signified a state of mind.

Jon and I were staying at the house where I usually stayed on rua Afonso Henriques. I could barely wait to get back and tell him about the incident at the Cardoso. He had spent the afternoon photographing the rubbish dump, and I let him tell me all about it before telling him about my afternoon at the pool.

I had first met Jon in London, when he'd come to my office to discuss some ideas for a documentary. His mop of black hair flopped into his eyes, and combined with his wicked smile and slight build, it made him appear boyish and much younger than his years. Both of us were fascinated by war. We'd come to Maputo to plan a film about South Africa's use of illegal ivory to finance its wars in the region, and were doing some research there before going on to make a film in Namibia.

Jon wasn't a filmmaker; he was a highly qualified surgeon who loved adventure and sometimes worked as a doctor in war zones. He had many interests, including journalism and photography, and this was to be his first excursion into documentary-making. He loved to talk about himself. In company, he entertained with a non-stop fund of hilarious adventures in which he always featured as the central figure. This had the strange effect of rendering me speechless, as if I had never been anywhere or done anything. He was quick to turn on the charm when there was someone present that he wanted to chat up, a technique he'd used successfully on me when we first got to know each other. However, at other times he was businesslike, treating me as a mere means to an end.

Jon had been excited by my story, and so the next evening he and I went to the Cardoso for a drink, to seek out Stefan. He was sitting alone in the garden and seemed surprised and pleased to see us. After a few beers, we wandered over to a nearby restaurant for dinner. We talked again about the possibilities of a trip to Ressano Garcia and, as far as we could tell, he was being quite genuine about it – 'if you can get permission.'

Jon tried to find out which battalions Stefan had served with, and where he had spent his time. Stefan's answers became increasingly evasive, but no less charming. He did tell us that he had been in the notorious 32 Battalion led by Colonel Jan Breytenbach, and seemed to be familiar with all the well-known baddies, like Craig Williamson. I wondered if I should mention my past.

Back at the house, Jon said with some excitement, 'That is one very bad man.'

That Monday I went to the Ministry of Information. I had known the director, Arlindo Lopes, for many years, and I told him my story.

'Arlindo, you will never guess who I met at the Cardoso pool.' Arlindo was cautious. 'Do you realise who this man is?' I told him what I suspected.

'Well, that's not all, this man was in Special Forces, and he was responsible for killing some of your friends, right here in Mozambique.'

'All the more reason that you should let me go with him.'

As a journalist, Arlindo knew the attraction of an opportunity like this, but as Director of Information, his duty was to dissuade me.

'Toni, we are very suspicious of these people. We have only given them permission to work here under certain conditions. Anyway, this has nothing to do with what you are here for.'

'I know, Arlindo, but come on, you would go if you had the chance.'

'And what do you expect? To meet Renamo?'

'Oh yes – please.'

'OK, Toni, we'll give you permission because we know you and trust you, and know of your courage. But will you be able to go and come back in one day?'

I reassured him we would, and explained about the armoured vehicle.

'All right,' he said reluctantly 'You have permission to go to Ressano Garcia on Wednesday, but only for the day. You must be back in Maputo by dark.' Arlindo paused, 'And then you must come and tell me everything.' He smiled broadly.

I stood over his secretary as she laboriously typed out the permission document. We could barely wait to get to the Cardoso with our bit of paper that evening, and await Stefan's appearance. He was clearly amazed that we had managed to get permission.

'You have friends in high places,' he said, but stayed quite cool about it.

The following evening, he had a man with him whom he introduced as his attorney. Gerald, an unsavoury-looking type from Pretoria, took an instant dislike to us, as we did to him. His leg was in plaster, the result of an injury sustained in an ambush on the road to the border in one of Stefan's Casspirs.

Gerald realised instantly that neither Jon nor I was English. 'You are South Africans, aren't you?' he asked. We admitted that we were. He turned to me: 'And when did you leave?'

'In the sixties.'

'Albie Sachs and Stephanie Kemp,' he said.

I shook my head. 'You're a few years too late.'

At that, Stefan looked at me hard and said, 'Rivonia, you are connected with Rivonia.' He was guessing, I suspected, but he'd managed to hit the nail on the head. Or had he known from the start who I really was? Was it *him* playing us along? I will never know for sure. Gerald began to whine. 'No, Stefan, man. Don't trust these people, they'll just get you into trouble. They know people here, you don't know what they're up to.' He then began baiting me about my background.

Stefan was having second thoughts about the trip and looked uncomfortable. The ease with which I had obtained the permission had filled him with doubt. He was nervous that the document didn't specify that we would be travelling with him. He seemed to think that we were trying to trap him, and that he might lose his contract to lift mines in Mozambique, so jeopardising future contracts. I could see he felt that Gerald could be right, and that we had been set up by the Mozambicans to spy on him.

In the end, I said it was up to him. He was obviously as fascinated by me as I was by him – and I knew things wouldn't end there.

From the start, he and I were compelled by each other. We needed a way to keep up the dialogue, so we met for drinks or dinner most evenings. That night, he turned up at a special birthday dinner I'd organised for Jon at the house. John had pulled out all the stops and bought aubergine, beans, fresh mangoes, and peaches from the market, and cooked 'loasty chicken' with gravy and rice. Stefan eyed the set-up and said again: 'You *do* have friends in high places.' I didn't reply. After dinner, we sat in the garden and hit the Stolichnaya bottle, and Stefan relaxed his formality a bit.

Before he left that evening, I said, 'I want you to understand that I am putting my life in your hands, so there has to be an element of trust here. You have my word that there is no motive behind this trip beyond curiosity.'

I don't know what decided him in the end. Certainly it wasn't Gerald. But he was there to fetch me and Jon at 6 a.m.

As with nearly every trip in Mozambique and Angola, there was a certain amount of *confusão* before we were able to leave. At the electricity station on the edge of town, we left Stefan's truck and got into the Casspir, together with his *escorte* of seven well-armed Mozambican soldiers. He joked with them in his basic Portuguese and I was struck by the rapport he had with them.

A young man called Francisco was with them. He was Stefan's translator, and spoke Portuguese and Afrikaans fluently. I was disconcerted by Francisco's cringing manner, rather like an abused dog – he was clearly just one more casualty of the endless conflict in the region. He had fought with the Portuguese during the liberation struggle and had been recruited by the CIA to work in Zaire and Northern Angola. He said that he had worked with CIA agent, John Stockwell, who'd recruited for Holden Roberto's FNLA. After that he was in Rhodesia, and then Namibia. Francisco had spent six years in prison in Mozambique and was now a Frelimo soldier.

By the time we hit the road southwards, the sun was up. Outside, it was already baking, and inside the confined metal box of the Casspir it was stifling. After we'd left the outskirts of Maputo, the road became empty, apart from the odd man on a bike or woman carrying a load of firewood. The combined heat and noise made conversation difficult and we travelled in silence. I was in the front with Stefan, and Jon was in the back with the soldiers.

This was the road that returning gold miners took to get home, once the train from Johannesburg stopped at the border. Usually, the miners brought with them two or three years' worth of pay, consumer goods, and food – mostly items that were unavailable in war-torn Mozambique. The trucks carrying them were constantly ambushed, and parts of the route were littered with the gruesome remains.

The road was bad, potholed, and slow. Moamba, a derelict little town, was the halfway point where we stopped to change Casspirs and pick up another soldier. The reasons for this were never explained. Beyond Moamba were ruined farmhouses, and the thick bush encroached on abandoned farmland.

The pathetic remains of the various convoy attacks were scattered along the roadside: an endless stream of burnt-out cars, buses and lorries, sometimes with the grisly remains of their occupants still lying there. Next to one vehicle a skeleton was still wearing faded plimsolls. It was too dangerous for people to stop and bury the dead. Stefan glanced at me from time to time to see my reactions. I had seen much worse, and in the context this was not especially shocking. Of more immediate interest were the numbers of blown-up pylons: no wonder the power supply had been so bad.

Inside the steel Casspir, the heat became unbearable, and the jolting and noise stopped most thought. Still, I wondered about all those men in all those wars, enduring stifling heat in one or other type of steel box.

After some time, Stefan shouted to me: 'We are entering an area known as ambush alley. I am always more on my guard going through here.' And indeed, the soldiers in the back were also more alert and cocked their guns, which they had pointed out of the portholes. I have never figured out in these situations whether I am hoping for an ambush, some action, or simply relieved when nothing happens. Maybe a bit of both.

Suddenly, Stefan half-turned his head, shouting something to the soldiers. In an instant, I was deafened by machine-gunfire. I remember my thoughts exactly: What the hell is this? Is it for real or a set-up? It's a set-up! And as that flashed through my mind I glanced at Stefan. He was looking at me to gauge my reaction, and grinned, saying, 'I love that smell of cordite,' and then burst out laughing. Our eyes met; I had passed his test, and I knew this wouldn't end when I left Mozambique at the end of the week.

At Ressano Garcia, Stefan left us for a couple of hours while he crossed into Komatipoort to do whatever it was that he did – pick up supplies, phone his wife, run guns, whatever.

Jon and I took the opportunity to walk around the town. It was like something out of a Vietnam War movie: a border town filled with crumbling buildings, underfed men, and crowds of miners returning from the gold mines of Johannesburg, all waiting for a convoy to make the deadly run down the road we had just travelled.

We visited the hospital run by Médecins sans Frontières and walked the main street, stopping to get a cold drink in a café frequented by prostitutes. A fey-looking blond boy came walking down the middle of the street towards us, holding a bottle of wine in one hand and a half-filled glass in the other. It was lunchtime and already he was quite drunk. He said he was a theological student from Pretoria, working for the Catholic Mission there, teaching boys.

Stefan fetched us and we drove back to Maputo in silence, parting at the place we had parked the cars. And that was all.

I think that we were both disappointed and relieved by the uneventfulness of the day. At the time, I must have been more aware of the danger than I remember, because years later I found a note I'd written in my journal for my family in case I was killed, explaining why I was going on this trip.

Later that week Eddie, a journalist friend from South Africa, arrived to investigate rumours that either Renamo or South Africa had used chemical weapons near Ressano Garcia. I took him to meet Z, who had interviewed the Lhanguene children in *Chain of Tears*.

I asked Eddie if he knew Stefan. He looked at me and said, 'Why do you want to know, and what do you think you are doing, hanging out with a person like that?' He told me that Stefan was being closely watched by Mozambican intelligence. He also told me about some of the operations Stefan had been involved in, including the raid on Matola, outside Maputo, where the South Africans had killed a number of ANC operatives in training.

Stefan and I had had several conversations during those days about who we were and why we were talking to each other. One night he said, 'I don't understand why you are talking to me. I don't understand why you have anything to do with me. I don't understand why you don't hate me, why you aren't bitter and twisted.'

I didn't understand either; I still don't, really. It seems that sometimes the enemy is more like us than we know, that the enemy can be closer to us than some of the friends we lived with in exile.

Stefan had told me that he'd been in the army since leaving school at eighteen, and that fighting his version of the enemy had been his whole life. Now it turned out that this enemy was about to take over the country, peacefully, and he didn't understand what the whole fight had really been about. He had always considered himself a loyal patriot – and now being a patriot meant being friends with the enemy. The changes had negated his whole reason for being; he felt confused, and was trying to process it all.

A week later, Jon and I left Maputo to start filming in Namibia. Just before we left for the airport, Stefan arrived.

'I had to come and say goodbye; I have never met anyone like you before. And I really don't understand why you bother to speak to me. But I wanted to tell you how amazing this has been for me.'

Knowing that I should be wary of him, I nevertheless found him remarkable too. Maybe he no longer wants to remember how he felt then, but I remember, and I remember it was amazing for me too.

# 5. FREE TO MOVE

> 'Things don't come in a blink of an eye, but I can say the changes are coming.'
>
> Alex Sangara, *Free to Move*, 1992

The king and queen lived in a traditional Ovambo homestead: a complex stockade of wooden corridors that led to a series of huts set in courtyards. We had to pay them a formal visit to request their permission to film in the area. Once we had that, we could attend a meeting at the community centre, to explain to the community what we had come to do and to ask their approval.

A messenger went ahead of us to announce our arrival and, after a short wait, we were led in to a courtyard with chairs set out under a tree. The king was a very genial Sam Nujoma lookalike, with a young queen and a stylish queen mother. A slightly formal but pleasant conversation took place, with Andreas, our handsome UNICEF driver, translating for us. The king told us that he was a SWAPO supporter. He was clearly a man of the people who was involved in, and encouraged, the various projects in the area.

He said that Queen Elizabeth and the Duke of Edinburgh had visited him here at his home last year when they had come to Namibia for the independence celebrations.

'Do you know dear Queen Elizabeth?' he asked.

I muttered that I did, but told him I hadn't visited her.

'Please give her my kind regards when you get back to England,' he said.

I promised to try. Jon had his head down, trying to hide his amusement by taking notes.

I'd gone back to Namibia in March 1992, exactly two years after it had become independent. I knew that South Africa would follow soon. The whole process of homecoming and transition fascinated me. I wanted to make an impressionistic film about a country in transition but I was hazy about the story – a bad sign, and probably the main reason why I'd been unable to raise sufficient money to do it properly.

The lack of funds brought all sorts of constraints and difficulties, one of which was that I'd have to shoot on video, a first for me. Video was much cheaper than working on film. It had been used for news-gathering for some time, but the technology was still in its early stages; cameras were large and cumbersome and tended to be temperamental, the sound recordist was no longer able to move around to get the best sound in any given situation, but was instead tethered by an umbilical lead to the camera; also, the editing was slow, inexact and painstaking.

I couldn't afford a British crew, so had agreed to work with a South African crew whom I barely knew. They had a rather more casual attitude to filmmaking than I was used to, and neither they nor Jon could give me the support and help that I needed. I should have known better than to go ahead with the project. In hindsight, it is clear that I had set myself up for a disaster.

Jon was totally inexperienced in film work, but was very sure of his medical expertise. While we were in Maputo, just before leaving for Namibia, we were talking about his work as a surgeon. 'Surgeons,' he said, 'are arrogant and tend to consider themselves above other medical disciplines. That's why I'm so sure of myself.'

He said it jokingly, but I had noticed that he hated being told to do anything by anyone at all, and I confronted him with this.

'Yes,' he agreed, 'and that is why I have been quite sharp with you at times. I'm used to being in charge, I expect people to do as I say. I'm not a team person.'

'Jon, if we're going to work together, you have to understand that making a film is a team effort, and that while I welcome everyone's input, there is only one director. *I* make the final decisions.'

Jon made a joke in response and we moved on to talk about something else – perhaps I should have taken more heed of this conversation.

Though I had some funding from a Finnish TV company, their stipulation was that the film must include something about Bushmen, although they weren't very clear about what that should be. In return for filming some of their projects in Ovamboland, UNICEF in Windhoek agreed to loan us a Land Cruiser and driver. I foolishly believed I could marry their varying needs with ideas of my own.

Andreas was far more than just a driver; he had a confident manner that most black Namibians didn't seem to have in the early years after independence.

'Were you in exile?' I asked him.

'Yes, I was a PLAN fighter. I was in charge of transport for SWAPO in Angola.'

He proved to be our best asset. He was quick to understand what the film was about and helped us enormously by explaining to locals what we were trying to do and why. He always introduced us as 'These people who are working with me'.

Andreas seemed either to be acquainted with, or related to, almost the entire population of Namibia, and was regarded as something of a hero. He was friendly to everyone except the police, whom he despised. He seemed to feel that his position in SWAPO, and his war record, made him superior to any policeman, and the fact that these were the new Namibian police cut no ice with him. He treated them all with contempt, particularly those who were stupid enough to pull over a UN vehicle at roadblocks.

When that happened, Andreas sat in the car, staring straight ahead while the policeman came to the window, then answering his questions in a bored monotone.

'Name?'

'Andreas Nkanala.'

'ID?'

'In the back.'

'Show me your papers.'

'This is a UN vehicle,' drumming fingers on the steering wheel.

Andreas never wavered. And we'd become obsequiously polite to try and make up for his rudeness.

During the course of the film we travelled the length of Namibia twice: first on the research trip, and then on the shoot.

We met the crew – Craig the cameraman and Robin the sound recordist – near the South African border at Luderitz. The last part of the drive from Windhoek had taken us through a desert of yellow sand dunes. We passed disused diamond mines with once-grand houses disappearing into the encroaching sands. Drifts of sand blew across the straight tarred road. On the rocky coast, where the desert ended and the sea began, stood

Luderitz. It was a strange town, full of Bavarian fantasy architecture.

I loved the scrubby bush and sandy desert, with nothing except power lines and telephone poles crossing the landscape. I loved the bare bones of this land that showed through as black rocks where the drifts of sand had blown away. As we approached Luderitz, a fog descended. This is the place where the cold Atlantic air meets the hot desert winds.

In the early morning we stood on the side of the road, waiting for a bus to loom out of the fog. Every day, a busload of young men from the north arrived in Luderitz to find work. The town had a fishing industry, factories and, not far inland, there were the fabled diamond mines. No one who made this journey wrote home to tell the sad truth. The diamond mines were now almost fully mechanised, and functioned with the minimum of labour; the crayfish were all but fished out; and the factories were laying people off. But these migrant workers stayed on in a squalid squatter camp called Benguela, while more and more people arrived each day.

Benguela was utterly demoralising. Tin shacks, made out of flattened paraffin cans, crowded one on top of the other up a rocky slope dotted about with human excrement. Many of the shacks were 'bars'. The more upmarket ones had a bench or a couple of plastic chairs outside. The beer was mainly a cloudy home brew that looked lethal. There was, of course, no running water, electricity, or sewage system.

A young man called Simon told us that he had come from Ovamboland looking for a job. 'Since I got here, jobs are very scarce. It is painful, life is very difficult, and I can't go home with no money.'

The fog vanished, as it did each day, and the sun glared

down relentlessly. As this happened, a bright red 1963 Chevy roared past us, turned round, and came by for a second look, skidding to a halt. It had been made into a convertible and was equipped with all sorts of additional exhausts, aerials, sound systems, and even a TV set. The windscreen had 'Dr Feelgood' emblazoned across it, and the number plate had 'Make my day' written above the number.

The driver introduced himself to us as Julius. He was as flashy as his car. Tall and good-looking, with a stylish shirt open to his chest that was adorned with medallions, he had his initials set in gold in his front teeth.

Julius was of mixed blood, mainly Ovambo. 'I'm a panel beater in Windhoek.' He told us once we had commented on his car. 'You should see my truck. You'd love it.'

We filmed Julius and his red car in this bizarre landscape, and then later again in Windhoek. We asked him what he felt about Namibia being independent.

'I'm happy, I feel all right now. Not like before, everything was not OK to me. Things are much better since independence, because I can drive anywhere without being hassled for papers. I am free to move,' he said.

*Free to Move* became the title of the film.

I had met Craig, the cameraman, with Tim in Mozambique. He was full of nervous energy and an impatience that caused tensions among the crew. He also had a worrying lack of stamina. From the start, he was unhappy about the film; he wanted to make his own story, not mine, and was only enthusiastic filming things that he liked.

Craig bordered on being racist, and he had a tendency to be rude to everyone – restaurant staff, curious bystanders, even people in authority. I had to keep telling him to cool it, to leave the talking to me. He took a dislike to Andreas from the start, and I could see the feeling was mutual. Thankfully, we had two vehicles: Craig's clapped-out Land Rover, which he and Robin, the easy-going sound recordist, travelled in with all the gear; and the Land Cruiser, for Dan, me and Andreas.

We had been warned that Namibia was notorious for fatal road accidents. We heard stories about people driving at high speed, head-on, into the only other vehicle on the dead straight, perfectly smooth roads; or otherwise they hit animals – cows or goats or buck; or they simply fell asleep and overturned the car. Mostly, these fatal accidents happened at night and the UN had forbidden their vehicles to drive after dark. On several occasions, we found ourselves in the middle of nowhere at dusk and ended up camping out or sleeping in unlikely spots that Andreas did not always approve of.

The road out of Luderitz took us across sensational desert landscapes, with vistas of mountains in the distance. We saw springbok, other small antelope and jackals. Late one evening, we were looking for somewhere to camp, when I saw a sign saying 'Hotel 4 km'. We found ourselves in Helmeringhausen, a tiny place lost in time, with donkey carts in the main street and Pegasus petrol signs from the 1940s or 1950s. *Mevrou*, who ran the hotel, made a delicious meal of schnitzel and fresh vegetables swimming in butter. In the bar, the local whites were friendly and quite matter-of-fact about Andreas eating and drinking with us.

'We have nothing to complain of since independence, it's just the drought that bothers us,' they told us.

Before going up north, we spent a week in Windhoek. At a small office where we were watching rushes, I met a young South African cameraman of Italian origin. Giulio was helping to train film technicians in Namibia. We were both desperate for new company as we found Windhoek limited and dreary, and took to each other instantly. It proved to be a fortuitous meeting: some years later, Giulio became my cameraman of choice. We travelled to many places together, and have become lifelong friends.

In Windhoek, we met up with Julius and his red car again and went to Katutura to film Annamarie, a Herero woman who ran a food stall that catered to passing taxi drivers on the outskirts of town. We accompanied her to buy meat. The market in Katutura made no concessions to hygiene – it was a street from a nightmare, lined with grinning skinned heads of cows, and hindquarters so thick with flies that they looked black.

Annamarie had a spot on the side of the road where she cooked over an open fire in potjies. Wearing the voluminous skirts of her elegant traditional dress, she crouched next to the fire and served us a meal that was delicious.

The Hereros came under German missionary influence in the nineteenth century, and their clothing is still based on Victorian dress. The dresses are ankle length with huge mutton-chop sleeves, and they're worn over a number of petticoats, which add fullness. Their hats are shaped to resemble the horns of their cattle.

At her home, I filmed Annamarie putting on her headdress and discovered, to my disappointment, that these were no longer elaborately tied each day, but came ready-made.

Her teenage son, Hammarskjöld – who preferred the nickname Samora – was operating a barber service in the back yard.

'I am only doing this for now,' he told me, 'I'm hoping to become a spy.'

'How do you become a spy?'

'I'm not sure, but I think you have to go to university or a school for spies,' he said.

'And what will you spy on?'

'Bad people.'

Everyone we filmed in Windhoek seemed to be more or less satisfied by the new government, and repeated the same phrase, 'We can't complain.' I was tempted to title the film *No Complaints*.

Driving north again, time seemed to stand still. The vehicle was moving but it was hard to know this, as we appeared to float above the heat haze, going nowhere. Our horizons were limited to the frame of the windows, and beyond that, the bush.

Most mornings Jon and I started off bright and chatty, but as the heat rose, we would fade. Jon dozed on the front seat next to Andreas, while I lay about in the back, losing any motivation to make sense of what I was doing.

The drive from Oshakati took us through a barren landscape. Donkeys, cattle, and goats wandered the road in the hot white light. A few people moved about slowly in the heat; there was no shade. The Ovamboland section of the filming was based in Tsandi, between Oshakati and Ruacana. Tsandi was no more than a collection of a few block-like buildings, some houses behind wooden fences, and of course the *cuca* shops.

I found it bleak and ugly, loathed the endless *cuca* shops, and was depressed by the stormy weather and by Ovamboland in general. The people were deeply suspicious of whites, as the rawness of the brutal South African occupation was still very fresh in their minds. It was only with returned exiles that it seemed possible to have any real communication.

Off the main road, people still lived in traditional Ovambo family stockades. Several huts were built in a sandy clearing: sleeping huts for various family members, a cooking hut, storage huts for grain, and a hut with a smooth floor and shallow depressions for pounding the millet. In the better-off households there was often a square, one-roomed house, sometimes with windows and a tin roof, where the parents slept.

The courtyards were normally well-swept sand, with a few small plants and a shade area for sitting. Each family surrounded its homestead with a tight wooden fence, often built in a labyrinthine manner so that one wound through a tight stockade before coming into the open courtyard area. Outside, there was another stockade for the cattle and goats.

All this fencing needed an enormous number of trees, which partly accounted for the deforestation of the area. Helvi, one of the SWAPO returnees we met, told me what it felt like to come home. 'I was so excited to arrive back from exile, but when I got to Ovamboland I cried. All the trees were gone. What had the people done?'

Life was hard here. Rains permitting, the locals grew millet and maize for themselves and their cattle to eat. The Ovambo were great cattle herders and there were numbers of scraggy cows trying to find something to graze. Unless they were lucky enough to have a well near their stockades, there was a long walk for water. Before school each morning, little groups of children trekked across the veld with buckets on their heads. When they had carried the water home, they walked several kilometres to school and back. The women pounded the millet by hand, enough each day for the porridge that made up the staple food. In the evenings little groups of boys gathered up the cows and took them to drink before heading home.

Yet despite the poverty and unemployment, there was a sense of hope and new beginnings. SWAPO members who had returned from exile with a good education were now in local government structures. A number of projects had begun, run both by government and NGOs. Many of these projects were aimed at raising the quality of women's lives. Women were still locked into a traditional dependency, both on men and the system of migrant labour, and many of them had to cope on their own while the men looked for jobs in Windhoek or on white farms further south.

UNICEF was training local women in simple health and hygiene. At a project to grow vegetables under shade cloth, we found the queen working alongside the other women. A small building, owned by a Dutch NGO, served as a community centre and office. They had started an income-generating project, teaching women to make bricks and wire fencing – a painstaking effort in the intense heat.

The men had at first scoffed at the women making bricks with a little hand machine, but now many of them wanted to join in, as they saw the women making money.

A team of men and women volunteers from surrounding villages were digging trenches across the sun-baked ground to lay a water pipe from the main road. Once they reached the main road, the government would connect them to the water mains, and three to four thousand people in the area would have access to piped water within a kilometre of their homes.

Digging on the pipeline didn't begin until late morning, as the volunteers had to do all their onerous household chores before walking seven or more kilometres to dig the trenches with pickaxes. Several of them wore sweaters while doing this back-breaking work in the heat.

'It is nearly winter,' they said, laughing at our astonishment.

'We feel the cold.'

Our living quarters in Tsandi were in a long concrete-block building, behind the 'Six Brothers' store. The shower and toilet had no door, which made for a number of embarrassing moments when we walked in on one another.

It had been raining non-stop and Ovamboland had turned green. Etosha, Ovamboland, and part of southern Angola were all once part of a vast lake, over forty metres deep in places, and when it rained like this, the water collected in the pans and depressions. So did the mosquitoes.

Living as we did in the community helped us to become accepted by the locals. The women we'd met on the research trip and who were part of the film liked being able to come by and visit me. They had greeted me with such warmth when I arrived back with the film crew that I soon changed my feelings about Ovambos being unfriendly. From my window I could watch the sky turn pink in the evenings, with black palm trees reflected in a great pool of water.

We had chosen three main women to film: Ailene, who ran the brick-making project; Wilhelmina, who was tall and thin with a friendly openness; and Eva Maria, who was older, the head of a large extended family.

Wilhelmina lived in a traditional Ovambo stockade, cleanly swept and planted with flowers. Her daily chores would both form part of the main film and also make a short film for UNICEF.

Her day started before dawn, pounding *mahungu*, millet, for the children's breakfast porridge that was cooked in an open kitchen area. She had a disarming way of talking directly to the camera as we filmed. 'I am sure you haven't cooked breakfast like this,' she said. 'Your kitchens are inside.'

Before school, the four oldest children went to fetch water, while Wilhelmina pounded maize for lunch and let the cattle out of the kraal.

When she had shooed them out to graze, she turned to us, saying, 'I am getting ready for work now,' and went into her hut, with its photograph of Nujoma, to wash and dress in her smartest clothes for the interview.

'I have five children and I have to do everything for them. My husband works in the south, in Okahandja. He is at a meat-packing company. He only comes home once a year on his annual leave, for Christmas.'

Wilhelmina planted and cared for the crops, saw to the cattle, fed and looked after the children, and did it all with enormous good humour and energy. She was attractive, intelligent and animated. Now she had a new role, as community health worker, and we filmed her striding off proudly with her UNICEF bag slung over her shoulder, to run a clinic at a neighbouring kraal.

She talked to the mothers about their babies and did simple health tasks like cleaning wounds and putting on dressings. Then she put up some posters and gave a talk about hygiene and what foods one should eat.

After the filming was over, Wilhelmina and I wrote to each other for a while. 'All my children are well, including my husband,' she wrote in one of her letters.

Being in Ovamboland, his home territory, and cooking around a fire, made Andreas chatty. One evening he told us about his days fighting with SWAPO in Angola. 'I was in charge of transport,' he said. 'Brigade Leader.'

When I told him that I had been at Cuito Cuanavale, he became quite excited, pleased at the way the South Africans were beaten there. He was particularly scathing about FAPLA. 'They are not motivated the way SWAPO was,' he said.

I had heard the same story, but the opposite way round, from my FAPLA friends in Angola.

UNITA he dismissed with a flick of his hand.

'They are nothing.'

From Ovamboland, we made our way to Rundu on the Okavango River, the border with Angola. It was one of those porous border towns, filled with the flotsam and jetsam of war. When Jon and I had been there on the research trip, it seemed to be full of fat, unsmiling Afrikaners and Portuguese. Rundu had been the point of entry for the smuggling of ivory and hardwoods run by the SADF during the war. It was not a place to spend the night and we had driven on, looking for somewhere else. After a while, we saw a crude wooden sign saying 'Lodge' and turned off the road onto the flood plain. More signs followed: 'Swiss and Italian cooking 2 kilometres' and 'Sarasunga Lodge 1 km'.

On the banks of the river we found a clearing with several peculiar, palm-thatched, wooden huts. A wooden sign said: 'Angola 30 metres, Berlin 12,000 kilometres'. Nearby, two dogs were tied up in the shade, with signs giving their names as 'Savimbi' and 'Mobutu'. A battered beach buggy was parked under a tree. A pretty young blonde woman approached us and we asked for accommodation.

'We are fully booked,' she said, speaking with a strong German accent. Jon and I exchanged glances. We asked if we could get some water and she pointed to a hut with a wooden board that said 'Bar'.

When our eyes had adjusted to the dark, we could make

out a man sitting at a table at the back. His sleeveless T-shirt showed off tanned and muscular arms, with a large ivory bangle on one wrist. His hair was held back by a headband and he was engrossed in a book called *Deep Water Yacht Navigation*.

Here we were on the Angolan border, pretty much in the middle of Africa and about as far from the coast as one could get. Rundu had been the centre of the ivory trade, and here was a guy looking as if he had stepped out of Vietnam in the 1970s, running a lodge where there was no available accommodation, right on the Angolan border.

'You will have to go back to Rundu. There is nowhere else to stay around here,' he said. 'We are expecting a group from Windhoek.'

It seemed unlikely that anyone would still be arriving this late but there was nothing for it, and as we drove away, Jon and I turned to each other.

'We *have* to stay here when we come back with the crew,' I said, but Jon had already made a note of the numbers and booked us in for our return.

A month later, there we were, back again with the crew. It proved to be all that Jon and I had fantasised about, and more. We each had a thatched bungalow with plaited straw walls. The bungalows had an inner room with a large double bed, and a mosquito-netted porch with a basin and table.

In the central shower block there was a notice, written in red and black felt-tipped pen: PLEASE KEEP THIS PLACE TIDY, WE DON'T TAKE FUCKING SHIT FROM ANYBODY.

In the bar at dinner, Volke, the owner, was still sitting at the same table. There was indeed 'Swiss and Italian cooking' in the form of real pizza and spaghetti Bolognese and salad, all cooked by Volke's blonde girl.

After dinner, Jon and I chatted with Volke. He had driven in the beach buggy from Hamburg in Germany to Cape Town, and later he'd moved to Windhoek.

'I came up here and built this place myself,' he said. 'I don't advertise, but people hear of it and come here.' *Deep Water Yacht Navigation* still lay open in front of him.

'What's with deep-water navigation?' Jon wanted to know.

'When I leave here I will build a yacht. I am planning to sail around the world.'

On the wall he had pinned up currency notes from various countries.

'I cleaned up during the UNTAG days,' he said. 'Made between fifteen and eighteen thousand a night.'

'Fifteen to eighteen thousand what?' we asked. 'Dollars, rands?'

'I accepted everything, dollars, rands, Finnish marks, Pakistani dinar. I just counted it at the end of the night and it always came to around fifteen or eighteen thousand.'

He told us that the tables in the bar were made of Angolan teak, bought off the Portuguese ivory and teak connection of the SADF.

'They used to come and make deals in my bar. I know everything that went on, but I closed my ears. I didn't want to get involved. It still goes on.'

Jon and I went outside to talk this over; we would dearly love to film here when we eventually did the ivory film. We sat on the banks of the river, looking at Angola on the other side where we knew there were now UN observers at UNITA bases. It was an incredibly peaceful spot.

In the morning Volke got up from his table to say goodbye, and for the first time we saw that his legs were paralysed; he was walking on crutches with much difficulty.

From Rundu, we left the tar road and took a bone-shaking track to the Caprivi Strip. Caprivi is a long finger of land in the far north of Namibia, pointing eastwards about 450 kilometres. It lies between Botswana to the south, Angola and Zambia to the north, and the Okavango region to the west. Bordering so many countries, it was of considerable military importance, seeing continual conflict between 1965 and 1994. The Okavango, Kwando, Chobe, and Zambezi rivers all border Caprivi and it is an area rich in wildlife.

The SADF bases in Caprivi had a fearsome reputation and history. Omega I was the home of 32 Battalion. It had been formed in 1975 by Colonel Jan Breytenbach, and was largely made up of defeated FNLA troops from Angola who had crossed into Namibia, serving under white South African officers and NCOs. The battalion had been mainly deployed in southern Angola, assisting UNITA, and it had fought at Cuito Cuanavale.

The Omega I camp was huge, but now it lay deserted and decaying. A quiet descended as we drove through the faded stone entrance, and we whispered to each other in the car. It had an eerie feel; the abandoned buildings had become overgrown with grass and bush. All the roofs were gone and the buildings were open to the elements; wooden structures were slowly sinking into the bush.

It must once have been a wonderful set-up, with magical views over the river. We stopped for a while to film and explore some of the buildings, but soon felt uncomfortable. I have been told that the camp remains untouched and decaying to this day, and has never been used by the Namibians.

There are certain places where great evil has taken place and which retain something of that evil for a very long time.

Wars may end, but their effects reverberate long afterwards. Their ghosts walk this earth. I felt it there, and have felt it before and since, including when filming in Croatia.

Andreas was unnerved by the place and wanted us to leave. We wandered around filming for a while, but soon climbed back into the vehicle. As we left, we passed a little cemetery. Nearly all the graves were of black Angolans who had fought with the South Africans against their own people. We tried to drive into it, but suddenly found our way blocked by a herd of exceptionally large elephants, which appeared as if from nowhere. They seemed to be guarding the graves and were angered by our presence, trumpeting and flapping their ears. We had a moment of fear as Andreas reversed the Land Cruiser in haste, with the engine whining and thorn branches scratching the sides.

Among its many infamous activities, 32 Battalion had been central to the slaughter of elephants for ivory, as well as the felling of huge teak forests in southern Angola. It seemed poignant, and possibly ironic, that the dead of the battalion, who had been so brutally involved in the slaughter of Angola's elephants, were now haunted, or guarded, by these enormous beasts.

Ivory and teak were given to the South Africans by UNITA as a form of payment for their help in the war against the MPLA. This was mirrored on the other side of the continent, where Renamo also gave the SADF huge quantities of ivory.

Later that year, working on *Spoils of War*, which exposed South Africa's ivory trade in Angola and Mozambique, we interviewed Colonel Breytenbach. He was a man who would stop at nothing to get rid of 'communists', but had been horrified by the elephant slaughter by his troops. He told us that at times they would go into Angola with helicopter gunships and simply mow down the herds. Then they would land at a village and direct the villagers to gather and clean up the tusks for later collection.

We left Omega I in the shimmering, white afternoon heat and had a blow-out at a treeless place on a rocky track. I stood on the side of the road, surrounded by huge buzzing flies, while Jon and Andreas struggled to change the wheel.

The last part of the drive took much longer than expected but had its reward. A herd of almost eighty elephants, from babies to huge old mothers, crossed the road ahead of us as we watched in awed silence. It was already 5 p.m. when we reached Kongola, on the Cuando River, where we were hoping to stay at a camp run by Nature Conservation. But we found it deserted, and had to try and find a safe place to camp.

Jon said he knew of a small house on the river, which had formerly been the weekend place of Colonel Breytenbach. It was a place he'd used to escape the war and occasionally to debrief his officers. The house had been known as Buffalo Lodge, but now it was owned by Nature Conservation. It was deserted when we arrived, but made a perfect campsite. We made a fire, brewed tea, and rigged up a shower for ourselves with a hose at an outside tap.

Andreas came and asked me where we were going to sleep.

'We'll sleep here, Andreas. You know we can't drive any further now, it's getting dark.'

'*Ek wil nie hier slaap nie, hierdie is 'n slegte plek.*' I won't sleep here, it's a bad place. Andreas turned and walked to the car, got in, then shut all the windows and locked the doors.

The rest of us unrolled our sleeping bags on the veranda and sat on the banks of the river, watching hippos and fireflies.

As we drove away in the cool, early morning, I asked Andreas if he knew who had once owned the house. He shook his head.

'It was the place of Colonel Breytenbach.' I told him.

'*Ek het gesê daardie was 'n slegte plek.*' I told you it was a bad place.

Before we could leave Caprivi and return to Windhoek, I needed to film some San. The San, sometimes called Bushmen, were the original inhabitants of southern Africa. Everyone they'd encountered had exploited them, and their hunter-gathering lifestyle had been largely destroyed. They were forced out of their traditional way of life and became increasingly marginalised.

Those living on the Namibian–Angolan border were caught up in the wars on both sides. Some were rounded up and moved into camps and villages where they were forced to try and learn farming, an alien lifestyle. Many of the men were inducted into the SADF in the fight against SWAPO. Their traditional tracking skills were highly prized by the various forces in the area.

Omega II, the other large base in Caprivi, had been the home of 31 Battalion, or Bushman Battalion. The new government had turned it into a small town and started an agricultural project. Huge fields had been cleared and planted with maize, cotton, and other crops that were withering in the drought. The project was largely run by development brigades made up of former PLAN fighters, and although there were still a number of San there, I found the relationships somewhat confusing.

The Ovambos by and large despised the San, and the people living at Omega II had all fought on opposite sides during the war. It was hard to know how well they were really working together. Stripped of their old hunting and gathering way of life, and unable to farm without proper help, the San appeared to have been discarded now that they were no longer of use. The place made me uneasy; it seemed doomed to fail.

At a place called Bagani, small plots had been given to some former Bushman fighters, and family groups were living in tents with their meagre possessions. They had cleared land and tried to plant crops, but the lack of rain had withered them. It was a pathetic scene. Accustomed to the paternalism of the South African army, these people were unable to return to their traditional lifestyle but seemed totally unable to manage on their own. Always marginal, they seemed even more so now, living pathetic lives among the filth and flies in the relentless heat. Everyone was hungry and listless, and many were sick with malnourishment, parasites, TB and malaria.

One of the men who had fought with the South Africans said, 'We have nothing. We can say that we played a game. Now the game is over, and these people who we fought have taken over the country.'

We went back to the little house on the river for our last two nights. Simon and Jack, the two Nature Conservation officials, were there to help us. Jon's ego got the better of him in the new company, and he regaled them with stories of the film 'he' was making.

In the morning we went off to find four young men who had recently been trained as an anti-poaching unit. They had been tracking poachers who had wounded an elephant, but hadn't managed to catch them. The anti-poaching unit comprised a mixed bunch of both ex-SWAPO and ex-SADF, all working happily together as Namibians. One of them, in particular, was a delight.

'Before independence, everything was tough, I may say. I had no freedom. You had to ask permission to do anything. Independence to me is great,' he said. 'Things don't come in an eye-blink, but I can say the changes are coming. Look, I can talk to you now and not have to say, "Yes, madam".'

Then, as I finished the interview and thanked him, he said, quite automatically, 'Thank you, madam.'

We all burst out laughing.

'It takes time,' he said through his laughter.

On the last night there was a full moon, and so Simon and Jack decided to go and look for elephants that had been damaging people's crops. The elephants apparently did this every night at that time of year, and seemed to do it for sheer fun. We drove to a nearby village and set off in single file through the bush to the fields, where we stood silently, without moving, for some time. No elephants appeared, though, and at midnight we went back to the camp. Filming was finished. Jon and I were leaving for Windhoek in the morning, while Craig and Robin were staying on a few days longer.

For some time now, there had been tensions within the crew, and that night we had one last quarrel. Craig's intensity would sometimes put us all on edge – he had never entirely approved of the film I was making and had his own ideas for a film in Namibia.

Jon's habit of trying to take over hadn't helped either. Perhaps we had just been together in the bush for too long.

As we climbed out of the Land Rover, Jon started giving Craig instructions as to what to shoot in the morning. I was almost speechless with rage, but waited for him to finish, and then said, 'As far as I know, I am still the director of this film.

I prefer to decide for myself what to shoot, and not have the researcher issuing the cameraman with instructions.'

I turned to Craig and told him quietly what I wanted him to do. Jon stormed off furiously to write in his journal, muttering 'drama queen' just loudly enough for me to hear.

On the road back to Windhoek the next day, Jon and I were both quiet for some time. It had been a difficult shoot. The heat had been wearying, the ongoing tension between myself, Jon and Craig had tested our loyalties to each other, and I was aware that the film itself was not what I'd wanted it to be. After a long while, Jon turned to me and said, 'What was that all about?'

I knew what he meant. Something had gone wrong with the interpersonal dynamics during the shoot. Individually, we were all friends and liked one another, but something had happened to crew relations early on. We discussed it for a while and Jon apologised for the previous night. We were friends again. But I would still be pleased to see the back of him once we went our separate ways.

In Windhoek I felt the need for a bit of luxury while I tied up the loose ends, and so I checked myself into the only decent hotel in town. In the foyer, I met Gillian who was working with the World Food Programme and had just returned from Angola. We had met each other briefly when she was working at Central Television in London. Like the meeting with Giulio, the meeting with Gillian proved to be fortuitous, and three years later we were working together.

But before that could happen, I needed to complete the film Jon and I were scheduled to make in Mozambique.

Author interviewing in Mozambique **1988**
Production Still

# PART FIVE

## 1992 SPOILS OF WAR

*We pay for aid with our diamonds, timber and ivory.*

**Jonas Savimbi, UNITA leader, 1988**

*The trucks went up with equipment and came back with ivory, rhino horn and wood.*

*The hundreds of thousands of elephants became thousands, the thousands became hundreds and the hundreds tens.*

**Colonel Jan Breytenbach, *Spoils of War*, 1992**

# 1. MEETING THE ENEMY 2

I was holding on for dear life. My arms were wrapped tightly around the plump man in front of me who was driving an off-road motorbike through dense bush. He was going too fast and I was clutching his stomach. I could hardly bear to look. If we had an accident here, what would happen? My mother had always told me not to go out with boys on motorbikes. I could see why. This was not going to be all right. I needed to get off – now.

I yelled in his ear, 'Mr President, we want to film you arriving at the airfield on your bike. But it will not look good on international television if you are seen to arrive with a white South African woman on the back of your bike.'

He braked in a cloud of dust, and left me to trudge the rest of the way to the airfield.

It was October 1992 and I was in Mozambique again, making the documentary Jon and I had been researching about South Africa's use of ivory to help fund its wars in Angola, Namibia and Mozambique. Our crew this time were Noel and Mel. Both were old hands at foreign documentaries for British television – professional and somewhat detached.

It proved to be a difficult, almost impossible, film to set up. We had information and evidence regarding the extent of the ivory trade in Angola, but the vicious war between UNITA and FAPLA in the south made filming there impossible. We had begun to investigate the story in both Namibia and Zimbabwe, but were warned off; there were people of influence involved, and filming would be dangerous. In the end we planned to do the bulk of the filming in Mozambique.

During the endless meetings with Channel Four and Central Television, it often seemed that the commissioning editors and I were talking about different stories. They wanted something that was not only not the film I intended to make, but most likely impossible. The commissioning editor seemed to think that poachers would simply lead us to elephant carcasses, although I never mentioned this as a possibility. When he came into the editing room months later he shouted, 'Where are the dead elephants? I want to see dead elephants!' The whole thing turned out to be a bitter experience. It was not my usual sort of story and I was struggling with it.

In Mozambique it seemed that the war had finally run out of steam. The Italians, with the help of the South Africans (who had backed Renamo in the first place), were trying to broker a ceasefire.

Afonso Dhlakama, the leader of Renamo, was not convinced that peace was necessary and so he flew back and forth to Rome, objecting to various clauses and holding up the agreement. While the negotiations stalled and restarted, Renamo launched offensives to try and capture territory that would give them a better deal. They claimed to hold vast swathes of the countryside, but had never held major towns and were delaying the peace while trying to gain some of the district capitals. When the peace was eventually signed in early October 1992, there was no outward sign of joy or celebration in Maputo; the long war and the drawn-out end to it had exhausted everyone.

By then it was possible to get to areas outside of Maputo that had been closed for years. However, the roads were mined and the UN peacekeeping force would not allow us to drive in ordinary cars. We needed armoured vehicles. I had phoned

Stefan from England and told him that I wanted to hire his Casspirs for a few days to go to Maputo Elephant Park near Ponto do Ouro, south of Maputo. No one had been there in years.

Like so many arrangements with Stefan, the initial agreement was retracted and renegotiated while he wavered between enthusiasm and reluctance. He, or his boss, wanted a huge fee in US dollars. Finally, a modest sum was agreed upon.

The filming in and near Maputo was planned for the end of our time in Mozambique before we went on to Swaziland and South Africa. Before that we would be travelling to the provincial town of Beira and then to Bazaruto Island.

For the first time it was possible to make contact with Renamo in Maputo. I wanted to interview Dhlakama about their involvement in the ivory trade. The Renamo representatives, and some of their international advisors, had moved to the Italian Club across from the beach, just outside of town. Its bar and swimming pool made it a popular meeting place on weekends, but it also had a group of thatched rondavels set in a secluded grove of trees where Renamo were able to keep a low profile. Days of phone calls and discussions finally found us standing nervously outside the Renamo rondavel, with a letter of introduction in our hands. We were about to meet the enemy.

We waited in an anteroom, where bodyguards sat all day watching television. It had been a special concession of the peace negotiations to bring the Renamo leadership and their entourage to the capital for meetings, but the government either didn't trust them, or else were worried that Maputo citizens might react with violence to their presence. Either way, they were forbidden to go into town.

Renamo's political representative, Anselmo Vitor, eventually came into the room to meet us. A typically soft-spoken Mozambican, he wore a mild expression. He was also rather plump, and was dressed casually in short sleeves and light trousers.

It takes a huge leap of imagination to stop thinking of the enemy as demons, and for them to appear in the guise of recognisable people. But here we were talking with the enemy, and they were just like anyone else. Anselmo Vitor and the others at the Italian Club may not personally have committed atrocities, yet they were the people responsible for the destruction of Mozambique's dreams of independence. They had let loose a terror on the land and had forced ordinary people to carry out unspeakable acts.

'*Bom dia*,' we greeted him. 'It is very kind of you to meet us.' We went through the usual explanations and pleasantries, and Vitor made noncommittal but polite replies. Conversation was hard going, but it did result in him giving us a somewhat nonspecific letter, which we hoped would enable us to get into Dhlakama's headquarters at Gorongosa. All we had to do was find a way to get there, and the only possibility would be an aid flight.

Fortunately for us, the International Red Cross and the World Food Programme were planning to start food aid flights from Beira once the ceasefire had been signed. Reports were coming in of thousands of people dying of starvation in the Renamo areas and the need to get food in to the population there was urgent. There was already an airstrip at Gorongosa, as this was how Renamo were supplied from South Africa. Although we had no guarantee of getting onto an aid flight, and no way of being sure that Dhlakama would be at his headquarters if and when we did get there, we decided in any case to go to Beira to try and reach him.

Central Mozambique and parts of Zimbabwe were in the grip of a fearsome drought. This should have been the beginning of the rainy season. But instead, each morning, the sun seemed to burst over the horizon, a fiery orange ball shooting straight up into the sky and burning its rays down relentlessly until it disappeared at dusk. Dust storms blew up out of nowhere, whirling scraps of paper and columns of dust through the air.

To make matters worse, Renamo had bombed Beira's pumping stations. Sanitation had broken down completely. People talked about *a guerra da agua*, the war of the water. Much of our time waiting in Beira to go to Dhlakama's headquarters in Gorongosa was spent trying to obtain water. Water to drink and water to wash with.

We had been lent a government flat that was adequate but not very comfortable. We were all sharing rooms, and in some cases beds, so there was nowhere to go to escape the heat or each other's company. As days passed and the possibility of a flight seemed to recede, the crew became bored and our nerves began to fray. One morning Jon came to the table later than the rest of us. He took a sip of coffee.

'Who put salt in my coffee?' he demanded.

It took a while to calm him and convince him that it was the brackish water that made his coffee salty, and that it wasn't a childish prank.

In desperation, I eventually struck a deal with a Rhodesian, an ex-Selous Scout who was not allowed into Zimbabwe and was wanted by the South African police for trading in endangered species, among other things. Somehow he had managed to set himself up with a timber mill outside Beira. We were interested in trying to speak to him, as we had evidence that he was involved in a company called Frama Inter-trading, which had been set up as a front company to handle the illegal movement of ivory and teak coming out of Angola. We spent several afternoons in the now completely derelict Don Carlos Hotel, spying on the various comings and goings at his heavily guarded house opposite. We learned nothing of interest, though.

One day we decided I should put a tiny microphone into my bra, then go to his house to get some sort of response from him. As soon as I entered the house I was overcome with terror, realising that he probably knew more about us than we suspected, and that he would know I had been bugged. So I didn't switch on the mike. However, I *was* able to negotiate a tanker of water to be delivered to our house.

It was wonderful, we all showered and flushed the toilet, but by the next day the water had all been used up and I had to go back and beg to buy yet another tanker. We soon discovered that, once the tank was switched on inside our flat, all the inhabitants of the small building had access to our water and were quick to drain it.

We devised a method of showering, whereby we all got undressed and stood in a line outside the bathroom. One person switched on the water and we ran into the shower in quick succession. Then we switched off the tank. After that, when we came home each day, the other inhabitants would be sitting hopefully with buckets and plastic bowls, waiting for us to arrive so that they could fill them in the time it took us all to shower and flush the toilet.

In an effort to get everyone out of the flat and working, I arranged for us to drive along part of the Beira corridor towards the Zimbabwean border to do some filming. The last time I had driven that route was in 1986 on *Destructive Engagement*, when it was still under constant attack and considered a dangerous expedition. Now Zimbabwean and Frelimo troops had secured the corridor, the oil pipeline was running, and so were food and other convoys.

The road, which had been all but deserted in 1986, had become a vast refugee camp, as people migrated closer to the road and railway line where they had access to food and protection. Nearly sixty per cent of the population of Manica and Sofala provinces had crowded into this corridor. At places, the huts stretched to the horizon. In the heat, the stink of raw sewage was pervasive, and dysentery and cholera were endemic.

At Dondo, about fifty kilometres from Beira, we filmed in a tent clinic filled with scrawny babies attached to drips, their mothers next to them on the floor, vainly shooing flies. In previous years I had seen people in Mozambique dying of hunger; now they were dying of thirst.

Queues at water pumps stretched for miles. Women and young girls would place a stone, or a bucket, or a plastic container in the line to hold their places, while at the head of the queue people took turns pumping a thin trickle of water, the sweat streaming off them as they did so. When the water ran out, squabbles erupted.

What had once been one of the most densely wooded areas of the country had been stripped bare of every possible source of wood to make cooking fires. Whole hillsides were denuded of trees, looking as though they had been napalmed. The normally lush bush had withered and dried; crops burned up under the sun.

Sometimes it felt like the end of the world. One day the heat was so intense that I tried to get shelter by standing in the cameraman's shadow. After Noel had stepped on me for the umpteenth time, he snapped, 'What the hell are you doing, Toni?'

'I am trying to stand in your shadow,' I said. 'My feet are burning.'

We gave up and went back to Beira to continue our own struggle to obtain water to wash with and give the toilet its daily flush.

One day we drove up past Chimoio, into the Vumba Mountains near the Zimbabwean border. For some time we went up a steep, sandy track that wound up into the forest. In normal years, these forested hills on the border are lush and green with abundant vegetation, but this year the trees were dry, with a few withered, brown leaves that rattled in the hot breeze. We came to the remains of what must once have been a farmhouse; now it was derelict, with broken windows and stucco peeling off the façade. In the neglected front garden, there were all sorts of exotic flowering bushes, now overgrown with brambles and small saplings. A man was guarding a car parked in the drive.

We had been told that there were many poachers in these hills, and we'd come to find them. Leaving the vehicle with the guard, we carried our equipment up a steep and narrow path that led us higher and higher. Dry leaves and twigs crackled underfoot. At a bend on the pathway we stopped to catch our breath, and out of the forest came three ragged men and a dog. All of them were carrying old guns.

'*Bom dia*,' we said politely, moving out of their way.

'*Bom dia*,' they greeted us and hurried off down the track.

'Wait a second,' someone said. 'Who were those guys? They had guns and a dog. They're poachers.'

We rushed off back down the track, but by the time we got

to the house they had driven away.

Apart from a man who came to our door one night offering to sell me small tusks, those were the only poachers I saw. They didn't seem like an evil syndicate to me, just hungry Mozambicans hunting for food.

At last the Red Cross food flights began, and we got a ride on one of the first Antonovs flying maize and cooking oil into Gorongosa. We sat on food sacks in the hold, staring out over monotonous brown bush and dried-up river beds.

Gorongosa had been the playground of Portuguese and Rhodesians; a game reserve to the north of Beira, it had once teemed with herds of buffalo, elephants and other game. Now, isolated by war, it had become a major Renamo base that had also served as a hunting ground for ivory. The lodges had all been destroyed, along with virtually all the animals.

Today it is a proper park again, restocked with animals, and the lodges rebuilt. It is run in accordance with modern techniques of eco-tourism, with a reforestation project and efforts to make sure that local communities benefit from the park. None of that was imaginable when we were there.

We landed in a clearing in a dry forest and jumped off the loading ramp at the back of the plane as thousands of people, dressed in bark and animal hides, surged towards the plane from the surrounding bush. They were strangely silent, with the desperate stares of the starving. All the women wore bizarre home-made cone-shaped brassieres constructed out of bits of rag; the ideas of decency imposed by America's right-wing Evangelical backers of Renamo still had currency among these desperate people. Snot-nosed children, with the huge bellies of the malnourished, dived to snatch up fallen grain as the food sacks were tossed out. In the heat, the smell of unwashed bodies was overpowering.

As the plane took off again, we were caught up in the hot blast of the engines and covered in a dust storm. The Russian pilots had told us they would be back in the afternoon with one more food drop. They would circle the strip once, and if we did not reach the plane by the time the food was unloaded, they would not wait for us.

A young man wearing a 'Viva Dhlakama' T-shirt pushed through the mob to greet us, as several motorbikes appeared out of the bush in a whirl of dust. This was our transport. I had heard that Dhlakama had all-terrain bikes. It had sounded crazy, but was a perfect form of transport for the bush. We clambered onto the back of the bikes, trying to balance the film equipment and holding on as we bumped over the rough ground and through the bush. In an apparent effort to confuse us, they seemed to take a long, circuitous route.

At a clearing in the forest, we were taken to one of several sturdy wood-and-thatch huts that were furnished with wooden benches, and told to rest.

'The President is coming from the mountains a long way off,' we were told.

An hour passed, and then another, as we sat, bored and anxious, beginning to wonder if Dhlakama really would arrive. Jon and I ventured out of our hut and peeped into some others. In one there was a radio receiver, and in another we found a South African Airways luggage tag on the ground.

Finally we were told that 'The President' was ready to receive us. We walked a short distance to another clearing, where tables and chairs had been set up in the shade. And there was Dhlakama, waiting to greet us. He was wearing his full uniform with four gold stars on each shoulder indicating his status as general. The large red epaulettes also bore three crossed arrows, a Spanish fascist symbol.

Dhlakama was smaller than I had expected from the television pictures that I had seen of him, a plump man with glasses and a round, smiling face. An older man, a senior advisor, hovered nearby and acted as interpreter, even though Dhlakama spoke good English. My questions were translated into Portuguese for him, giving him time to consider his answers. After a cordial exchange of greetings, and feeling rather obsequious, I asked him not to be offended if some of my questions about his role were provocative.

Dhlakama didn't get angry or begin to rave. He handled the interview professionally, answering carefully with a pleasant and smiling demeanour. In rational tones, he explained that the death of elephants was anathema to Renamo. 'Renamo are dedicated to wildlife,' he said. 'Our soldiers were instructed during the war not to kill animals; not only elephants, but even trees.'

I told him about the testimony given to us by a senior South African officer of the 'arms for ivory' operation run by Military Intelligence, and the film of piles of tusks and guns after one of his bases was taken by Frelimo. Then I showed him the captured Renamo documents detailing ivory prices per kilo and its exchange rate for weapons.

'It is all propaganda,' he explained. 'Frelimo planted it. It was the Zimbabweans and government troops who killed the elephants and stole all the ivory. Furthermore, the population do not flee from Renamo, but they flee from the Zimbabweans, Malawians and Tanzanians.'

He was enjoying the interview and so, feeling more courageous, I moved from wildlife to humans. I asked him about the atrocities against women and children that Renamo had consistently been accused of. I told him that I had filmed and interviewed many of these victims, over several years, in Mozambican hospitals and elsewhere in the country.

It was simple, Dhlakama explained. 'The lady journalist must have interviewed many people without legs who said they'd been injured by Renamo. Frelimo prepared all these people. Put them in beds, so they could say to journalists: "Look at all the atrocities committed by Renamo."'

I quoted from an American State Department report that described Renamo as waging a 'systematic and brutal war of terror against innocent civilians ... beatings, rape, looting, burning of villages, abductions ... One of the most brutal holocausts against ordinary human beings since World War Two.'

Facing me squarely, and without hesitating, Dhlakama denied each allegation at length, claiming that this was proof of a disinformation campaign being waged against Renamo.

I went on to ask him about the use of child soldiers and children forced to commit horrible acts. I told him that, when filming *Chain of Tears* in 1988, I had spent time at a special centre in Maputo that had been set up for these children.

Dhlakama was not shaken. He found this easy to dismiss. 'The first thing Frelimo does when a journalist arrives in Maputo is to present a crowd of children who say: "I was a soldier. My mother was killed. Renamo gave us a gun and forced us to fight."'

I pressed this issue; I was very sure of my ground. 'Mr President, I have spent much time with these damaged children, I have filmed them and interviewed them, and I know that their stories were true. I was very affected by it all.'

This annoyed Dhlakama, and for a moment he lost his careful tone. 'My mother is dead, Renamo gave me a gun,

Renamo made me fight,' he said, imitating the whine of a child.

This was not a foot soldier carrying out orders, but one of the architects of Renamo's policies. He was head of the force responsible for the destruction of Mozambique's dreams for independence as well as the mutilations, deaths and displacement of so many millions. He may not personally have lifted a finger – the men who give the orders rarely have to but they cannot deny that they know what is done in their name. Despite his soft voice and pleasant demeanour, this was clearly an ambitious man, ruthless enough to have eliminated any rivals in the quest for leadership. The real face of evil, he was impervious to the evidence I presented to him.

After the interview, we were offered lunch. This was a fairly formal affair with tablecloths, china plates, fresh water, and cooked food. All through lunch Dhlakama talked. On and on he went about the great conspiracy against Renamo.

'All the frontline states are against us,' he complained. He was concerned about Renamo's poor image, especially in Britain. 'I feel this is caused by Frelimo's communist propaganda.'

Then he asked me how best to change this poor image. He seemed to feel that he had already won the war: 'Renamo stands for multi-party democracy.'

When he talked about 'Frelimo's Marxist love affair with Maggie Thatcher,' I had to keep from catching the eye of anyone else on the crew for fear of collapsing into giggles. But there was no eye to meet. Jon had his head down, trying to capture every word that Dhlakama uttered in his notebook. Noel, the cameraman, was staring off into space. However, Mel, the sound recordist, appeared to be completely enthralled and was enthusiastically agreeing with everything that Dhlakama said. We were being carefully watched by the canny senior advisor/translator. Unable to argue against Dhlakama for fear of losing the interview that we had shot, and yet unable to perjure myself further by agreeing, I sat and nodded and smiled and nodded.

Although he had clearly been coached in the right phrases, Dhlakama was far more than the puppet I had expected. But despite his charm and the gracious way we had been received, the flashes of wild megalomania and paranoia that came through his talk were disturbing. This was the man who wanted to be president of Mozambique.

It was late, and I was beginning to get anxious. Dhlakama was enjoying himself with us and seemingly had no other pressing engagements. I began to wonder if we'd been kidnapped and were being held there for his amusement. After an interminable period of time, I heard the Antonov circle. I tried to break into the flow of talk, saying we had to leave.

'No hurry, no hurry,' he said, keeping us for tense minutes after we had heard the plane land, while he wound up his talk and his aides were sent off to fetch Dhlakama badges and Renamo flags for us. Eventually he called for the motorbikes and we were whipped off to the airstrip.

Dhlakama insisted that I ride pillion with him. It was the last thing in the world that I wanted but, arms tight around his ample middle, we shot through the bush. I was too terrified to realise how ridiculous we must have looked.

I got off near the airstrip, and the crew filmed him driving onto the strip. A mass of ragged people had crowded around the ramp of the aircraft, oblivious to their leader in their desperation to get at the food sacks.

A Renamo soldier shouted and got the crowd to join in a rhythmic clapping as Dhlakama climbed onto the mound of sacks and addressed the people, telling them that he had brought them the food.

We had to shove our way through the sea of people to scramble into the hold of the Antonov. The Russian pilots were anxious, beginning to taxi before the ramp was fully raised; one of the aircrew was still pushing away people who were trying to cling to the ramp as take-off began.

Once in the air, we relaxed, and hysteria took hold. We were all shouting and laughing at once.

'Jesus,' Jon said. 'Did you hear what he said about Maggie Thatcher's "Marxist love affair with Chissano"?'

'I really thought he was going to keep us there,' I said. 'I thought we wouldn't be allowed to get to the plane in time.'

'Mel, you seemed very impressed by Dhlakama,' we teased. 'You were hanging on his every word and agreeing with him: "Yes, Mr President, you are right, Mr President." Looks like you were totally taken in by him.'

I wasn't actually sure that Mel hadn't genuinely been impressed by Dhlakama's ravings. However, he was indignant. 'Well, someone had to nod him yes,' he said 'None of you lot were prepared to do it, and it was obvious that unless someone agreed with him, we'd all be held hostage.'

Back in Beira, where a sea breeze made it marginally cooler than the baking bush of Gorongosa, I phoned the British TV company to tell them that I had a unique interview with Dhlakama at his bush headquarters, and that we should try and sell it to Channel Four News. We had high hopes.

But the interview was never broadcast. The peace had been signed; Mozambique, which was never high on the media agenda anyway, was no longer news. And Dhlakama was no longer a rebel leader, simply someone who would be standing for president in the coming UN-organised elections.

My dealings with Renamo, with Dhlakama and other disreputable characters in Beira, made me feel contaminated. Also, I felt bad about the fact that I'd intended to use the material against them, that I had not been totally honest with them. This was not my way, and not the way I liked to operate.

Flying over Mozambique **1986**
*Photograph by:* Ivan Strasburg

## 2. NO DEAD ELEPHANTS

I was lying at the pool at the Cardoso hotel in Maputo, reading my book, when suddenly a dark shadow blotted out the sun. I turned over and looked up. It was Piet, or Gert. I never could tell them apart.

'We don't like you,' he said with menace in his thick accent, 'and we don't like your crew. We don't want to take you with us. But when Stefan trusts, we all trust. When Stefan doesn't trust, we don't trust.'

Then he smiled, or was it a grimace? And walked away. He had made it sound like a threat.

Back in Maputo, we were getting ready for our trip to Maputo Elephant Park with Stefan. He spent a lot of time with his two ex-Koevoet mates, drinking with them and hanging out with Mozambican girls. The two men had been part of the landmine clearance team, and this was the first time I'd met them.

Stefan was more taciturn than he'd been earlier in the year. Third Force violence in South Africa had escalated, and Inkatha, in particular, was running a low-level war almost identical to Renamo's in Mozambique. He told us that a South African journalist had written a story about him in the Sunday papers. It disclosed Stefan's involvement in smuggling guns to Inkatha from Renamo, using his white Casspirs as cover. Stefan felt he was in big trouble. His boss was certainly in trouble.

It was on this trip that Eddie, my journalist friend from South Africa, phoned to say he was investigating the murder of a high-profile activist in the Eastern Cape, and he believed that Stefan had been involved. He asked me to find out about an identifying mark on his body.

Stefan seemed to feel at the time that his life was at an end, that he was being unfairly accused. He could see no way out and was moody and depressed. He had already begun to try to understand and reconcile himself with his past, and this was one of the things that always attracted me to him. His companions, the Piets and Gerts of this world, didn't have the same ability to question and analyse – people like that are just trained killers. Stefan was also a trained killer, but he was something more than just that.

I have often asked myself why I continued my friendship with him. And the only answer I have is that, beyond the mutual attraction, the instant curiosity, the excitement of meeting the enemy, it was his self-questioning, and his efforts to come to terms with his life, that interested me. I felt that we had begun to trust one another.

Now, though, I wonder about this trust. Stefan had been specifically trained to gain trust from the enemy. That was what he did. He had told me about it often. He told me how he would spend weeks and weeks alone with someone they had captured, gaining their trust just to get them to talk. Not hurting them or torturing them, just being alone together with them.

But whatever the truth was, I believe that Stefan trusted me at the time. Now, he was the one on shaky ground, the tables had turned, and maybe he saw me as his link with the new order. Later on though, I think he just needed to talk with me, and maybe he felt he owed me something.

Stefan was the perfect gentleman. He was kind and couteous in an old-fashioned way and never swore in front of women – my bad language really seemed to shock him. He went out of his way to help. On one occasion, when the car didn't arrive to take my crew to the airport, he brought them himself in the very early morning, and then waited for me so that we would have a moment together.

The arrangements to go to the Elephant Park became complicated. We had found a one-time elephant hunter, now hanging out in Mozambique, who would accompany us. He had a chequered past and seemed to be a rather dodgy character, but he now appeared to be in favour with the Mozambicans, and had become totally sold on conservation.

During that trip, I learned that many of the 'conservationists' we came across around the region were ex-military – traumatised men from the wars in Rhodesia, Vietnam and elsewhere, who couldn't live with people, or without guns. They were at home in the bush and were able to love animals in a way that they couldn't love humans. Remote and isolated places allowed them to continue their lifestyles in a manner that they couldn't do elsewhere.

Stefan proposed bringing someone else along, and the person turned out to be a terrifying Portuguese guy who was trying to reclaim a family farm that was on the way to the park. His family had abandoned it when Frelimo came to power in 1975, and now he wanted it back. To make things worse, he'd previously been in trouble with the government because of his pro-Renamo sympathies.

We all met up at the Cardoso. Jon and I instantly told Stefan that we neither wanted nor needed this man along with us. We felt that he would jeopardise the filming, that he might even compromise us, and cause the government to retract our permissions. But for some reason, Stefan insisted that he would be useful to us. We argued. Actually, it felt more like blackmail than argument; although it was never spelled out, the implication was that this bloke either accompanied us, or the trip was off.

The man boasted about guns and killing. So far, I'd avoided talking to him, but now I turned to him and said, 'We are a film crew and this is our trip. Under no circumstances are there to be any guns on the vehicles that I am paying for.' I drummed it in, over and over: 'I refuse to ever have guns around my crew, unless I am accompanied by the army, and I am not changing my rules now. I don't care how "dangerous" you think the situation is.'

The arguments went on all afternoon but eventually, things were resolved. Stefan would take the gun he normally had in his vehicle; other than that, no one else would have guns, except, of course, for the Mozambican *escorte*. The Portuguese guy would come with us unarmed.

I know there was another agenda here that I never fully figured out. The permissions we had to travel, and the fact that we needed to hire the Casspirs, gave Stefan and the weird characters that he hung around with a legitimate excuse to do other things as well; but I never worked out what exactly the Portuguese guy was up to. Was he just using the security we provided with the Casspirs to visit his farm? Or did he want to show something to Stefan?

At the compound where we transferred into the Casspirs – both of them, this time – the Portuguese guy arrived with his guns. I went crazy and shouted at him, 'I was serious the other day, and unless you get rid of those guns right now, none of us will leave.'

I stormed off. Eventually, they were discarded.

I travelled with Stefan in his vehicle, together with Noel and Mel. In the other vehicle, driven by Gert, or Piet, were the elephant man, the Portuguese guy and Jon.

It took time to get clear of the outskirts of the city. Stefan was in a happy mood; he always was when he was going into the bush. 'This is where your friends hung out,' he said as we passed Matola, acknowledging that I knew of his involvement in attacking the ANC. In January 1981, the SADF had carried out a raid on ANC houses in the suburb of Matola; they killed sixteen people.

We stopped for a break near a dam. Stefan and his guys stood in a huddle while we tried to film them standing around the Casspirs. They kept walking out of shot; they were very careful not to get in front of the cameras.

Our next stop was at the farm the Portuguese guy was reclaiming. He wanted to make breakfast, which we refused to allow; so he strode around screaming at what seemed to be a group of workers. I was angry about the hold-up and refused to get out of the vehicle. Finally, we moved on.

After that, we were in fairly remote country. There were few signs of people and it seemed that not many vehicles had been along this road since the war had come to an end. A couple of ancient tanks marked Changalane, the last government-held point. After that, the road passed through thick bush. Occasionally, we passed abandoned farms with burnt-out buildings and overgrown fields. Our escort soldiers became more alert. One of them shouted out, '*Bandido*,' as we passed a man with a gun, who stood watching us.

I thought nothing of it, but Stefan said, 'They have seen us pass now, they might mine the road, knowing we must come back this way.'

The road took us through bush thick after recent rains. The going was hard and took several hours. At the entrance to the Elephant Park, the warden was waiting for us – a shy

Mozambican who had tried to do what he could with very little outside contact during the war. He was happy to see us, greeting us by saying that we were the first 'visitors' in years. With the help of his careful guidance along barely visible wheel tracks, we drove to what had once been offices and a field school. Nothing was left other than crumbling walls, charred rafters, and rubble.

Watched over by our *escorte* who sat on top of the Casspirs, we roamed around, finding used cartridges and old bones in the rubble. We ate our lunch sitting against a wall.

I have one photograph of that trip: Stefan and I propped against the wall, with his gun between us, and on our right the old elephant hunter. I am looking straight ahead and Stefan is gazing directly at me.

After lunch, we drove through thick bush and grassland and saw no game at all, nor any sign of it. Certainly, there were no elephants around. The plan had been to spend the night there in order to film again the next day, but there was nothing to film except waving grass. We decided to return to Maputo.

The sun was low and we were in danger of being on the road after dark, breaking that cardinal rule of conflict zones. We were driving fast and, as we flashed around a bend near where we had seen the *bandido* in the morning, a couple jumped out of the road and into a ditch. Stefan waved, the man returned the wave, but the old woman dropped the bundle she was carrying and stood with her hands over her ears.

With a jerk, Stefan pulled the wheel to one side and the Casspir leapt onto the bank, hitting young trees as we lurched along. A few yards on, he swerved back onto the road. Behind us, the second vehicle performed the same bucking manoeuvre. Noel, the cameraman, hit his head on the steel top of the vehicle and our gear flew about in the back.

The crew began to shout angrily, 'What the fuck are you doing?'

'Landmine in the road,' Stefan said. 'I could see that the tracks we'd made in the morning had been dug up and then smoothed over. When the old woman put her hands to her ears I knew she expected a bang. They knew we'd be coming back this way, so they'd have put in something like an anti-tank mine.'

It all happened so quickly that I had no time to be aware of danger. Stefan had saved all our lives.

When we reached the outskirts of Maputo we relaxed. We were stuck in a long line of returning trucks and cars, many of them loaded with wood, which was needed by the many displaced people in the city.

Now that we were out of danger, Stefan started to talk. The dreadful shootings at the Bisho stadium in the Ciskei had taken place not long before.

'What do you think about what the ANC did at Bisho?' he asked me, and went on to criticise a prominent ANC official.

'Be careful what you say about him,' I said. 'He is one of our oldest friends.'

We had lived opposite the family in exile in London, and our children had grown up together. Stefan became so excited at the idea that I knew this man that he took his eyes off the road for a moment and hit the back of a wood lorry. My cameraman bumped his head for the second time that afternoon.

'Fucking hell,' Noel shouted. 'Watch what you are doing.' He wasn't having fun.

It was then that I first suggested to Stefan that I'd like to make a film about him.

'No way. I know how Afrikaners come over on film.'

But, months later, he agreed that he would do the film sometime – but only with me.

When he dropped us off, Stefan joked, 'I thought we were going to get the chance to spend the night together. I had my pyjamas all packed.'

I was disappointed too.

Unlike Maputo Elephant Park, Tembe Elephant Park on the South African side of the border was teeming with elephants. Today, both parks are part of a transfrontier park and the elephants can cross freely between them. These elephants are reputed to be the largest in the world.

Tembe was not yet open to tourists; at that time, one of the people in charge was a rather strange American. He had fought in Vietnam, and when that war finished he needed more war, so he volunteered to fight for the Rhodesians. In Africa he had developed a love of wildlife and now here he was, working with elephants at Tembe.

'I'll show you lots of elephants,' he said to us. 'Be ready at midday tomorrow and I'll take you.'

Midday is not normally the time for game viewing, so we decided that this American knew nothing about game. However, the following day he took us to a platform high up in a tree, above a river-crossing. At midday a huge herd of elephants, from the smallest babies up to huge old cows, came to the river to bathe. It was one of those moments of sheer magic.

In the Kruger National Park, the park authorities allowed us to film an extraordinary scene. Every week they drove a truck piled high with flour, washing powder and other goods to a section of the park fence that bordered Mozambique. The dirt track on the Kruger side ran parallel with the fence. On the Mozambican side stood a ragged crowd of people. Many of them had heaps of wood in front of them. The game wardens opened a small hole that had been cut into the fence at ground level.

Several people at a time were allowed to crawl through the fence with their little piles of wood, and then gather round the truck.

'What's going on?' I asked.

'These people have nothing,' the white game warden said. 'There is war in their country, so we are helping them.'

I still didn't get it.

'But what are they doing?'

'Well, they chop down trees on their side and we buy the wood to sell to tourists in the park for firewood. We pay them in rand,' he explained.

Once all the wood had been bought, the Mozambicans were again allowed to crawl through the fence.

'OK, but now what's happening?' I wanted to know.

'Now they are buying things they need, like food and soap, from us.'

So the Mozambicans deforested their border area to sell the wood to the South Africans, who immediately took the money back in exchange for consumer goods. From the South African point of view, it seemed to be a useful system. They were saved from deforesting their side of the border, while their cash was returned immediately. The game warden seemed to have no idea that this was in any way exploitative, or that forcing people to crawl back and forth through a hole in the fence was an undignified and humiliating way of conducting these exchanges.

But there were other things that went on at that fence, which was why we were filming it. We were now seeing wood and consumer goods crossing, but during the war, this had been where Renamo and the South Africans exchanged ivory for guns. These vast, wild areas were the secret shipment points for ivory, arms, and men, throughout Mozambique's protracted war.

In Johannesburg we interviewed Colonel Jan Breytenbach of 32 Battalion. We told him that Dhlakama denied that Renamo had anything to do with the slaughter of elephants, or that they had received aid from South Africa.

'Rubbish! Absolute rubbish!' he exploded. 'That I know for a fact. I trained his troops after Nkomati. I trained him, and that's a fact, that's not speculation.

'That border was controlled by military personnel troops. They could go anywhere, freeze an area, as it were.' He explained, 'Military Intelligence would move in with their equipment, hand it over the fence to Renamo, and get the ivory. It is easy to do, because there's nobody there. I trained Renamo and a lot of them were smuggled out via the Kruger Park.'

He believed that the whole ivory smuggling operation from both Angola and Mozambique had been given the green light at the highest level. 'Perhaps even at the Minister of Defence level,' he said.

Breytenbach told us about a gift that UNITA leader Jonas Savimbi had presented to the then-president of South Africa, P. W. Botha: a perfect replica of an AK-47 carved out of a giant tusk. We later filmed it at the museum in George, where it was being kept.

Soon afterwards, I went to Washington where I did

an interview with Craig van Note of the Environmental Investigation Agency. He'd spent many months undercover in northern Namibia investigating South Africa's trade in ivory and teak.

'In the 1980s we uncovered the "South African Connection",' he told me. That was the poaching and smuggling pipeline run by the SADF whereby over one hundred thousand elephants and tens of thousands of rhinos were killed in order to finance the wars in Angola and Mozambique. 'You can see the devastation of Angola's teak forests on satellite photos. In my view, the trade in illegal wildlife is connected to the same mafias that run drugs and arms. When the ivory is gone, when the teak is gone – and it will be, soon – southern Africa will see an influx of drugs, guns and other smuggling.'

Everything that Van Note predicted in that interview has since materialised.

The shoot, the gathering of material, is in many ways the easiest part of filmmaking – and it's fun too, especially if you have done your research well. But there comes the time when all those many feet of film and video need to be edited and a story constructed. Editing is hard work and can make or break a documentary. Deciding what goes in and what is redundant, which bits work together to drive the story forward and allow the characters to develop, is a skilled job. After that come all the specialist bits: cutting to music, putting in graphics and subtitles, and doing the sound mix. And there are times when it doesn't all come together as it should.

When the film was complete months later, it was a disaster. The commissioning editor was angry that I had failed to film dead elephants. But dead elephants are hard to find, and missing elephants are hardly riveting material. The

Mozambicans hated the film because the war was now over and they were trying to reconcile the country. The South Africans hated it because South Africa was moving towards its own democratic elections and did not want to deal with the crimes of its past at this point. I hated it too. It was not the kind of story I should ever have embarked on. I knew that I had to stick to what I did well – films about people.

Every time I allowed male commissioning editors to bully me into their way, whenever I attempted to imitate what I felt was the male-oriented style of reportage filmmaking, it turned into a disaster. I had to learn to follow my instincts.

I was tired of war. Southern Africa was moving on and I needed to find a way to leave the pain and suffering behind and find more positive stories to film. I was jaded, I no longer believed that my films made any real difference; they were something people watched in between lighter television. I needed to stop for a while. I needed to do something that felt more constructive, and consider what sort of documentaries I wanted to make in the future.

In the meantime, I worked as a consultant on a survey of landmines in Mozambique, and felt that I was making a contribution to helping the country recover from the war years. Then in 1993 I became an observer with the United Nations Observer Mission in South Africa (UNOMSA), where I was deployed in the Eastern Cape and stayed on as a UN election observer. Later that year I did the same thing with the United Nations Operation in Mozambique (UNOMOZ). It was exciting to be on the ground as these historic elections took place in both countries. I felt that I had, in a very small way, contributed to the process, and could feel my way back into South Africa.

It also gave me a chance to reassess how I wanted to

express myself on film. I returned to filmmaking in 1995 – but by then I had a fuller sense of my own capacities and the confidence to express myself in my own voice.

Girl Mozambique, **1995**
Production Still

# PART SIX

## 1995 CHAIN OF HOPE

*I think children affected by war can get back part of their opportunities which were denied to them because of the conflict. I am not sure whether we can give them back the sense of childhood.*

**Graça Machel, *Chain of Tears*, 1988**

# 1. FINDING FRANISSE

During the years following *Chain of Tears*, I had tried to keep up with the children I had filmed, particularly the ones in Mozambique. I wanted to make a film following what had happened to these children, but had found it impossible to raise the finance. Once the war had ended, Mozambique, never high on the Western agenda, had sunk into complete oblivion.

Now, together with Gillian, whom I had met in Namibia in 1992, I managed to raise the money and we were about to start filming a follow-up. It was refreshing to work with a female producer and not to be travelling with an all-male crew. It made for a better balance between all of us and it was helpful to have female support.

Gillian was younger than me, and her good looks and long dark hair attracted plenty of male attention. I soon began to experience a strange phenomenon; I seemed to have become invisible. At first I was not quite sure what was happening. People still greeted me, but seemed generally to ignore my presence. Gradually it began to dawn on me. I had become an older woman.

It was 1995 and a good moment to be making this film. Mozambique had held its first democratic elections only months after South Africa had gone to the polls in 1994, and the United Nations Angola Verification Mission (UNAVEM) was in Angola to try and broker elections. There was a lull in the fighting and hope that the war would soon end.

This time I wanted to use a regional crew, and chose

Giulio – whom I had also met in Namibia – as the cameraman. Of Italian origin, Giulio was easy-going, with a naughty sense of humour. We got on well together, and he was enthusiastic and completely involved in the project. We have worked together many times since then and remain close friends.

Gabriel a Mozambican, was doing the sound. He was a Shangaan, and I'd known him for some time as we'd worked together on previous films that I'd made in Mozambique. Pedro, another old friend from Maputo, was the local producer. He was experienced in filmmaking; he was also something of a diplomat, good at cooling down fraught situations, and I was grateful to have him with us. It turned out to be a happy choice of crew. Gillian had done well with the budget and we had enough to pay a local researcher in Johannesburg to help me; Gillian dealt with the Angolan research, and Pedro worked on Mozambique.

The days of shooting documentary on film were over, so we would be shooting on video, which had come a long way since I'd made *Free to Move* in March 1992. Video editing had also progressed. With the event of digital editing, even films shot on conventional film were edited in this new way. It was extremely fast and gave directors and editors tremendous leeway in making radical changes quickly and with no extra costs.

Speed also brought disadvantages, though. Because changes could be made so fast, broadcasters had cut the number of weeks allotted to the editing process. Working under this sort of pressure took away valuable time needed to think and process what one was doing. I always insisted on having a week's break in the middle of an edit, simply to have time to reassess and think about where the film was going.

Peace had changed Maputo. Contrary to expectations, many refugees from the countryside had not gone back to the rural areas, but had stayed on in the city in the now-sprawling *barrios*. It was still shabby and run-down, but there were shops and supermarkets, consumer goods of all sorts from South Africa, new buildings going up and restaurants opening. It was also possible to travel to many places by road.

Aid agencies had burgeoned with the misery of war, famine, displacement, and poverty. During the war they had been a necessity, but since UNOMOZ had overseen the elections in 1994, the aid agencies seemed to have taken over the country. White Land Cruisers, with logos of the various agencies on their sides, cruised the streets of Maputo and sped around the rural areas. Local people with the right kinds of skills left jobs in government and public service to work for the dollar salaries paid by many agencies. Some aid workers had an inflated sense of importance, and strutted around as if they were there to save the country, as if the Mozambicans couldn't do anything for themselves. Of course, many were doing good and useful work, but I wondered how many of them came offering solutions without fully understanding the problems. I hoped that they weren't creating yet another African beggar state. However, the UN agencies in particular did help us enormously with transport and access.

Working with war-traumatised children was one of those areas where the Mozambican government worked closely with aid agencies. Even while the war was still on, the government had started to make efforts to reunite children separated from their families. In the late 1980s, more and more children were coming to the attention of the authorities, often when an area was recaptured by Frelimo, and they were faced with what to do with these children.

Together with UNICEF, Save the Children Fund (SCF), and other NGOs, the Directorate of Social Action started a programme to try and trace the families, or at least the communities, of these children. Details were taken from those who were old enough, or able, to remember their own names and names of family members, or at least the name of the village or district they came from. A Polaroid photograph was taken of each child, and these were then pinned to trees in the villages by local workers. Sometimes the children's voices were recorded and broadcast over the radio. It didn't take long for people to come forward and identify children.

Once they were identified, it was possible to return these children to their communities. If the parents had been killed or had moved away, then the extended family could be found. In some cases, the community would take the child in. In this way, Mozambique was able to avoid the expense of having large orphanages of separated or orphaned children and all the attendant problems. When a child was identified, the whole village would rejoice.

Later on, this system of family tracing was extended to the former Renamo areas. It was a simple and remarkably effective system.

The Llanghuene Centre had been disbanded, and the children we had filmed there had been reintegrated with their families or communities. Some of the older boys were grown up and working now.

The child I was most keen to contact was Franisse, the little boy from the Lhanguene Centre who had been forced to kill his parents and was mute. His story had been the one that most disturbed and saddened us during the making of *Chain of Tears* in 1988. I had heard in the meantime that he had recovered his health and begun speaking again and had gone to live with the family of Pedro, one of the other Lhanguene children.

Gillian and I were at the Mozambican Save the Children office in Maputo, trying to find out Franisse's whereabouts, when Senhor Horacio, one of the people working there, called me over.

'Look at these photos,' he said, holding up Polaroid pictures of two little girls. 'We have been working on tracing their families for some time. Renamo abducted them when their villages came under attack, and they were taken to a Renamo base and later given to families living there. We have finally confirmed their families, and are going to fetch them next week to take them home.'

Although these little girls had not appeared in *Chain of Tears*, the story was too good to miss and was surely a positive outcome of the end of the war. Coincidentally, the area where they were being held was not too far away from where we would be going to find Franisse. It was agreed that we would meet Senhor Horacio and his team in Chokwe, on our way back from filming Franisse, and accompany him to fetch the girls.

There was a muddle over the vehicle that Gillian had arranged for us from the World Food Programme, so we started out from Maputo later than intended. By the time we arrived in Manjacaze to pick up the social worker assigned to Franisse's family, it was already mid-afternoon. Gabriel and Pedro went off to look for her.

'The good news,' Gabriel announced, 'is that we have found Donna Bemvida. It is indeed a good day for us,' he smiled, playing on her name, which means 'good day'. Then he paused. 'But the bad news is that she is two ladies rolled into one.' He stood against the car chucking to himself.

The Land Cruiser had a double cab and open back. With Pedro and Cobra, the driver, in the front, and the rest of us squeezed snugly in the back, it had felt reasonably comfortable. The film gear was packed in the rear under the canvas tent that Cobra had insisted on bringing along. Cobra, now a World Food Programme driver, had once been a basketball player with the Mozambican national team and was hugely popular and fun to have with us.

We weren't that keen on the tent as it took up a lot of space, and anyway we had no intention of spending a night in the open. For this reason, we had not brought any food along either, although at the last minute the ever-mindful Giulio had packed a few tins of tuna and beans, and put a raw onion from the lunch table into his pocket.

Before leaving Maputo, Gabriel and Giulio had gone into town to buy clothes, blankets and other goods as presents for the families of children we were going to film, and had also bought a case of beer. Pedro had his bottle of whisky. We called these the 'boosters' and the 'blaster'.

Donna Bemvida was indeed a very large and jolly lady. Squeezing her into the back of the vehicle meant that someone had to sit on top of the tent on the open back. It turned out that she had no more idea of the directions than we did, though she did have a suggestion: 'There is an old man who comes from a village near to where we are going. If you give him a lift back to his village, he will be able to help us find the way.'

No one seemed to have a clue about the distance or the time it would take to cover it. Any enquiries elicited the answer: 'It is still far. Very, very far.'

The tarmac ended outside the town, and for a while we drove on a dirt road that wound through groves of cashew trees. But soon we had to turn off and put the vehicle into four-wheel drive, as we took a sandy track into a gloomy forest. There were no signs of life, either human or animal. It was eerie.

We drove in silence. At first it felt exciting, then it became tedious, and finally, hugely uncomfortable. Time passed, the forest grew darker, the track was barely visible, and the discomfort eventually became insupportable.

In desperation, Giulio burst out: 'Doesn't anyone know how much farther we have to go?'

Gabriel asked the old man.

'Still far,' came the reply in Shangaan.

It had begun to rain, and by now it was really dark – the kind of blackness you only experience out in the bush when there is no moon. The dense trees seemed to crowd us as we moved at a virtual crawl.

We seemed to have been driving for hours. We had. This was ridiculous. We shouldn't be driving around in the bush after dark. Eventually, at a fork in what was now no more than a path, we stopped.

'Which way?' Cobra asked. No one knew.

'Let the old man walk ahead of the vehicle,' Gabriel suggested, 'and he can guide us.'

'He'll get cold,' Cobra said.

'We'll give him one of the blankets we brought as presents,' Gabriel said.

But the old man demurred. 'It's too dark to see the path.'

On our trips, we all carried Maglites – small strong torches – and we were very possessive of them.

'Someone give him a Maglite,' I said. But everyone claimed that theirs were packed away with the equipment. They all knew that I carried mine in my bag. I gave it to the old man.

Wrapped in a blanket, carrying my Maglite, the old man walked ahead of the vehicle with the air of someone who had been forced at gunpoint to do something. He crashed around in the bush with Cobra trying to follow him, while we were thrown around in the back of the vehicle as the trees scratched and tore at the sides.

None of this felt like a good idea. We were off the road; the old man and Gabriel were worrying about wild animals, armed men and spirits, while Gillian and I worried about landmines.

We seemed to be driving round in circles. Several times we saw the light of fires in the bush.

'There must be people there. Let's go and ask them.' I suggested.

Apparently this was a stupid idea. Although the war was over, one didn't approach strangers in the bush at night. 'They could be bandits,' chorused the Mozambicans.

We stopped and argued. 'This is pointless. Let's just stop here and sleep until it gets light.'

'We can't be far. We must go on. It's too dangerous to sleep in the bush.'

Cobra managed to get us back to where the track had forked. The path widened, and we were driving in our own tyre tracks. Then the clouds parted and the Southern Cross shone directly ahead of us, visible through the windshield. The village we were heading for was north and we were driving due south, back in the direction from which we had come. Pedro was adamant that we were on the right track.

'We can't be,' I said pointing at the Southern Cross. 'Look

at it, it points south, we should be going north.'

'What do you know about stars, Toni?' Gabriel and Pedro mocked me. I pulled out my compass to prove that we were going south instead of north.

'White man's magic,' said Gabriel, dismissing it.

We were standing in the road, in a sort of Mozambican *confusão*, shouting at each other.

I pointed to the ground. 'These are our tracks, how many other vehicles have you seen in the last many hours?'

Gillian had been nervously whispering to me for some time about landmine protocol. She was right. I had had enough and insisted that we go no further.

'We will sleep right here, in the middle of the road,' I said. 'We will stay ahead of the vehicle on our own tracks where we know there aren't mines.'

Gillian was relieved and backed me up, although this was not a popular decision with the others.

'No one is to step off the road and into the bush,' I insisted. In the end, even this anarchic lot were nervous enough to obey. With some hilarity, the tent was pitched in the middle of the sandy road and we discovered that Cobra had brought some camp beds as well. We collected firewood and sat around the fire wrapped in the blankets we had intended as presents.

'Where are the boosters?' Gabriel asked, and the beers were brought out. Giulio started opening the tins of tuna and beans, and cutting up the onion from his pocket into the cans. We passed them round, each of us making do with the little we had.

Later, Guilio complained bitterly that whenever he was about to eat something, I would say, 'Has anyone given the can to the old man?' So in the end, the old man ate more than any of us.

Relaxed by the beers and food, Gabriel started telling stories. His gift for languages and storytelling made an easy bridge between us and Donna Bemvida and the old man. It felt quite jolly around the fire, until he began to tell us about men who turned into beasts at night.

'There are people who can change themselves into flying lions,' he said in a serious voice. The more we scoffed at this idea, the more serious he became. 'You don't believe me, but it is true. At night certain people turn into lions and can fly through the bush. They are very dangerous.'

'We all have a totem,' he explained, and told us what his was. Then he asked around. The old man and Pedro knew their totems and appeared to be in full agreement with Gabriel.

'What is your totem, Toni?'

'I don't know,' I said. 'We don't have totems in my culture.'

'I think it's a black cat,' Gabriel decided.

The more the talk of totems and spirits went on, fed mainly by Gabriel but vigorously backed up by the old man, the more frightened Gabriel became. By now, they had moved from the boosters to the blaster, and for much of the time Gabriel seemed to have a booster in one hand and the blaster in the other.

Gillian and I left them to it and, along with Donna Bemvida, went into the tent. Gabriel thought that it was probably best to stay awake all night to keep off the flying lions, and Pedro and Giulio preferred to sleep outside. Donna Bemvida settled her huge bulk onto one of the flimsy camp beds, which instantly collapsed. It collapsed several more times during the night, and each time she would set it up again, roaring with laughter.

Gabriel was famous among film crews for his stories, which he would tell with equal facility in Shangaan, Portuguese or English. Whichever language he was using, he had an idiosyncratic turn of phrase that turned the ordinary into something hilarious. I have now heard his version of the story of our night in the bush from several sources. Of course, each time it is an embellished version.

'Toni was the person who cruelly forced the poor old man out of the Land Cruiser, to walk in front of us in the danger of the night. She was the director and we had to obey her. If it hadn't been for the kindness of us in the crew, she wouldn't have allowed him a blanket or a torch.

'Not only that,' he would say, 'she was so frightened of stuff like landmines, that she put us all in danger of being eaten by wild beasts.' And so on.

Three years later, I was in Harare teaching a film workshop. I stayed at the Bronte Hotel, where the rooms faced onto a pretty garden with several resident cats roaming about. The first night at the Bronte, as I was falling asleep, a black cat came through the window, jumped onto my bed, and slept at my feet. In the morning it was gone.

It came every night that I was there and yet I never saw a black cat in the garden during the day. I questioned the staff and they told me that there weren't any black cats living at the hotel. Maybe Gabriel had been right about my totem. Maybe there are indeed flying lions in the bush in Mozambique at night.

In the early dawn light we all looked the worse for wear – those who had been on the boosters and blasters more so than the rest. The old man had become disorientated in the dark, and we found that we were only a few kilometres from the village we had been trying to get to.

Once there, several 'Franisses' were brought to me for inspection, and although it was seven years since I had seen him as a traumatised and malnourished six-year-old, I knew that none of these was the right one.

Someone offered to guide us to a family living a little distance away, whose son had been captured by the bandits. So, leaving the others with the vehicle, Giulio, Gabriel and I set off. It was a forty-minute hike down a narrow track through dense bush. The film equipment became heavier and more cumbersome with every stumbling step. The bush was full of scratching and biting things, and the heat and humidity had sweat dripping off our faces and into our eyes, attracting flies and other insects. We were dusty and dirty from the previous twenty-four hours, and none of us had had any breakfast. It all felt like a wild goose chase.

When we were just about ready to give up, we came across a woman digging a small vegetable patch at the side of the track. On the assumption that this could be Franisse's mother, Gabriel asked if we could film her. While Giulio began filming Gabriel questioned her in Shangaan, and we went through a confusing period where she claimed not to know anyone called Franisse. She had been startled by our arrival out of the bush, but eventually we established that she was indeed the mother of the boy we were seeking, although he no longer went by the name Franisse. She led us to a clearing where the family had three shabby huts and a small field of maize.

Once we were sure we had the right family, we sent someone to fetch Gillian, Pedro and Donna Bemvida to come and join us, and we were able to introduce ourselves properly and explain why we were there.

The woman told us that Franisse was a name that either Renamo had given to her son after he was kidnapped, or one that he'd given to himself. 'He told me about the people who came to film at the school when he was little. I am pleased for you to come and see him again.' He was at school right now, she told us, but would be home shortly. We met the rest of the family: his older brother, a married sister, and her two small children.

While we were talking to them, a child came running into the clearing, followed by Franisse. It was a heart-stopping moment as we instantly recognised each other and he gave me a huge grin. It was one of those rare instances of film luck that make the whole business worthwhile.

'When you are attacked you don't know where to run. You each go a different way. That is how we got separated,' Franisse's mother told us. 'I managed to escape with some of the other children, but the boy and his father didn't make it. There are two more of my daughters who I have never seen again. Maybe they were killed.'

We asked about the story that Franisse had told at Lhanguene about setting fire to the hut and eating meat from his father's body.

'Yes, it's true,' she said. 'The bandits made him set the hut alight, but we had already run away. The fire didn't kill us, but he didn't know that. They told him that to frighten him.

'Of course worried, I lost count of how long he'd been missing. I couldn't believe he was still alive, I thought he was dead. I only believed it when I saw and spoke to him. All these years I lived, believing this child was dead.' Overcome by her story, she turned away and began sweeping the yard.

'We were both taken by Renamo,' Franisse's brother told us in a low voice, looking at the ground as he spoke. 'Mainly, they used us as porters and servants. Then one day I injured my foot and they left me behind.'

We were unable to establish exactly what had happened after that. His foot was still a mess and the boy had difficulty walking. His mother and surviving sister had also been captured at some point, and were 'used' by Renamo. Generally this meant that they were made 'wives' of the bandits.

While Franisse was living with his friend Pedro's family, someone was able to make contact with his village, and had discovered that several of his family members were still alive.

His brother put it poignantly. 'He was just a little kid, involved with guns, away from his mother and brothers. It was best to keep silent. Who would care for a young boy? But he feels better now he's found me and his sister and mother. His heart has cooled down.'

This seemed to me an almost miraculous outcome, and as near to a happy ending as possible. Franisse had begun to talk again, although he was too shy to say more than a few words to us.

'I thought my family had been killed in the bush. I didn't know where they were.' Franisse had realistic expectations of life. 'When I am grown up,' he said, 'I want to be able to get a bit more land. I want to continue growing enough to eat.'

His family was living at subsistence level, growing just about enough to eat. They didn't even own one of the ubiquitous plastic buckets and basins. Before we left, we gave the family the gifts we had brought them, minus the blanket that the old man had taken. In turn, they gave Donna Bemvida two live chickens to take home, something they could ill afford to spare. We put the chickens in a shady place on the back of the Land Cruiser.

At Manjacaze, on our way back, we dropped Donna Bemvida off, and then made our way to Chokwe for our assignment with Senhor Horacio.

At the Hotel Limpopo in Chokwe, we found yet another

miracle of the return to normality in Mozambique: hot showers.

For the few days we used the hotel as our base, the crew would gather in someone's room after dinner to drink a few whiskys, smoke some dope, and talk. We learned about each other's families, and hopes, and dreams. Gabriel, the storyteller, entertained us each night with tales from his travels as part of President Machel's news crew.

By this time I'd come to realise that, as a director, it was best to be clear about what I wanted and to keep friendly with everyone – but to keep myself to myself.

## 2. ROSITA'S RETURN

The drive from Chokwe to find the two little girls took us along sandy tracks across the Limpopo plain, which was just as Kipling had described it: 'all dotted about with fever trees.' Now and again I glanced at the Polaroid photos of the girls, Rosita and Delphina.

At the end of the track we stopped, and Horacio got out to ask directions from a pregnant woman who had a baby on her back and two toddlers hanging onto the *capulana* tied around her waist. She pointed into the bush. The road ended here. Horacio would have to walk to find Delphina. We watched him vanish into the trees and long grass and then drove off to find Rosita, together with Victor, Horacio's Save the Children Fund (SCF) colleague.

The track became narrower and the bush denser. We had to be very careful not to stray off the edges of the track, as this area was known to be mined. There was no place to stop, turn around, or step out of the cars.

It was afternoon when we eventually reached our destination, and we hadn't seen another vehicle since leaving Chokwe hours before. By then, I was no longer thinking of Rosita because, faced with the difficult and urgent problem of where to pee, I was wishing that I had been born a man.

By the time the war ended, the authorities had extended the system of family-tracing throughout the country. As early as 1992, the system already had a network of fourteen thousand volunteers and had succeeded in reuniting twelve thousand children with their families. Much of this was due to the initiatives of the communities themselves.

Every one of these children had suffered severe trauma, and many of them had been abused both physically and emotionally. Torn from their villages and marched for days to distant districts, they had witnessed attacks and all sorts of death and destruction. Often, the families they were placed with had used the children as servants. For many years, the children had no contact with their parents, and they had no idea if their families were still alive.

Remote areas and villages didn't have postal services or telephones; families lived scattered over huge areas of bush where frequently there were no roads. Agencies like SCF had few vehicles and had to perform a Herculean task, which they nevertheless did with great dedication.

No child returned home without bringing a gift: a box of food, maize, sugar, oil, soap, perhaps a hoe and some seeds or a *capulana*. Each child was placed in a school and, wherever possible, a social worker tried to follow the progress of the child.

In the rush to leave Chokwe in the morning there had been no time to explain to Horacio and Victor how film crews work. Nor did we get to tell them to keep us informed of what they'd be doing before they just went ahead and did it.

It takes time for camera and sound equipment to be up and running, which means that the people we're filming usually have to wait while we get ready. And often we have to ask people to repeat an action so that the cameraman can get a better shot or angle on it, but in situations like these, that would be unthinkable.

Fetching abducted children was hardly an action I could request the SCF people to repeat, so it was going to be very much a case of filming what we could, where we could, and hoping for the best. We followed Victor into a clearing where there were two huts in a neatly swept yard under some trees. On one of the trees, out of reach of the dogs, hung some bits of meat from a small animal. A teenaged girl was sitting on a reed mat under the tree and a much younger child was in the yard. Unusually, there were no other children around. Families in rural Mozambique tended to have many children. Later, we were told that this place had been part of a Renamo base, so few proper families lived there.

A painfully thin couple were talking with Victor in subdued tones. The woman wore a faded but neatly tied *capulana* and headscarf. Her sad, lined face showed evidence of her life. They had not been expecting SCF today, although they had been warned some months previously that Rosita would be taken away.

Horacio had visited the couple twice in the past: once when the initial contact was made and Polaroids taken, and later when Rosita's family had been traced and he had brought their pictures to see if she recognised them. The sheer numbers of families that had to be visited, combined with the problems of getting transport, and then the distance and inaccessibility of places such as this, meant that there was no definite time or day, or even week, scheduled for these events.

Rosita was small for her seven years, and very pretty. Without saying a word and without looking at us, she went to fetch a basin of water from a plastic barrel at the edge of the clearing. She stood there, tiny and alone, washing herself and putting on a clean dress. Everything took place in total silence, as if it was happening in slow motion. Giulio filmed on a long lens in order not to be too intrusive, while the rest of us stood back.

Still without speaking, Rosita went over and sat next to the girl under the tree for a minute. Although neither of them said anything to each other, it was her way of saying goodbye. Then the couple walked her to the Land Cruiser, and said a very brief goodbye. She was too small to climb in by herself, and after a moment's hesitation, the woman stepped forward, picked her up, and put her inside. I think it was the first time that Rosita had ever been in a car. She seemed to be in a frozen state.

The couple looked grief-stricken as they talked to us. 'I've looked after her since she was a small child,' the woman, Amelia, said. 'But I wanted her father to find her. I'd ask her, "Don't you have any other family?" We want to visit her, because she was with us for so long. We can't forget her just because she's going home.' She wiped a tear away with the end of her scarf.

Her husband, Antonio, said, 'I can't feel anything because she is going to her family. I cared for her because she had no one. She is my daughter too.'

And then we drove off, leaving them standing in the middle of the road, looking forlorn as they watched us disappear in a cloud of dust.

None of us was able to imagine that this could possibly be a good solution for the child – who had been with the family for five years – or for the family that had clearly cared for her.

Some miles back along the track, we met up with Horacio, marching along with Delphina in tow. They had walked a long way, and were hot and tired.

'It was five kilometres there and then five kilometres, with this child.' He said, 'She walks well. The bush was thick and the heat too much.'

Later, we spoke to Horacio and told him that we found it

all very worrying.

'Of course, we do worry,' he said. 'We are sad at separating a family, but we can't avoid it. The children do better back with their own parents. We try to heal the wounds caused by separation and establish contacts. We do encourage links between the two families, and sometimes it works.' He went on, 'Reuniting people solves the problems of forced separation for both the family and the child.'

As we got nearer to town, the extreme poverty and isolation of the ex-Renamo areas we had driven through gave way again to evidence of Mozambique's return to life after the war.

Chokwe is in Gaza province, in southern Mozambique, and many of the men there had been, or still were, migratory workers on the South African gold mines. The money they earned gave them access to all sorts of consumer goods. Men had bicycles and most homesteads had various plastic goods like buckets and basins lying about. Some of the huts had elaborate three-piece lounge suites, set up outside in the sun. Many of the men and women working in the fields were wearing the badge of honour from the Johannesburg gold mines: hard plastic miners' helmets in various colours.

The sun set as we forded the river. In the glorious evening light, we stopped to film scenes of women washing, cattle being driven home, men walking by, and little boys swimming and fishing. The tranquillity and beauty made it hard to imagine the years of war here.

While Giulio filmed the SCF Land Cruiser splashing across the ford with the two little girls in the back, I leaned against the back of our vehicle, enjoying the lovely scene. Suddenly I became aware of faint clucking sounds. At the same moment, Gabriel, who was standing nearby, pulled off his headphones and looked at me angrily. He thought I had been making chicken noises to spoil the evening sounds he was recording. Then we started pulling gear off the back of the Land Cruiser, and found the two chickens Franisse's mother had given to Donna Bemvida.

Incredibly, they were still alive after two days. Gabriel fed them rice left over from our lunch and some water. After that, he looked after them carefully until we returned to Maputo. He named them Donna Bemvida and Franisse, and promised us that they would never be eaten. They lived out the rest of their lives in his back yard.

In the morning, Horacio took Delphina and Rosita shopping for presents to take home. Rosita still moved about like a zombie, without speaking. Horacio very gently helped her choose a *capulana*. The children would present these, together with the other gifts that returning children brought to their families.

Delphina's village was a large one, not far from Chokwe. The contrast with the poverty of the Renamo areas we had been in yesterday was startling. Here, the huts were in good repair, and the community had a school and a small clinic. Farming was on a far larger scale than mere subsistence level, with fields of cotton nearby.

Word had gone ahead of Delphina's arrival, and the villagers crowded around as we stopped in front of the hut where her older sister stood. Accompanied by Horacio, she went to her sister and handed her the folded *capulana*.

'She has grown so tall!' the sister remarked to the assembled crowd.

One of the elders came forward and made a little speech of thanks. Several little girls ran up to Delphina to touch her hand. There was real joy at the arrival of this child.

Horacio and Victor guided the events without seeming intrusive. Delphina was overcome with embarrassment and stood picking her nose. Horacio took her by the hand and asked her quietly, 'Delphina, do you know her?' He pointed at her sister. She smiled and turned away.

'Be serious,' he said. 'Do you want to stay here? Or do you want us to take you back?'

'Stay here,' she whispered.

While the adults completed the paperwork, Delphina was led away by one of the little girls. We followed, and Gabriel gently asked them about what had happened.

Delphina made patterns in the dust with a little twig, not looking at us as she spoke. 'I was kidnapped with my mother and some sisters. I tried to follow them, but then they escaped. When I looked around, I saw my mother had run away. I thought I'd die there. I didn't know I would see my family again.'

'Do you know who this is?' Gabriel asked, indicating the child next to her.

'I know her, but I can't remember her name,' she said.

'I am Cremelda,' the child said, taking Delphina's hand. 'We used to play together. My friend has come back. I'm happy; I didn't think I would see her again. We'd heard that the kidnapped people were killed, so I didn't think she was alive. I thought she was dead like the others.'

When we left, Delphina already had her sister's baby on her back and seemed ready to take her place in the village. Cremelda would probably be the key to helping Delphina readjust.

Rosita's homecoming was less joyful. Her aunt – who had two-year-old twins scrambling on her lap – and an older woman were sitting outside a dilapidated hut. There were one or two other women around and ten ragged children, covered in flies, milled about. Two of them were apparently Rosita's brothers.

The aunt took Rosita from Horacio's arms and sat her on her lap. Then she cried and cried and cried, wiping her tears on her headscarf. All the while, the two babies fought to get back onto her lap and grab hold of her breasts. The older woman, who turned out to be Rosita's grandmother, also wept noisily. Rosita seemed unable to react at all, until at last all the weeping became too much and she too started to howl. We all cried too.

Horacio beckoned to us and we stood back for a while to let the scene play out. Then he gathered them all together to take Polaroids and do the necessary paperwork, and spoke gently. 'Don't cry,' he said to the family. 'We have brought her home for you today.'

The aunt thanked him profusely.

We left to return to Maputo, shocked by the double trauma that little Rosita had been through, and wondering if this was really the best thing for her.

Horacio could see that we were uneasy with what had happened. 'I believe Rosita will get over this trauma,' he told us. 'In my experience, she will definitely settle, and with the family's help, and our help, she'll be a changed child.

'The difficult part is finding the relations. The most exciting, happy part is bringing them together. When we reunite the family and the child it's an emotional moment after years of separation. We feel we've done something important.'

I couldn't imagine that we would be able show the footage of Rosita being taken from the Renamo family, or the reunion with a family she didn't recognise, on European TV. It would be far too shocking, and would raise too many questions about how to handle such children.

We all wanted to go back to do some follow-up to see what the outcome would be. None of us could bear to leave matters like this, so we changed the filming schedule to accommodate it.

Nine days later, we arrived in Delphina's village. She ran to greet us, dressed in the new *capulana*. Delphina was happier and more self-possessed than when we had last seen her, and seemed to have settled into the community. She and Cremelda had become inseparable. Yet these were early days. Delphina seemed still to have a very short attention span, and much to deal with, but it did seem that the community would help her settle down properly.

This was a rich farming area, and on the road we passed a convoy of SADF armoured vehicles. This was a sign of the times: South African farmers were buying land here. I wondered who would benefit from this new form of colonisation.

Our second visit to Rosita's family started off badly. The place where we had filmed the reunion was deserted, and neighbours told us conflicting stories.

'Rosita has been taken to hospital,' one said.

'No, she hasn't,' another contradicted. 'Rosita's father has fetched her to go to a funeral.'

We struggled to get directions to find the family. At last we came to a fairly prosperous-looking village, where we found an old woman watching Rosita and some other small children. The family had gone to a funeral, she told us. We needed permission to film here, so we sat and waited for someone from the family to turn up.

Rosita had changed. She was no longer in a state of shock

but looked cleaner and brighter as she played with the other children. Once she glanced up at us and smiled shyly.

A man arrived and introduced himself as Rosita's uncle. He was an educated man, good-looking and with a sympathetic personality. He told us Rosita's story. 'When the village was attacked, Rosita's mother was killed and the little girl was abducted. Of course the rest of the family thought that the child had died too.'

'Rosita's father is still alive, but he is an old man now. I am aware of what this child has been through. I was in the army myself and know what went on.' He continued, 'She is still very shy, but she is getting used to us. We will absorb her into the family and she will be all right.'

He went on to tell us that they would be holding a special ceremony in three days' time, when the whole family would gather to give thanks for Rosita's return. 'We will be honoured if you film people would attend, as you were with Rosita when she was brought back to us.'

Mozambique did not hold a Truth and Reconciliation Commission, as South Africa did, and it wasn't a country with a tradition of western psychological methods. There were few counselling facilities, no child guidance clinics, and in any case, the numbers of people needing help were enormous. So, instead, people used traditional ceremonies as a way of cleansing people of war crimes and integrating them back into fractured communities.

On the day of the ceremony, we drove out to Rosita's home one last time. A cow and goat had been slaughtered, and under a tarpaulin that had been erected on an area of raked sand, a kitchen had been set up for cooking. The younger men were chopping up the meat, while women came from all around with huge pots of food.

The elders sat on plastic chairs, drinking. The case of beer that we had contributed was gladly accepted. Children ran about everywhere. Rosita was sitting with the older women on reed mats. All morning, more people arrived, dressed in their best *capulanas* or suits, all making a very colourful scene.

Later, Rosita was taken away and dressed in the new *capulana* that Horacio had chosen in Chokwe. She sat on the mat, smiling and eating, very clearly aware that she was the star of the show, aware that this ceremony was being held to celebrate her return.

Her uncle said to us, 'Look at her. Even after a few days, there is such a big difference. She plays and talks to her friends. We want to help her get rid of the things in her head.'

Many studies that were done at the time showed that the majority of children settled back into their communities. In cases where this did not happen, it was found that there had usually been family discord or other problems before the separation.

In Maputo I interviewed Graça Machel once more. By then she was an internationally recognised figure and was working on a UN study of the effects of war on children. It was published in 1996 under the title *Impact of Armed Conflict on Children*. I used her interview to link the countries and issues in *Chain of Hope*, and I also used an edited version of her interview in a short film for UNICEF.

We had managed to find almost all of the Mozambican children who had appeared in *Chain of Tears*. It was a success story. All of them seemed to be doing reasonably well.

Instead of using a conventional map to introduce the different countries in the film, we'd decided to get children to make their own map of Africa and then outline their country. To help them, we gave them a map of Africa to copy. In Maputo, we took a group of street children to the beach, and after some argument about where exactly the horn of Africa was located, they drew a huge map of Africa in the sand and outlined Mozambique with coloured stones.

Our shoot in Mozambique was a success story as well, with a good-natured and pleasant crew, and mostly free from tensions. With Pedro and Gillian organising everything, I was freed from dealing with practical matters and had the luxury of being able to concentrate on the content and look of the film.

## 3. THE LOST GENERATION

Journal entry: **Johannesburg, 3 July 1995**

*Fucking difficult day. I've got to a non-sleeping stage and seem to have too much admin to get through here. The crew were late and disorganised, lunch late. Late at Wits for a meeting, late to pick up a guy called Jomo who is supposed to help us in Soweto, who said yes when he meant no. Traffic. Rising anger and frustration.*

*Giulio not functioning, because he and his girlfriend have broken up for the umpteenth time, Gabriel in culture shock. And it is grey and cold and dull. Soweto looked ugly.*

*I find it harder and harder to go away now and leave all the threads of my life to tangle up behind me. Yet when I get here, there are things pulling me in every direction too; how to make a quality film with such budget constraints and working on video? I want this film to be outstanding.*

*Got into a long row with the committee that decides on who is and isn't allowed to work in South Africa. They couldn't get their heads around my wanting to bring a Mozambican sound-recordist to South Africa for two weeks to work on a British documentary. I had to go through the third degree. This remains a thoroughly authoritarian country with people still unable to think for themselves.*

After the 1994 elections in South Africa, Johannesburg had replaced Harare as our travel base for the region. We were there to do the South African leg of the filming on *Chain of Hope*.

It was disconcerting returning to South Africa after a spell in Mozambique. The good roads, working traffic lights, and general tidiness of the city always came as something of a shock. Despite the effects of the war and the shambling beginnings of reconstruction, there was a lively energy in Mozambique that was lacking in South Africa. But for me, it still felt exciting to be there. People had begun to open up, enjoying the feeling of being part of the rest of the world again after so many years. Real change had begun.

July in Johannesburg is midwinter. Despite the sunshine, the cold was raw, and biting wind blew grit and dust everywhere. It was so dry that skin cracked and eyes burned. To make matters worse, people didn't have proper heating and it felt far colder indoors than I was used to after all my years in London with central heating.

After the violence that had preceded the elections, South Africa was moving into a new era and called itself the 'Rainbow Nation'. Expectations were high, and people were happy. The black population had achieved equality and majority rule at last, while many whites who had feared the worst when the ANC came to power found that their fears were groundless. There was a new mood in the country.

In Soweto, a group of girls at a play centre painted a large map of Africa on the wall of the building and carefully filled in South Africa in the colours of the South African flag. It was beautiful.

'I will be an artist when I grow up,' Thandi, one of the children, told us.

These children were beginning to feel that the world was open to them. They had a happy innocence that their older brothers and sisters had lost long before, and they had ambitions that had not been possible for them even to imagine a few years earlier.

But some things hadn't changed.

I was unable to find a policeman who would acknowledge, on film, that a system that arrested and tortured children was immoral. In fact, it was hard to find anyone who had ever supported apartheid.

The original children from *Chain of Tears* were adults now, and were difficult to trace. They had been filmed clandestinely in 1988, and we never knew their real names. So instead, we were documenting the aftermath of the school protests that had taken place in the 1980s and early 1990s, which had left a whole generation who never completed their education. They were known as the 'lost generation'. This was a legacy that would haunt the country for years to come.

One of them, Lerato, was working in an office in a seedy part of downtown Johannesburg. Ostensibly, it was some kind of local NGO to 'help the community', but there were a number of suspicious characters around who were aggressive and unpleasant to us.

Lerato told us that the first time he was detained, 'it was an accident, not something I went into.' He explained, 'We were still young and it was very, very fucking frightening in there. Especially when you heard people screaming in the cells.' Speaking slowly, he went on, 'The worst that can happen is that in your mind you think that you are not going to get out of that place. It made me very, very angry.'

He was trying to study for a degree part-time, but said that he still had problems. 'It affected me, killed me mentally,' he said. 'I have problems with concentration and found it hard to integrate back into the community.' His dream was of a society free of violence.

Tina was faring better. She had a job at a large store in an upmarket shopping mall and was also studying part-time. She had been arrested as a young teenager and spent a year in prison where she had been given electric shock torture. 'Growing up suppressed, you don't have a sense of ownership,' she told us, 'so we acted in a negative way.'

Sometime after her release she became depressed and was unable to cope, but she did manage to see a counsellor. 'I see myself as one of the lucky ones,' she said, 'because many of my friends who were detained are not able to live normal lives.'

At Katlehong, we filmed at a trauma clinic for young children; the therapy sessions were held in a temporary Portakabin in the grounds of a large hospital. Katlehong is a sprawling township east of Johannesburg. It had seen extreme violence, and in 1995 it seemed that this was not yet quite over. There were rows of dismal low-cost houses, the streets were unpaved and full of potholes and rubbish, and all the shops had iron grilles over the windows. It was a depressing place.

Some of the children were tiny and undernourished, and among them were three-year-olds who had been raped, and children who had seen their older brothers or fathers shot in front of them.

Although South Africa had not had a war in the same way as Mozambique or Angola, people were nevertheless damaged by the repressive and inhumane system of apartheid. Years of deprivation, rioting, imprisonment and hatred had left a huge scar across society. The task facing the new government seemed overwhelming, but among the children, with their positive views and ambitions, I felt we'd glimpsed the beginnings of a very different South Africa.

Our next stop would be Angola. I had grown to love being in South Africa and was sorry to leave, as I felt I could really make a difference there. The day before we flew to Luanda, Gillian and I visited the consumer paradise of Sandton City, a huge, hideous shopping mall. I bought a beautiful pair of lightweight Italian canvas boots with heavy rubber soles. That evening I jettisoned my old boots in favour of these wonderful things.

At the duty-free shop at the airport, Gillian bought two large bottles of whisky. Giulio, believing these were to help us through the rigours of Angola, was happy to carry them for her.

# 4. LARIAM DAYS

Luanda again. I had said I would never come back, and yet here I was. The war over, we no longer had to work through the Press Centre, and were free to move around on our own. Giulio and Gabriel would be staying with Katia, whom we'd worked with in 1988. The feisty Finn was now renting out rooms to visiting journalists and photographers, and, true to form, she had organised filming permissions and a driver to meet us at the airport.

Gillian had arranged for the two of us to stay with a friend of hers who worked for the World Food Programme (WFP), but before we could go to the apartment we had to pay some calls and check on arrangements for filming outside Luanda.

Everything seemed to be going surprisingly well, in a most non-Angolan way. At the UNICEF offices, we were told that we were expected in both Huambo and Kuito Bie, and that they had arranged vehicles and accommodation for us at the UNICEF houses in both places. At the WFP office we made arrangements to fly to Huambo on an aid flight leaving in two days' time. While we were there, Gillian picked up the key for the apartment where we would be staying.

The UN housed its foreign personnel in an apartment block in the centre of Luanda. From previous experience, I knew that the front door of each flat opened directly into a kitchen and open living area. There were two bedrooms, one on either side of a short corridor, with a bathroom next to one of them. I was surprised to be greeted by two large Alsatian dogs, which almost knocked us over as we opened the door. Two young women were sitting in front of a blaring

TV, braiding each other's hair. They barely looked up to acknowledge us. One of the dogs had recently had puppies, and they, and their mess, were all over the living room. A sinking Angolan feeling began to set in as I followed Gillian to one of the bedrooms. I put my luggage down and looked around. It had twin beds, but its rather lived-in look suggested that it was not really a spare room.

'Who are those girls?' I asked.

'One is Mercedes's maid, the other must be her friend. They don't speak any English.'

'OK, well I'm going to unpack. Where can I put my clothes?'

'Just leave everything until Mercedes comes home. I'm not sure where everyone is sleeping.' Gillian had become evasive, not making eye contact with me. Everyone, I thought to myself. Who is everyone? There was something here that I wasn't being told.

We sat in an uneasy silence, waiting for Mercedes to arrive. I was tired and irritated. I wanted to unpack, have a shower and relax. The two young women continued to ignore us and the dogs kept pestering me. I couldn't imagine why anyone would choose to keep such large dogs in a small, fifth-floor apartment in downtown Luanda.

Eventually, Mercedes arrived home. For a moment I was completely taken aback, embarrassed and shocked that Gillian had not told me in advance that Mercedes was a dwarf. When I saw her, I realised that Mercedes needed a live-in maid to help her, as the UN apartments could not be modified and she was unable to reach work surfaces, wash basins and so on.

She was friendly and very pleased to see Gillian. 'Have you put your things in my room?' she asked Gillian as she went to open a bottle of vodka Gillian had brought her.

I still couldn't work out the sleeping arrangements. 'Where am I going to sleep?' I asked.

'Gillian will share with me, and you can sleep on the living room floor, Toni,' Mercedes said gaily, as she and Gillian got stuck into the vodka. 'The dogs will be fine.'

The dogs will be fine? I was furious. No wonder Gillian hadn't told me the full story – she knew I would never have agreed to this set-up. It was too late now to find somewhere else to stay and I felt constrained. There was nothing I could say that wouldn't appear rude in front of Mercedes, someone I had only just met and who had kindly agreed to share her apartment with us. I felt a strong sense of foreboding that there were likely to be a number of other things in the coming days that would come as horrible surprises, and very likely they'd have more to do with the actual filming.

At dinner, I took Gillian aside. 'Get me into a hotel from tomorrow,' I said, and left it at that.

Luanda looked much the same: filthy and broken, street kids and *mutilados* – amputees – were everywhere. Nowadays, though, the Ilha was full of restaurants and bars and prostitutes. We all went to one of the restaurants for dinner. Gabriel was wide-eyed at the corruption and mess of Luanda, but was happy to be able to communicate in Portuguese again.

Angola was corrupt on a scale with which Mozambique couldn't compete, and Luanda was a chaos of poverty, filth, and oil money. Fat Angolans, dressed to the nines, drove around in flashy cars; elegant women dripped with gold jewellery; and ragged children, displaced by war, begged on every corner. Luanda always elicited strong reactions, and I think that this was the moment when I knew I would never cover another war.

It was in Luanda that we finally worked out why we all had a day in the middle of each week when we just didn't function properly.

At lunchtime on a Tuesday, we took our weekly dose of anti-malarials, and for the following twenty-four hours suffered what we started to call our 'Lariam days'. Everyone felt slightly unwell in one way or another. Giulio became slow and grumpy, and he and Gabriel would bicker over trifles. We were all tired and short-tempered, and I suffered more often from migraines.

Mefloquine, also known as Lariam, is no longer prescribed; there are newer and better drugs now. The side effects of Mefloquine were described in the package insert, which warned of 'permanent adverse side effects ... severe depression, anxiety, paranoia, aggression, nightmares, insomnia, seizures, birth defects, peripheral motor-sensory neuropathy, headaches.'

Soon, we were on our way to Huambo. The town had been under siege for two months in 1993, and it seemed that every building that remained standing was pockmarked by bullet holes.

Savimbi had refused to accept the outcome of the elections in 1992 and retreated to the Central Highlands, threatening to turn Angola into another Somalia. The war broke out again with a vengeance. This time, there were no outside forces involved, as the South Africans and Cubans had both left. The Cold War was over; Namibia was independent, and in South Africa Mandela had been released from prison. The world no longer had any real interest in Angola, and the war took on a savagery that surpassed anything that had happened in the previous decades of fighting.

The Central Highlands were traditionally UNITA territory and it was here that the fighting was most vicious. In Huambo, UNITA and government forces had battled over territory; the shelling had reduced the town to rubble and left the population starving. Whole neighbourhoods of Huambo had been razed as they were held by first one and then the other side. The destruction was far greater than even the worst times of the South African army invasions and air strikes.

'Don't walk off the pavements,' we were warned, 'and never go into any house. Most places have not been de-mined.'

One of the casualties was the Huambo library and museum building, which had been wrecked by the shelling, and all its documents and artefacts ransacked. Apparently, papers and books still showed up in the market sometimes, but essentially, the historical documentation of the central plateau of Angola of the last century and more had been lost.

By the time we arrived in 1995, a ceasefire had held for six months, and there were UN observers in the city. Maybe this time the war really was over, although many didn't believe it. There was too much evidence that both sides were using this period to re-equip their forces.

We had no sooner arrived at the UNICEF house from the airport than we had to race back again. Médecins sans Frontières had a small plane arriving from Benguela, with two boys who were going to be reunited with their families. We were told that we could film the whole reunion.

Two teenaged boys climbed down the steps from the small plane and stood, lost and bewildered. Denis and Pinto had been separated from their families in the endless bombardment and fighting during the two-month siege in 1993. During those months, the sound of gunfire never stopped. The residents of Huambo dug underground bunkers and lived on what they had stored. The wounded and dying had lain for days with no one to help them. UNITA refused all access to the Red Cross and other agencies. It was estimated that over a hundred thousand civilians died during the siege.

Just before Huambo fell to UNITA, long columns of near-starving civilians and government soldiers fled the city. These boys became part of the exodus. With about a hundred thousand others, they had walked 150 kilometres over mined roads and through the bush. All the bridges had been blown up and, although the soldiers helped people to cross the rivers, many refugees drowned. Many others simply died of hunger and exhaustion along the way, especially the old and the very young. After nearly three weeks, the survivors reached Benguela, which was in government hands. Some estimates say that nearly four hundred thousand people fled the city during the siege.

Many of the children who survived this horror march were taken to an orphanage in the coastal city of Lobito. Since arriving there, they had had no contact with their families. Their parents hadn't known that the children were still alive until Save the Children began a family-tracing programme similar to the one in Mozambique.

A small crowd had gathered on the pavement outside the SCF house, where their parents were waiting for the boys. As we drove up, the two mothers ran out, grabbing the boys and crying and laughing. Far messier and less controlled than the process in Mozambique, it was a very emotional moment.

After the formalities were over, we accompanied the boys home. Pinto was a small, smiling boy, good-looking and self-contained. His home was in a mud *barrio* on the edge of town, and he was led to his house by a crowd of women and children who ran along the narrow streets behind him and his mother.

There was much crying and many shouts of joy, and all the while Pinto beamed with happiness. A sister, grandmother, and collection of aunts and cousins were waiting at the house to greet him. The family was poor, but there was clearly an income from somewhere.

By contrast, Denis's parents and sister were thin with hunger and very subdued. We left them all at the entrance of a bombed-out public building, where there was no one else around at all. The father turned to us and said pathetically, 'What will we do? We have nothing to give him.'

Unlike the family reunifications in Mozambique, the children here did not receive gifts to bring to their families.

Later that day we went back to Bomba Alta, the Red Cross prosthesis facility, only to find that it too had been destroyed in the fighting. UNITA had shelled and then looted it, taking everything that had not been destroyed. After asking around the neighbourhood, we managed to trace Armando Jamba, the physiotherapist whom we had interviewed with Josefa in *Chain of Tears*.

'Troops came here to the centre,' he told us, 'and they began taking everything they wanted, even the cables and orthopaedic material. From then on we had no way of working here, and the amputees aren't being rehabilitated.'

Recently, though, the Red Cross had started rebuilding Bomba Alta, and Armando was able to give us news of Josefa. 'Not long after you left here she went to her family in Lubango. I have heard that she is still doing well.'

The UNICEF house where we were staying was clean and relatively comfortable, with a functioning well in the yard so that we had access to water. The problem was Silvio, the UNICEF representative. He was an unsavoury-looking

Brazilian, with a droopy moustache, greasy hair, and high-heeled boots – one of those minor officials who loved to exercise their power. Over dinner, I tackled him about the arrangements for driving to Kuito in two days' time. The Luanda office had told us that they had instructed him to provide us with a driver and Land Rover to take us there.

He was quick to say that, no matter what UNICEF in Luanda told us, 'That will not happen. You can't drive to Kuito, the road is mined.'

'But we have been told that it has recently been de-mined and it's OK.'

'You don't know anything, only last week someone stepped on one.'

I wondered if this was true.

'I am in charge here in Huambo,' he went on, 'and you will be beholden to me for all permissions.'

Gillian tried to argue with him in a flirtatious manner, but he wouldn't listen.

'Luanda is wrong,' he said. 'There are no cars available for you.'

'But Gillian arranged this when she was in Luanda last month,' I argued. Gillian looked uncomfortable. She was being very cagey about exactly what arrangements she had made for the Kuito trip. I knew she was dissembling.

'No,' snapped Silvio. 'I will not be making the car available until maybe Sunday. I want it for something.' He stalked out of the room. This was not the first time that Gillian had not been entirely honest with me about arrangements she was supposed to have made during her research trip. Several times now I had watched her use her good looks to try and solve a tricky situation It didn't always work and then I would have to step in and try and salvage the situation.

Luanda was a long way off, and the only communications were by shortwave radio that worked very intermittently. I tried calling on the radio but couldn't get through. So instead, I suggested that we go to some of the other agencies to see if we could get them to lend or hire us a car for a few days. Gillian and I walked in silence, first to the SCF house, and then the World Food Programme house, to see if either of them could loan us a car but they couldn't.

'Go to UNAVEM,' they told us. 'They have plenty of vehicles and are always up and down that road.' So we went to the UN Angolan Verification Mission, and at their compound, Gillian tried flirting with the UNAVEM major, but it got us nowhere.

We were stuck. The only way to get to Kuito Bie would be to try and get an aid flight back to Luanda, and then another one to Kuito – but there were no flights to Luanda until the following week. There were no phone lines either in this part of the country, and we were unable to get Luanda UNICEF on the radio.

I knew I shouldn't panic; by Angolan standards things had gone amazingly well until now, and there were still a couple of days before we had to be in Kuito. But still, my spirits sank; my fear was that we would run out of time before we finished the Angolan part of the shoot.

In the morning, Silvio was not around. But the car was, and we set off to film around the city. Many of the children that we saw in the streets had the red hair and distended bellies of kwashiorkor. Yet there were some signs of recovery: the market was thriving, and there seemed to be plenty of food available to those who could buy it. Also, efforts were being made to clear up some of the war rubble.

While we were filming the wreckage, a little boy came up to

us and said, 'I want to talk to you on the film.'

'OK,' we said.

'You have to hurry,' he instructed us. 'I've only got fifteen minutes. I must go to school.'

We sat him on the shell of a car and he poured out his story. 'My name is Simeo,' he began like a professional. 'I was in Huambo when the war started. It was Saturday and I couldn't get out because of the enemy, so I had to stay on my own, because my mother hadn't come back.' He went on, 'When UNITA was attacking it was terrible, there were terrible things in the street.'

Simeo proceeded to tell us a confusing story in which bombing, shooting, people dying, and him searching for his mother, were all jumbled up.

'We suffered a lot and many people died,' he said. 'We had no food and no water.' He paused, and then he concluded, 'When I grow up I would like to be a footballer, or maybe a journalist, and walk around the street filming people.'

Then he jumped off the car and ran away, shouting, 'I have to go; I don't want to be late.'

Simeo was one of several children we spoke to in the streets that day. Mostly, they were unable to express the things that they had experienced in words other than 'everyone suffered', and 'it was terrible'. No doubt they carried many scars, but at that moment they simply wanted to play and get on with their lives.

In the late afternoon, Giulio and Gabriel decided to take a walk around the neighbourhood to see if there was anything worth filming. Gillian and I went to sit in the sun and talk to the UNICEF driver, João. He had lived in Huambo throughout the siege and was telling us how he had managed.

'It went like this. I worked for whoever was in control, and that was how I kept going. First it was FAPLA, then UNITA and then FAPLA again. They all needed drivers.'

Right then, a blast ripped through the neighbourhood. My stomach sank sickeningly as, without a word, we all ran to the car. The streets were quiet as we drove around frantically. I told myself that Gabriel and Giulio knew to stay on the road, not to enter deserted houses or any grassy space, but still, my heart was beating frantically.

We stopped an old man and asked if he had seen two men with film equipment, but he hadn't. He pointed in the direction of the blast. 'Maybe a goat stood on a mine in that empty plot,' he said.

We circled around the blocks once more before making our way back to the house. As we rounded the last corner, there they were, safe and sound.

Only two days, and Huambo was already getting to me. Filming, war, and the haphazard arrangements all combined to make me utterly paranoid. On the surface, Huambo seemed friendly, but I had always felt deeply unsafe here. The city was dead, people had no work, they were living in ruins; there was hunger and a sense of hopelessness. Also, the peace seemed far too fragile.

Later on, at the market, we bought some maize, sugar and soap as gifts for the families of the two boys who had returned from Lobito. We found Denis sitting with his family in the forecourt of the building where they lived, in the cellar.

'We live in a cave,' his father said. 'It is dark, we have no light at all. We sit outside, even when it is cold.'

He told us that he had a job, but for a long time hadn't been paid, so he spent part of his day walking around Huambo, looking for food.

Denis wanted to see Pinto again, so we took him and his sister along with us. Pinto's family lived in a *barrio* that was full of life and people. His family were pleased to see us again; they seemed to think that we were in some way responsible for bringing him home. Pinto was delighted to see his friend again and we left them together.

We still had the problem of getting to Kuito. If we went by road we would have to cross two UNITA areas and they might be suspicious of a film crew coming through. UNITA had a history of kidnapping foreigners. Also, we were still unsure about Silvio's warning of mines on the road.

Later that same day, Silvio's secretary informed me that we'd received UNAVEM clearance to make the trip. But she had not yet received clearance from UNITA because there had been fighting the day before. I went to Giulio and Gabriel to tell them what we had heard and to see how they felt about driving there.

'If you don't feel comfortable driving through UNITA checkpoints then we will just drop the whole thing and go back to Luanda,' I said. I didn't want to lose the Kuito part of the shoot, but I had to make their safety a priority. We sat discussing it. Giulio looked doubtful, and he glanced at Gabriel to see his reaction.

'But of course we have to do it,' Gabriel said. 'We have to go. Anyway, we haven't had any *adrenalino* on this trip. We need the *adrenalino*.'

So it was settled then – if we could pin down Silvio. Gillian took Giulio aside and asked for the two bottles of whisky she had bought at Johannesburg airport. Giulio was still under the illusion that these were our bottles, so he told Gillian he'd left the whisky in Luanda, for our return.

Gillian was irate. She had brought these bottles as gifts for the people we were to stay with, one for those in Huambo, the other for the Kuito people. But now she needed the Huambo whisky – as a gift, or bribe, for Silvio.

A fierce, whispered exchange took place between them, and Gillian angrily turned on her heel. It was only years later that Giulio told me what this had all been about, and he claimed that Gillian loathed him from that moment on.

After dinner that evening, Gillian told us to leave her alone with Silvio, she would sort it out. But the more she tried to get rid of me, the more I wanted to see what she was going to do. I'd been irritated by Gillian's behaviour ever since we'd arrived in Angola. I felt that she hadn't made enough effort to confirm the promises made to her in Luanda during the research period, and I didn't trust what she was getting up to with Silvio.

I have no idea what went on downstairs after the rest of us went to bed, but in the morning the car and driver were ready for us, and we were on the road.

## 5. HEROES OF KUITO

We crossed several checkpoints without incident; the soldiers on both sides were no more than teenagers. At the last UNITA point, a soldier stuck his head into the car.

'Who are these people?' he demanded.

Without missing a beat, João, the driver replied, '*Nord Americanos.*'

North Americans? Oh no, please. No way do I want to be a North American. As it turned out, though, the soldier didn't believe João.

'I give you one more chance to answer,' he said, waving his gun around, 'Who are these people?'

'Swiss,' said the driver.

I could see that we were in trouble. 'Say something, for God's sake,' I muttered at Gabriel, the only native Portuguese speaker among us. He glared at me. We had been given strict instructions not to say a word at the UNITA checkpoints – the driver would deal with things, and we must just leave things in his hands.

'Gabriel!' I hissed, jabbing him with my elbow.

'Well, officer,' he started, 'you must understand that this man here is only a driver, he doesn't know anything. He doesn't even know where we are from. While it is true that some of us could be North Americans, equally we may not be, and then again some of us could be Swiss, but not all of us. In fact, we come from various countries, some of which may even be in Africa or Europe.'

Disgusted, or maybe just bored, the soldier turned his back and waved us on. It was a tricky moment on an already tense drive.

We bounced against each other in the back of the Land Rover, as the driver tried to avoid the potholes and craters caused by bombing and shelling. Although the road had been cleared of mines there was no guarantee that it was safe; we dared not deviate from the central tracks.

The arrangement was that João would take us to a small town that was the halfway point between Huambo and Kuito, where the UNICEF vehicle from Kuito would be waiting to take us the rest of the way.

The countryside seemed deserted apart from a few women and children in the fields or carrying firewood along the road. I saw so much that I wanted to film, but the driver had been told not to stop along the way. We did stop once, but only because a lorry had broken down ahead of us. It was filled almost to tipping point with an enormous pile of goods, and was being pushed by a group of very young soldiers. After that, I managed to persuade João to stop once again so that we could film a group of women and children walking down the middle of the road, seemingly on their way from nowhere to nowhere in a wide and deserted landscape.

This part of the country had once been rich agricultural land. But it had reverted to the most basic subsistence farming, with no infrastructure at all, no health care, no schools, nothing. The war had been going on for so long – the destruction so total, and the suffering so terrible – that no one seemed to care enough to end it.

The halfway point was a small and utterly ruined town, where we said goodbye to João and got into the waiting UNICEF van from Kuito. We reached Kuito in the late afternoon, exhausted, filthy and hungry. The last time I had been there was in 1988, during *Chain of Tears*, when we had filmed the street of orphanages, the hospital, and a rehabilitation centre for amputees. At the time I'd thought the effects of war couldn't get much worse, but I was wrong.

In Kuito the siege had lasted nine months, killing a third of the population either by shelling or starvation. According to journalists reporting from Angola, even after UNITA finally allowed UN planes into Kuito, they still prevented the sick and injured from leaving.

The UNICEF house was in a small street of houses that seemed to have survived the siege more or less intact, although it had neither water nor electricity. In the bathroom stood a large drum of brown water, with buckets to scoop water for washing and to flush the toilet.

The kitchen was overrun by huge cockroaches and rats. Luckily, Giulio took over the food department, painstakingly picking over weevil-infested beans and rice, before soaking them and slow-cooking them. At least we had something to come home to at night.

The first thing I did when I got inside was to remove my boots. Those pretty Italian boots had rubbed my heel raw and so I'd limped around Huambo the whole time we had been there. I dumped my bag and lay down on the bed, unable to move.

Half-dozing, I heard Gillian say, 'Donna Evangelista is here from the orphanage. We must go and film now, they've been waiting for us all afternoon.' I had met Donna Evangelista Charmarle previously, while filming *Chain of Tears* in Kuito.

'Well, we aren't filming now. We've only just arrived, we've been travelling all day without food or water, and everyone is exhausted. The boys need to rest and there is no way I can ask them to unpack all the gear and get sorted now. Tell them we'll film in the morning.'

What happened next was one of those dreadful breakdowns in communication, caused by either poor translation, or simple misunderstanding on the part of both our hosts and us. My lack of grace and understanding at that moment still haunts me.

Reluctantly, I got up and went into the living room where the driver and Donna Evangelista were sitting. We had no one to translate for us. Donna Evangelista didn't speak any English, and the driver spoke very little. Neither Gillian nor I spoke enough Portuguese to fully understand what we were being told.

What made my unintentional rudeness even worse was that it took me several days to understand that Nango, whom I had assumed was a particularly well-informed driver, was in fact a medical doctor – only he was too modest to say so. There had been no UNICEF driver available to make the dangerous trip halfway to Huambo on a Saturday, so Nango had volunteered. When I did find out about his status, I was mortified. Heaven alone knows how many other gaffes like this I have made all over the region.

Not being fluent in the language of the country we were filming in always left me dependent on translators, and this inevitably led to misunderstandings. It also made it difficult to get below the surface in interviews, to understand the nuances. Over the years, I had developed an instinct for finding the right person to interview and had also learned how to ask the sort of questions that elicited a natural response, but that day we arrived in Kuito I was just not really picking up on what was going on.

I tried to explain that we needed to rest, that we weren't ready to film, but that we would do so tomorrow. Slowly, dimly, I began to perceive that UNICEF in Luanda had told the local people that we were looking for child amputees to film, and that a group of these children had been rounded up and were waiting for us at the orphanage. In the end, Gillian and I walked over to meet and talk to them.

When we had filmed this street years before, in *Chain of Tears*, every house had been an orphanage. Now it was unrecognisable. Only one house was left partially intact. The rest had been bombed to piles of rubble. I was too stressed by the journey, and too disoriented by Kuito at that moment, to fully comprehend the horror of what must have happened here. It took several days for the reality to hit me.

In a concrete yard at the side of the house was a group of recent amputees, patiently awaiting the film crew. I sat and chatted to them, trying to explain what we were doing, and why we couldn't film all of them but would have to choose only a few.

'Which of you would like to talk to us, and tell the camera your story so that we can show it to children in other countries?' I asked. And on the basis of their responses, I chose the least shy among the group, asking them to come back the next day.

Caught up in my own difficulties, I didn't realise that Donna Evangelista had given up part of her weekend to find these children, get them to come here on their crutches and poor prosthetics, and then sit and wait for us to arrive. Without even properly thanking her and her staff, I had gone there with bad grace, spoken to them for a mere twenty minutes, and told the chosen few to make the journey again the next day.

Gabriel and Giulio were slow to get moving the next day. Somehow, amid the ruins of Kuito, they had managed to find a disco, where they stayed drinking until the early hours.

They both thought it hilarious that the favourite song of the evening, played again and again, was something to do with Bosnia, and sang the chorus, shouting 'Sarajevo, Sarajevo' constantly over the next few days.

Kuito shocked me. I no longer had any stomach for this amount of suffering. In my journal I wrote:

### Kuito, July 1995

*This country is an inflamed, suppurating sore that could explode at any moment, like the blister on my heel. My new boots have rubbed my one heel raw and now it is infected, like this country. I know I have chosen to do this, but God help me, I never want to see another filthy, begging, little war victim again. Save me from the hungry, the mutilated, and the traumatised, I can no longer deal with this amount of misery. It is literally grit your teeth and hang on till the end now. I was counting the days and now I am counting the hours.*

We had arrived on a Sunday and we hoped to get a flight out on the Wednesday. Then there would be only four days left in Luanda until we left. I was counting down to the end.

It was hard to think about how to film in this devastated place, especially for a film that was supposed to be largely positive. Not a single building was untouched by the fighting. Whole floors of buildings had been blown away, others had gaping mortar wounds, and everything was peppered with bullet holes. Craters in the road still contained unexploded shells.

For six months of the nine-month siege, the frontline ran through the centre of town; fighting was literally house-to-house, moving down the streets. People couldn't get out to bury their dead; they had to wait for a lull in the fighting to dig shallow graves in their gardens. In their hunger, people ate dogs and cats and rats, maybe worse.

Of the three baroque pink-and-white government buildings in the town square, only one was still standing, and that was in ruins. A ruined church stood on the other side of the square. What was once a little park, with swings and flowerbeds in a town square, was now a pathetic little cemetery. The graves were so shallow that, here and there, bones were sticking out of the soil; in one place there was a whole skull. Small wooden crosses and a few flowers had been planted.

I wanted to film in a block of flats where only the lower floors were intact, but the stench was too overpowering. The apartments had no bathrooms and the people used the stairs as a toilet. There were even some families living in the filth on the stairs.

Among the remains of what was once a suburban house, we found two young women with a group of snotty, malnourished children, squatting on empty tins in the blackened ruins. Other than the tins and a blackened pot standing on a small fire in the corner, these people had nothing at all. They had come here from the countryside to escape 'the enemy'. Some of the children had died during the siege and were buried in the garden.

For all this, though, and extraordinary as it seemed, there were signs of renewed life starting up here and there. In the mornings, streams of children of all ages walked through the streets to school, carrying empty powdered-milk tins to sit on. There were no chairs or desks. Some of the schools had only a few useable rooms. Classrooms had no doors or windows, some had gaping holes in the sides, but teaching still took place. A theatre group was in town doing little plays in parks and schools to teach landmine awareness.

Nigel and Rupert from the Halo Trust, a British de-mining group who were training local de-miners, came looking for us. They were ex-British army, very public school, and kind and helpful. They had come to tell us that they had found some mines in a field behind the hospital and were about to lift them, would we like to film it? We crept tensely through the plastic tape with its 'Danger – Mines' warning that cordoned off the minefield, and watched as they probed, dragged, and finally defused the mine.

In the only remaining house in the street of orphanages, Donna Evangelista was waiting for us in her 'office' on the second floor. The building had no roof and there were only gaps where the windows had once been, so the desks and typewriters were in the open. On what was left of the walls, the staff had pinned up photographs of children whose families they were trying to trace.

Donna Evangelista and her five helpers were the only people in the entire city dealing with the flood of orphaned children.

'Everyone in this region is traumatised,' she told us. 'We can't counsel everyone, so we concentrate on orphanages.' She said she couldn't even count the numbers of orphans and amputees in the city.

'Many of the children have nightmares. They dream of bombs, of bones, of their fathers dying, or their brothers. They wake up screaming.' She slowly tapped her pen on the desk. 'I think the effects of the war will go on; I don't know about the future for these children. They will only feel safe if we can really help them to overcome this trauma, otherwise the future will be difficult for them.' Then she sighed, 'Not all of them will have a happy future. It's hard.'

Downstairs, a number of small children were crowded into one room. Many of them were babies, some sleeping on blankets on the floor, while others sat motionless. They barely registered the crew and camera. They didn't look like babies to me, but like very old people.

Outside, several children were playing on a lone swing. A hand-painted sign said: 'Infancia Herois de Kuito' – Infant Heroes of Kuito. Poor little heroes.

Gabriel and Giulio had managed to find a very scrawny chicken and a fresh pineapple. We took them to the Halo Trust house, where Nigel and Rupert supplied beer. It was a relatively jolly evening.

The blister on my heel was infected. I couldn't walk the foul and broken streets of Kuito in flip-flops, so I limped through the remaining days.

We drove to nearby Kunje to film at a Médecins sans Frontières feeding centre for children. The road there was littered with the detritus of war: blown-up tanks and lorries, flattened houses. Huge army tents had been erected to house the thousands of refugees. Really, there was very little in this part of Angola that gave us any feeling of hope.

Every evening after filming, we checked in at the WFP office to make sure we were still on the flight manifesto for Wednesday. We were not the only people desperate to get out of Kuito; there were several aid workers trying to fight their way onto the passenger list.

At night we were driven crazy by the mosquitoes and scratching mice. Our sleep was broken by shooting; and my own Kuito nightmares, of the children we had seen, woke me up screaming.

Luanda's mess and chaos seemed no worse than any other city when we got back. At last I could remove my boots and try to treat my now suppurating heel.

Katia told us that the government wanted to rebuild Kuito at an entirely new site, but that the people didn't want that. They defended 'this Kuito', and they wanted it built right where it had always been. I couldn't help feeling sceptical.

At a school for displaced children, where a windowless, wheel-less bus served as a classroom, some of the children made us a huge map of Africa in the dust of their playground. Angola, outlined in whitewashed stones, was several times its actual size. The children always made their own country larger than reality, dominating southern Africa.

Manuel and I sat in his garden on the Ilha without saying much. Life had been hard for him these last few years. It felt like an ending to me.

Before I left, Ulienge brought me a photograph that we had taken at a hot, February Sunday lunch in 1986, nearly ten years before. There we all were, sitting in bathing suits around a food-laden table in the garden. Uli and Nyela looked little and cute, their mother looked pretty and happy, Manuel was far less grey and care-worn than today. Ivan, Christian, and I were tanned and lean.

The day had been cool and slightly oppressive; nothing moved and the bay looked like a mirror. On the way back into town, the sun appeared briefly in the slate-grey sky and dropped like an orange stone into the flat sea, turning it momentarily blue.

For me, the war was over. I wanted to tell stories of peace.

But for Angola, the war only ended with Savimbi's death in February 2002. By 1998, the country had exploded again. In this final phase, another million people fled their homes, joining the refugee population that already made up a quarter of Angola's population. Once again, UNITA shelled the government-held cities of Huambo, Kuito and Malanje, killing hundreds more people. The government bombed rebel-controlled towns. This time, no one was watching. The major powers had left Angola; no one was interested in the death throes of this conflict.

*Chain of Hope* was a successful – and ultimately positive – film. We had caught up with many of the children from *Chain of Tears* and discovered that, with few resources, real strides could be made to help children recover from the traumas of war. Even in Angola, we had found hopeful stories of children who were resilient and recovering against all the odds.

What I had filmed and witnessed over the years were things that would be with me forever. But it was time for me to move on. To leave war behind and find other stories to tell.

# GLOSSARY OF ACRONYMS

| | |
|---|---|
| ANC | African National Congress, South Africa |
| CIAM | Centre Impressa Annibal di Melo (Press Centre) |
| COD | Congress of Democrats |
| FAPLA | Forças Armadas Populares de Libertação de Angola (People's Armed Forces for the Liberation of Angola) |
| Frelimo | Frente de Libertação de Moçambique (Liberation Front of Mozambique) |
| IFP | Inkatha Freedom Party, political party in South Africa formed by Mangosuthu Buthelezi; originally Inkatha Cultural Liberation Movement |
| Koevoet | ('Crowbar') South West Africa Police Counter-Insurgency Unit |
| MK | Umkhonto we Sizwe (Spear of the Nation), the military wing of the African National Congress |
| MNR | Mozambican National Resistance |
| MPLA | Popular Movement for the Liberation of Angola (Movimento Popular de Libertação de Angola) |
| OMA | Organisation of Angolan Women |
| Oxfam | Oxford Committee for Famine Relief |
| PLAN | People's Liberation Army of Namibia |
| Renamo | Resistência Nacional Moçambicana |
| SACP | South African Communist Party |
| SADCC | Southern African Development Coordination Conference |

| | |
|---|---|
| SADF | South African Defence Force |
| SCF | Save the Children Fund |
| SWAPO | South West Africa People's Organisation |
| UNAVEM | United Nations Angolan Verification Mission |
| UNDRO | United Nations Disaster Relief Organisation |
| UNICEF | United Nations Children's Fund |
| UNOMOZ | United Nations Operation in Mozambique |
| UNOMSA | United Nations Observer Mission in South Africa |
| UNTAG | United Nations Transition Assistance Group |
| WFP | World Food Programme |
| ZAPU | Zimbabwean People's Union |

# REFERENCES

Aghostinho, Marmande, Peter Easton & Ahmed Zuber. *Repairing the Ravages of War* (World Bank: IK Notes, 2001)

Bernstein, Rusty. *Memory against Forgetting* (London: Viking, 1999)

Bernstein, Hilda. *The World that was Ours* (London: Heinemann, 1967)

Bernstein, Hilda. *The Rift* (London: Jonathan Cape, 1994)

Bernstein, Keith & Toni Strasburg. *Frontline Southern Africa* (London: Christopher Helm, 1988)

Boothby, Neil, Jennifer Crawford & Aghostinho Marmade. *Mozambican Child Soldier Life Outcome Study* (USA: Global Health, 2006)

Ellis, Stephen. 'Of Elephants and Men: Politics and Nature Conservation in South Africa' (*Journal of Southern African Studies*, Vol. 20, March 1994)

Harding, Jeremy. *Small Wars, Small Mercies* (London: Viking, 1993)

Hanlon, Joseph. *Beggar Your Neighbour* (London: CIIR, 1986)

Hanlon, Joseph. *Mozambique: The Revolution under Fire* (London: Zed Press, 1984)

Herr, Michael. *Dispatches* (New York: Alfred Knopf, 1977)

Kaplan, Jonathan. *The Dressing Station* (London: Picador, 2001)

Kaplan, Jonathan. *Contact Wounds* (New York: Grove Atlantic, 2005)

Kapuscinski, Ryzard. *Another Day of Life* (London: Pan, 1987)

Kasrils, Ronnie. *Cuito Cuanavale: A Paradox of History* (Transcript of address delivered in Havana, Cuba, April 2008)

Kerr Conway, Jill. *When Memory Speaks.* (New York: Random House, 1998)

Kipling, Rudyard. *Just So Stories* (1902; republished London: Everyman Library, 1992)

Justice Kumleben Commission of Enquiry (South Africa: 1996)

Meier, Karl. *Angola: Promises and Lies* (London: Serif, 2007)

Minter, William. *Apartheid's Contras* (London: Zed, 1994)

McGrath, Rae. *Landmines and Unexploded Ordnance* (London: Pluto, 2000)

Martin, David, & Phyllis Johnson. *Destructive Engagement, Southern Africa at War* (Harare: Zimbabwe Publishing House, 1986)

Pierce, Justin *An Outbreak of Peace* (South Africa: David Philip, 2005)

Reno, William. *The Real (War) Economy of Angola* (Evanston, Il.: Northwestern University, 1999)

Said, Edward. *Reflections on Exile* (Cambridge, MA: Harvard University Press, 2001)

Shubin, Valdimir. *The Hot Cold War* (London: Pluto, 2008)

Sontag, Susan. *On Photography* (London: Penguin, 1977)

Strasburg, Toni. Transcripts of Film Interviews (unpublished)

Tochman, Wojcieh. *Like Eating a Stone* (London: Portobello, 2008)

Van Vuuren, Hennie. *Apartheid Grand Corruption* (Institute for Security Studies, Cape Town, May 2006)

Zinesser, William (ed.). *Inventing the Truth: The Art and Craft of Memoir* (New York: Mariner Books, 1998)

# ABOUT THE AUTHOR

Toni Strasburg was born in South Africa and was exiled to Britain in 1965. She studied at London University and worked in various jobs before becoming a filmmaker.

She has documented apartheid-era wars in southern Africa concentrating largely on the effects on women and children. Her award-winning films include *Chain of Tears* and its sequel, *Chain of Hope, The Other Bomb, An Act of Faith* and *A South African Love Story.*

She has served as an International Peace Monitor and Election Observer for the United Nations and has run training workshops and been a consultant for UNESCO and other NGO's in southern Africa.

www.tonistrasburg.com

## Other Non-Fiction titles published by Modjaji Books

*Hemispheres* by Karen Lazar

*Eloquent Body* by Dawn Garisch

*Jabulani means Rejoice* by Phumzile Simelane Kalumba

*Swimming with Cobras* by Rosemary Smith

*Undisciplined Heart* by Jane Katjavivi

*Reclaiming the L-Word* edited by Alleyn Diesel

*My First Time* edited by Jennifer Thorpe

*Invisible Earthquake* by Malika Ndlovu

www.ingramcontent.com/pod-product-compliance
Lightning Source LLC
Chambersburg PA
CBHW011721220426
43664CB00022B/2888